MIDWEST
GARDENER'S HANDBOOK

Brimming with creative inspiration, how-to projects, and useful information to enrich your everyday life, Quarto Knows is a favorite destination for those pursuing their interests and passions. Visit our site and dig deeper with our books into your area of interest: Quarto Creates, Quarto Cooks, Quarto Homes, Quarto Lives, Quarto Drives, Quarto Explores, Quarto Gifts, or Quarto Kids.

© 2013 Quarto Publishing Group USA Inc.
Text © Melinda Myers 2013

First published in 2013 by Cool Springs Press, an imprint of The Quarto Group, 401 Second Avenue North, Suite 310, Minneapolis, MN 55401 USA. T (612) 344-8100 F (612) 344-8692 www.QuartoKnows.com

Cool Springs Press titles are also available at discount for retail, wholesale, promotional, and bulk purchase. For details, contact the Special Sales Manager by email at specialsales@quarto.com or by mail at The Quarto Group, Attn: Special Sales Manager, 401 Second Avenue North, Suite 310, Minneapolis, MN 55401 USA.

10 9 8 7

Library of Congress Cataloging-in-Publication Data

Myers, Melinda.
  Midwest gardener's handbook : your complete guide : select, plan, plant, maintain, problem-solve / Melinda Myers.
    p. cm.
  Includes bibliographical references and index.
  ISBN 978-1-59186-568-1 (softcover)
  1. Gardening--Middle West. 2. Plants--Middle West. I. Title.

SB453.2.M53M94 2013
635.0977--dc23

                    2013026161

Acquisitions Editor: Billie Brownell
Design Manager: Cindy Samargia Laun
Layout: Kim Winscher
Horticultural Editor: Lee C. Hansen

Printed in China

MIDWEST
GARDENER'S HANDBOOK

ILLINOIS, INDIANA, IOWA, KANSAS, MICHIGAN, MINNESOTA, MISSOURI,
NEBRASKA, NORTH DAKOTA, OHIO, SOUTH DAKOTA, WISCONSIN

YOUR COMPLETE GUIDE:
SELECT • PLAN • PLANT • MAINTAIN • PROBLEM-SOLVE

MELINDA MYERS

COOL
SPRINGS
PRESS

DEDICATION

To Maya and Sammy, my grandchildren and the next generation of gardeners in the family.

ACKNOWLEDGMENTS

I want to thank all the Cool Spring Press authors, especially those in the Midwest, who have been inspiring and educating gardeners for years. James Fizzell of Illinois introduced me to Cool Springs. Cathy Wilkinson-Barash of Iowa and I co-authored a book and then, as her life became busier, she allowed me to revise that book and expand into it to cover the Dakotas and Nebraska. Thanks also to JoEllen Meyers Sharp of Indiana, who also shares her gifts of writing and gardening through the State-by-State garden magazines. Others include Mike Miller of Missouri; Denny McKeown, who covers my home state of Ohio; and Laura Colt, Marty Hair, and Tim Boland of Michigan.

Thanks to all the botanical gardens, their staff, and volunteers who create a great environment for teachers, plant geeks, and new gardeners to learn and experience the beauty of gardening. If you haven't visited one lately go do so. It is good for your body, mind, and spirit.

Thanks to the horticulture professionals across the country. You generously share your knowledge and enthusiasm with many. Your websites, publications, and lectures are a great gift to those of us that depend on your research and all of us who benefit from your efforts.

Thanks to the Master Gardeners who donate their time and talents to educate gardeners of all ages.

I would like to thank my family. My parents, John and Betty, gave me love, support, and the courage to follow my dreams. My daughter, Nevada, is an inspiration and delight, and is there with me to laugh our way through life's challenges. My grandchildren Maya and Sammy make me smile and keep me young in spirit, if not body. And Pete, my new partner in life; I am looking forward to building our dream together.

Thanks to my amazing team who is helping grow our company so we can inspire and educate more gardeners to have fun and be successful in their garden. Diana does everything from keeping me on target—not easy—to syndicating *Melinda's Garden Moments* on television and radio. Thanks to Dawn, who is a horticulturist and graphic designer who always amazes me with her creative designs in print and electronic media, and to Mark Brothen, who is helping Pete and me create a sustainable learning center to share our passion and knowledge with others.

Thanks to my advisory team of Heather, Dave, Dennis, Jim, and Terry. Your insight and wisdom has been invaluable to me personally and professionally.

And of course my friends; you know who you are. You have been my cheerleaders, support and most importantly, people I can laugh with.

Thanks also to Billie Brownell, Tracy Stanley, and the folks at Cool Springs Press and Quarto Publishing for this opportunity.

CONTENTS

FEATURED PLANTS

WELCOME TO GARDENING

in the Midwest

Whether you are new to gardening or just new to gardening in the Midwest, use this book to help you create, maintain, and enjoy your landscape. Selecting plants suited to the diverse and often challenging Midwest garden climate is the first step to success. Team that with some monthly tips and helpful hints to remind and inspire. Together they will eliminate much of the guesswork to creating the garden you desire.

This book is just a starting point. Use the basic information I provide along with your own experience to increase your gardening success. Start keeping a garden journal to record your experiences. It doesn't have to be fancy. It's just a place to record your gardening successes and failures. All gardeners learn as much if not more from their failures as gardening successes. Record significant weather events. The impact of droughts, floods, and extreme heat and cold can show up years later. Buy a weather calendar or almanac and let the meteorologists keep track of some of the climate data for you.

Thomas Jefferson, a horticulturist as well as our third president, kept a garden journal for fifty years, entering the name, date, and source of every plant he purchased; how it grew; and when and why it was removed.

With all that said, the most important thing is to relax and have fun! If a plant dies (and it happens to every gardener), look at this as an opportunity to try something new. If you put a plant in the wrong spot, move it to a new location. Gardening should be enjoyable, not a weekly chore. And when you get discouraged, think about what Thomas Jefferson said: "Though an old man, I am but a young gardener."

THE GARDEN ENVIRONMENT

Every Midwest gardener seems to say, "If you don't like the weather, wait five minutes and it will change." They are right. The Midwest's weather is variable and often challenging for gardeners.

We base our plant selection and care on average weather conditions and expected extremes. Then weather exceptions like drought, flood,

A PERENNIAL GARDEN

May snowstorms, and too many others to list come along.

There seems to be no "normal" Midwest weather. There always seems to be some type of weather extreme to keep gardeners and horticulturists challenged and humble. An overview of our average weather conditions, however, may help you better plan and care for your garden.

Let's start with frost dates. On the back of every seed packet and throughout this book you will read, "Start seeds "X" number of weeks prior to the last spring frost." Use the zone map information on pages 244-245 to determine frost information for your area.

Now, count the days between the last spring frost and the first fall frost. That will give you the number of growing days for your region. Soil temperature and the frost tolerance of each plant should determine your planting date.

Average growing temperatures and seasonal extremes will influence plant growth and development. Some plants need warm temperatures to thrive and flower. Others become stressed or stop flowering in hot weather. Winter temperature extremes are among the major factors that influence winter survival. The U.S. Department of Agriculture hardiness zones are based on the average annual minimum temperatures. See the USDA Cold Hardiness Zones for the Midwest on pages 244-245 of this book.

Rainfall is also important for growing healthy plants. Most plants need an average of 1 inch of water each week. Plants need more water during the hot, dry days of summer and less during cooler periods. The type of plants grown and the care you provide influences the amount and frequency of watering. Some plants, like yucca and coneflowers, are more drought tolerant and can go longer between watering. Others, like astilbe and hostas, need moist soil and will scorch if the soil dries. Select more drought-tolerant plants if you are unable to water during dry periods. Mulching will also reduce the need to water by keeping the soil cool and moist.

Select plants that tolerate your landscape's climate to increase survival and minimize maintenance. But what about those gardeners who like to push plants to the extremes? Well, we can't change the weather, but we can modify it by creating microclimates or modifying our gardening practices.

SUNLIGHT

Light is always at the forefront or at least on your list of criteria when selecting plants.

Plant tags and this book are filled with symbols identifying how much sun a particular plant needs to thrive. But how many hours is full sun? And how many hours of light does your garden really receive.

Monitor light throughout the day, season, and year. The amount of sunlight changes as trees develop and lose leaves, sheds are added, and plants mature. As the angle of the sun changes throughout the year; the amount of sunlight reaching various parts of your landscape also changes.

In this book full sun means eight hours or more, including midday. Part sun means six to eight hours, not midday. Part shade means four or six hours, preferably morning. Shade means less than four hours of sun. Some plants can be grown in more than one range of sun, so you will sometimes see more than one sun symbol. This is a starting point. As with all gardening you will find exceptions in your gardening experience.

Full Sun   Part Sun   Part Shade   Shade

MODIFYING THE CLIMATE

Microclimates are small areas that have slightly different growing conditions than the surrounding areas. Large bodies of water and nearby vegetation can alter frost dates and moderate temperatures. Gardens near large bodies of water or in large urban centers are among the last to freeze. On the other hand, cold air sinks, creating frost pockets in valleys and other low areas. Woodlands and shelterbelts can block the northwest winter winds and reduce winter damage to sensitive plants. These areas can also shade the landscape, keeping temperatures cooler.

Use the following ideas to create microclimates. Plant windbreaks or install decorative fencing to block damaging winter winds. Grow heat-loving plants near brick buildings and walls. Even a flat warming stone in the perennial garden can add warmth for a nearby plant. Use an outdoor thermometer to track the temperatures in different parts of your garden. Record this information for future use.

Mulch can also be used effectively. Organic mulch used on the soil keeps roots cooler in the summer and warmer in the winter and minimizes soil temperature fluctuations that can stress plants. Winter mulches can be used to protect the aboveground portion of the plant. Roses, rhododendrons, and other tender plants are frequently mulched for winter protection. Apply weed-free straw, marsh hay, or evergreen branches once the ground lightly freezes. The purpose is to keep the soil temperature consistent throughout the winter. This prevents early sprouting that often occurs during our frequent, but short, midwinter thaws. Mulching also prevents drying of stems and evergreen leaves. The mulch blocks winter wind and sun to reduce moisture loss. Northern gardeners have access to the best winter mulch: a reliable snow cover. Even as you tire of shoveling this winter, remember that all that white stuff is protecting your plants.

Or maybe it's extreme heat that is limiting your gardening success. Look for heat and drought-tolerant plants that are better-equipped to survive these conditions. Add a vine covered trellis or a shade tree to provide some cooling shade for you and your plants to enjoy. Add a groundcover under trees and shrubs and mulch all your plants with shredded leaves, evergreen needles, woodchips, or other organic mulch to keep the soil cool and moist.

Maybe it's not the heat or cold winter that limits your gardening, but rather the length of the growing season. You can easily lengthen the growing season by several weeks or even a month or more. Gardeners traditionally use cold frames to get a jump on the growing season. These structures require talent to build and room to store, and they also need venting and watering. There never seems to be enough time to do all that. Season-extending fabrics such as Reemay and other spun-bonded fabrics can make this task easier. Plant annuals or frost-sensitive perennials outside several weeks earlier than normal and loosely cover the planting bed with a season-extending fabric. The covers keep the plants warm and protect them from spring frost. Air, light, and water can all pass through the fabric, so it doesn't need to be removed for watering or ventilation. Remove the covering once the danger of frost has passed. You can also use these fabrics, bed sheets, or other material to protect plants from the first fall frost. Cover plants in the late afternoon or

early evening when there is a threat of frost. Remove the frost protection in the morning. The season-extending fabric can be left in place day and night if the meteorologists predict several days of cold, frosty weather. The first fall frost is often followed by two weeks of sunny, warm weather. Providing frost protection will give you a few more weeks of enjoyment before our long winter arrives.

SOIL

Soil is the foundation of our landscape. Not many gardeners enjoy spending the time, energy, or money it can take to build this foundation. It's more fun to show someone a new plant than to show off properly prepared soil. But building productive soil will result in a beautiful and productive garden worth showing off.

Most gardeners do not start with the ideal. They may be battling poorly drained clay or dry rocky soil. And many have what plant and soil scientists refer to as "disturbed materials," not soil. When homes are constructed, the topsoil is scraped off the lot and removed. Once the basements are dug, much of the clay, sand, or gravel subsoil is spread over the lot. Some of the building materials, many of them made from limestone, accidentally get mixed into this "soil." An inch or two of topsoil is spread, sod is laid—the yard is ready to be landscaped. Not at all. This conglomeration is usually poorly drained, very alkaline or acidic, and hard on most plants. Fortunately, many municipalities and customers are requiring builders to stockpile the topsoil for reapplication to the site.

MODIFYING THE SOIL

Given all this information, what do you need to do to improve your soil? Start with a soil test. Contact your local university Extension office necessary forms and information for soil testing, or contact a state-certified soil-testing laboratory.

Take separate soil samples for each type of planting: one for the lawn, another for flowers, and a third for trees and shrubs. Spread the cost over time by starting with new planting beds or struggling gardens. Then start testing existing beds

Good garden soil that is loose, friable, and rich in organic matter is the foundation for successful gardening. Take the necessary time to get it right before planting.

every few years to get a better understanding of your soil.

Take a representative sample. Remove several plugs of soil from the garden area to be tested. Take the soil from the top 4 to 6 inches, removing any surface mulch first, from different areas throughout the garden. Mix these soil plugs together and allow the mixture to dry. Send 1 cup of this soil mix to the lab for analysis. Your results will be in the mail within two to three weeks.

The soil test report tells you how much and what type of fertilizer to use for the type of plants you are growing. It also tells you the soil pH and what, if anything, should be done to adjust it.

Adding 2 to 4 inches of organic matter such as compost, peat moss, or aged manure will improve the drainage of heavy clay soil and increase the water-holding capacity of sandy soil. Work this material into the top 6 to 12 inches of soil. Improve the soil whenever you establish a new garden, plant your annuals and perennials, or transplant perennial flowers and groundcovers.

Do not add sand to clay soil. You need an inch of sand for every inch of soil you are trying to amend. If you add less than that, you will end up with concrete. Don't add lime to improve the drainage of alkaline soil. Lime improves drainage, but it also raises the soil pH. That increases problems with nutrient deficiencies in alkaline soil.

Gardeners growing plants in poorly drained, disturbed sites have a bigger challenge. These soils will take years to repair. Many gardeners give up and bring in additional topsoil. Make sure the topsoil you buy is better than that you already have. Purchase a blended or garden mix. Many garden centers and nurseries sell small quantities of topsoil. For large quantities, contact a company that specializes in topsoil. Friends, relatives, or a landscape professional may be able to recommend a reliable firm. Otherwise, check the telephone pages listings under Soil or Topsoil.

A 2-inch layer of good topsoil spread over disturbed material will not help much; water drains through the good soil and stops when it hits the bad material. A better solution is to create planting beds throughout the landscape. Large, raised planting beds and berms at least 12 inches high will give plants a good place to start growing.

COMPOSTING

Make your own organic matter (compost) by recycling all your pest-free plant debris. It is as simple as putting it into a heap and letting it rot. The more effort you put into the process, the sooner you get compost.

Start with green debris. Shred fallen leaves, add herbicide-free grass clippings, and include other plant debris. Do not add meat and animal products that can attract rodents. Do add soil and enough water to moisten the pile. Make it at least 3 feet tall and wide for quicker results. Turn the pile occasionally to speed up decomposition.

Start a holding pile. Use the second pile to store plant debris until you have enough to make a new pile. The first pile will decompose faster if fresh materials are not continually being added.

Use finished compost to amend new and existing gardens. Try mixing it with topsoil to create a well-drained potting mix for container gardens. Or topdress by spreading a thin layer of compost over the soil surface in lawns, perennial gardens, and groundcover plantings.

AMENDING SOIL PH

Soil pH affects nutrient availability. Iron and manganese are not readily available in these high-pH soils. The nutrients are in the soil; they are just not available to the plants. That creates problems for acid-loving plants such as rhododendrons, red maples, and white oaks. It is very difficult to lower

A compost bin contains the pile and can improve the view.

Irrigation systems offer many different types of fittings, including the spray head shown here. This allows you to direct water exactly where it's needed.

in each chapter to learn how and when to plant trees, shrubs, flowers, and all the other plants in your landscape.

WATERING

Summer droughts and spring floods remind us of the value of water and watering properly. The garden hose can be a great help or a detriment to landscape plants. Consider the plant, soils, and weather when watering the landscape. Each plant profile lists watering needs and the chapter introduction provides water management strategies for that group of plants throughout the year. Use these guidelines to help conserve water and reduce the risk of over- and underwatering your plants.

Adjust watering to fit the weather, soil, and plant. Water more frequently during the hot, dry days of July and August. Decrease watering during the cool days of spring and fall. And always consider rainfall when calculating water needs. Nature often provides regular—sometimes too regular—irrigation for our planting.

Water gardens growing in clay soil thoroughly but less frequently than those growing in sandy and rocky soils. Clay soil holds the moisture longer. Wait until the top few inches start to dry, about every seven to ten days, before watering again. Water thoroughly, wetting the total root zone. Apply needed water to sandy soils in two applications. Water thoroughly so that the root zone is moist. Wait three to five days and water again if the top few inches have begun to dry.

New plants need more frequent watering to get established. Check them several times a week, and water often enough to keep their roots moist. Gradually decrease watering frequency to encourage deep, drought-tolerant roots. Give established plants a helping hand during extended dry periods. Their extensive root system allows them to find and use water from a large area for most of the season. Help maintain growth, improve productivity, and minimize pest problems through proper watering.

Water plants early in the morning to reduce the risk of disease and foliar burn. Keeping leaves

the soil pH. Incorporating elemental sulfur and organic matter can slightly lower the pH. Using acidifying fertilizers, chelated iron and manganese, and organic mulch will help. But all of these methods can take years to lower the pH and have a minimal impact. It is much easier on you and the plant to grow species adapted to high-pH soils.

In acidic, low-pH soils, the phosphorus, calcium, and magnesium are tied up in the soil and are unavailable to the plants. Many gardeners add lime to raise the soil pH. Follow soil test recommendations carefully. It takes years to correct improperly limed soils. Never lime alkaline soils.

PLANTING

Proper planting is important to establishing a healthy, long-lived plant. There is more to it than making sure the green side points up. Preparing the site, digging the hole, and planting at the proper depth and time will increase your transplanting and gardening success. Follow the planting guidelines

The first number on a fertilizer package represents the percent by weight of nitrogen; the second phosphorous; and the third potassium.

dry at night helps prevent the development and spread of fungal leaf spots and blight. Allowing leaves to dry before the heat of midday reduces water lost to evaporation and damage caused by the bright sun shining on wet leaves.

Use soaker hoses or drip irrigation to place the water on the soil right where it is needed. You will waste less water and save time if you don't have to drag hoses and set up sprinklers.

Use shredded leaves, evergreen needles, and woodchips as a mulch to reduce watering needs. A thin layer of these materials over the soil surface will conserve moisture, reduce weeds, and gradually improve the soil.

Consider installing rain barrels to capture water for use on containers and during dry periods. And install a rain garden to filter water through plant roots and soil instead of overwhelming our storm sewers. This is a beautiful solution to flooding problems many homeowners and municipalities face.

SELECTING A FERTILIZER

A trip to the garden center and down the fertilizer aisle can be overwhelming. There seems to be a bag and formulation for every plant you can imagine. It is difficult to decide which product is best for your garden situation.

Start by reading the front label. Look at the three numbers on the bag. These represent the amount of nitrogen, phosphorus, and potassium in the fertilizer. The first number on the left is nitrogen. It is essential to plant growth and is used to grow leaves and stems. It is used in relatively large amounts by the plants. This mobile element moves through the soil quickly. You can use slow-release forms to provide plants with small amounts of nitrogen over a longer period of time. These products also reduce the risk of fertilizer burn. Excess nitrogen encourages leafy growth and discourages flowering. It also leaches through the soil, harming our lakes, streams, and groundwater.

Phosphorus is the middle number on the bag. Phosphorus stimulates root development and flowering. This nutrient is used in small amounts by the plants and moves very slowly through the soil. Excess phosphorus can interfere with the uptake of other nutrients and damage our lakes and streams.

Potassium is used in even smaller amounts by plants. It is essential in many plant processes and helps the plants prepare for winter.

Many Midwest soils tend to be high in phosphorus and potassium. That comes from years of using complete fertilizers, like 10-10-10 and 12-12-12. Excessive amounts of one nutrient can interfere with the uptake of other nutrients. You can't remove the excess nutrients, but you can stop adding to the problem by following your soil test recommendations. Several Midwest states, municipalities, and lakeside communities have banned or limited the use of phosphorous containing fertilizers to protect water quality. It also saves you money and can improve your gardening success.

Select the fertilizer formulation recommended by your soil test. Or check the fertilizer recommendations in each chapter for the plant you are trying to grow. These are based on general plant needs for the Midwest.

Now decide on liquid or dry fertilizers. Liquid fertilizers can be applied with a sprinkling can, garden hose, or spray tank. Dry fertilizers are spread on the soil surface. Apply dry fertilizers to the soil using a small shaker, hand-held spreader, or push-type spreader.

Look for the words slow-release or fast-release on the bag. Use slow-release fertilizers to provide a constant supply of nutrients over a long period of time. Fast-release fertilizers provide a quick fix but must be applied several times throughout the garden season.

Choose between an organic or inorganic form of fertilizer. Inorganic fertilizers come in a variety of formulations and are in a form ready for the plants to use. Organic fertilizers improve the soil structure, while providing small amounts of nutrients over a long period of time.

Select the fertilizer that best suits the plants, soil, and your gardening style. Use the fertilizer recommended by your soil test report.

Test your soil every three to five years, or as problems arise. That will allow you to adjust your fertilizer program to your soil and the plants you are growing. This practice will save you money, improve plant growth, and help our environment.

PRUNING

Keep your plants healthy and attractive with proper pruning. Train young plants, develop a strong framework, encourage flowers and fruiting, or repair damage. Know why you are pruning before you make the first cut. A plan will help you achieve your goals and maintain the health of the plant.

Pruning also includes deadheading, pinching back, and other related grooming techniques. Pinch back leggy plants to encourage fuller, more compact growth. Deadhead faded flowers to encourage rebloom and discourage reseeding. Prune some young perennials to control height and bloom time.

Check each chapter introduction and plant profiles to find out when and what to prune for the results you desire. And see pages 236 to 239 for additional information.

PEST MANAGEMENT

Once your plants are growing, some unwelcome visitors may enter the landscape. These pests come in the form of weeds, diseases, insects, and plant-devouring wildlife. A healthy plant is your best defense against pests. Even with proper planting and care, you may need to intercede to help plants through difficult times.

Use a Plant Health Care approach (the horticulturist's version of IPM, Integrated Pest Management) to manage your landscape. It starts with proper plant selection and care and ends by managing pest problems using a variety of the most environmentally sound techniques, with chemicals as a last resort.

Select the most pest-resistant varieties available and grow them in the proper location. This helps you avoid many pest problems, eliminating the need for control. Provide proper care, such as watering, fertilizing, and pruning, based upon the plant's needs.

Monitor the garden throughout the growing season. Finding pests early can mean the difference between picking off a few sick leaves and spraying a plant throughout the season. Look under the leaves, along the stems, and on the ground for signs of insects, disease, and wildlife.

Remove weeds as soon as they appear. Not only do they compete with your garden plants for water and nutrients, but they also harbor insects and disease. Remove them before they have a chance to set seed and infect the soil for next season. Mulch to prevent weeds.

Follow the planting and care guidelines in this book to keep your plants healthy and more resistant to pests. Cover the plants, hand pick, or trap insects to minimize the negative attack on the good insects, fungi, and wildlife in our environment. Properly identify all pests before reaching for a pesticide. Sometimes the pest we see is not causing the damage. Other times the damage is done, the pest is gone, and there is no need to treat. Always find out what is causing the damage and if control is needed to maintain the health of the plant. Consult my website, your local university Extension office, or garden center for advice. It is important to use the

Remove the entire root system or rhizome of a weed, but be careful not to uproot neighboring plants. Use a weeding tool to get leverage, if needed.

right product or technique at the right time to maximize effectiveness and minimize the negative impact on the environment.

Consider all control options and their impact on the plant, your health, and the environment. Select the most environmentally friendly method that fits your gardening style and the plants' needs. Always read and follow all label directions before using any product in your landscape. Make sure it is labeled to control the pest on the plant you want to treat. Wear any protective clothing recommended or required by the label.

Evaluate the success of control measures used and record this in your journal. Mark next year's calendar and review this book's monthly pest management sections to help reduce and control problems next season.

WEED CONTROL

You will simplify your life by eliminating existing weeds before planting. They can be removed with

regular cultivation one season prior to planting. Another option is to solarize the garden. Edge the bed and cover the planting area with clear plastic for six to eight weeks during the hottest part of the growing season to kill the weeds and many of the seeds. A more attractive method involves woodchips and newspaper. Edge the area, and cut the weeds and existing grass short. Then spread several layers of newspaper or a layer of cardboard covered with woodchips over it. The newspaper helps smother the weeds, but eventually breaks down and improves the soil.

Or use a total vegetation killer such as Roundup® for quicker results. You can plant treated areas in one to two weeks. Remember, these products will kill any green plant they contact. Be sure to read and carefully follow label directions.

Mulch the soil after planting. This step will prevent many weed seeds from sprouting. Any that do grow through will be easy to pull. Heavily mulched soils may need some additional nitrogen fertilizer. Cultivation with a hoe or weeding tool will also work to control weeds. Be careful not to damage the roots of your garden plants.

DEALING WITH DISEASES

Leaf spots, stem rots, mildew, and blights are just a few of the diseases found on plants. Growing the right plant in the right location will reduce the risk of infection. Proper soil preparation will help reduce rot problems. Remove infected leaves as soon as they appear. Fall cleanup will reduce disease infection the following season. Most disease problems develop in response to the weather. You will have problems some years and not others. Plants are usually more tolerant of these problems than the gardener. Contact your local university Extension service, certified arborists, or other landscape professionals for help in identifying and controlling these problems.

MANAGING INSECTS

As you battle the insects, remember that less than 3 percent of all the insects throughout the world are classified as pests. Many more are beneficial and desirable to have in your garden. Keep in mind insecticides also kill the caterpillars that turn into beautiful butterflies and kill aphid-eating ladybugs. Try some environmental (and often fun) control techniques before reaching for the spray can. Always read and follow label directions carefully before using any pesticide.

Here are some of the more common insects that attack a wide range of plants:

Aphids are small teardrop-shaped insects that come in a variety of colors. They suck the plant juices causing the leaves to yellow, wilt, brown, curl, and become distorted. They also secrete a clear sticky substance on the leaves called honeydew. It doesn't hurt the plant but a black fungus, called sooty mold, may develop on the honeydew. You can wait and let the ladybugs move in and devour this pest or try spraying the plants with a strong blast of water. You can also use insecticidal soap, which is effective for killing soft bodied insects but is gentle on the plant and the environment. You may need several applications to control large populations.

Mites cause similar damage. You need a hand lens to see these pests. Like aphids, they suck plant juices and cause leaves to bronze, wilt, and brown. Don't wait to see the webs before you treat the mites. Sprays of water and insecticidal soap will help control this pest.

Slugs are slimy creatures that eat holes in the leaves of hostas and other garden plants. They feed at night, so you will notice the damage before you see the slugs. Slugs love cool, dark, damp locations and multiply quickly in wet weather. Stale beer in a shallow dish makes a great slug trap. Or lay a partially filled beer bottle on its side in the garden. Tuck it out of sight under the plant leaves. The bottle keeps the beer from being diluted by rain, so it won't need frequent replacing. The slugs really do crawl in the small hole, drown in the beer, and die. Commercial slug baits are also available, but most have very toxic materials. Slug control products, such as Sluggo™, contain iron phosphate that is effective at killing slugs, but are not harmful to birds and wildlife.

Japanese beetles feed on several hundred different plants. Healthy plants can tolerate the damage but most gardeners can't. Knock these voracious beetles into a can of soapy water. You won't eliminate them but this will help reduce their population and feeding damage. Several insecticides are labeled for use on Japanese beetles.

Unfortunately many are harmful to beneficial insects including honeybees. Soil applied insecticides are absorbed by the plants and concentrate in the leaves and stems, not the flowers. These are applied the previous fall or in the spring a month or more before the beetles start feeding. Don't use traps as they attract more beetles into your garden.

ANIMALS IN THE GARDEN

Wildlife can be a nice addition to the landscape— until they start eating all the plants. Start by eliminating hiding and nesting areas, such as brush

Deer can be a major problem for Midwest gardeners. Try surrounding your garden with fishing line at several different heights to keep the deer out.

piles. Fence desirable plants. Sink fencing several inches into the ground to keep out voles. This rodent kills young plantings by feeding on the trunks of trees and shrubs and the crowns of some perennials. Fences must be at least 4 feet high to keep out rabbits and over 10 feet high to keep out deer. This type of deer fencing is not very practical. Many gardeners are having luck fencing small planting beds with 5-foot-tall deer fencing. You can see through to the garden while keeping out the deer, which tend to avoid small, fenced areas.

Scare tactics and repellents may provide some control, but urban wildlife is exposed to and is very tolerant of the sounds and smells of humans. Apply repellents before the animals start feeding. It will be easier than trying to break the habit once they start dining on your landscape. Vary the repellents and scare tactics for better results. And work with your neighbors—make sure one of you isn't feeding the wildlife while the other is trying to eliminate it from the neighborhood.

WINTER CARE

Some plants need a little help surviving our winters. Snow is the best mulch, but it often arrives too late, melts too soon, or comes and goes throughout the winter.

Apply winter mulches of evergreen boughs, straw, or marsh hay to the ground after it freezes. The goal is to keep the soil constantly cold throughout the winter. Fluctuating soil temperatures cause early sprouting and frost heaving. Early sprouting results in damaged leaves and flowers when the normal cold temperatures return. Frost heaving causes the soil to shift, damaging roots and often pushing perennials and bulbs right out of the ground.

Use discarded holiday trees, decorative fencing, burlap, or other items to create windbreaks and shade for tender plants and broadleaf evergreens. Place them on the windward and sunny sides of the plant. The screening reduces the wind and sun that reaches the plants and dries the leaves.

See the plant profiles and chapter introductions for more specifics. A little preventative action in the fall can save a lot of time repairing damage and money spent replacing damaged plants.

THERE'S ALWAYS NEXT YEAR

If all these methods fail, there is always next year. Someone once shared this definition of a green thumb gardener: The green thumb gardener is someone who grows a lot of plants, kills a few without mentioning it to others, and keeps on planting! So, take heart. If you've lost a few plants, you're on your way to a green thumb.

ANNUALS
for the Midwest

Grow them in a pot, in the ground, intermingled with your vegetables or tucked in amongst your perennials. Use annuals to brighten the landscape from spring through fall. Include traditional favorites and try some of the new varieties to add a little pizzazz to your landscape and make gardening with annuals even more fun. Botanically speaking, annuals are plants that complete their life cycle (from seed to producing seeds) in a single season. Horticulturally speaking, they can be true annuals or nonhardy perennials that are replanted each year. Creating an attractive annual garden involves planning, proper planting, and a little follow-up care.

CREATING A PLAN

Start with a plan. Going to the garden center in spring is like going to the grocery store hungry. Most Midwest gardeners can't resist buying bargain plants or hard-to-resist selections, instead of the right plant for the intended location. Try planning your gardens all year-round. Visit botanical gardens, attend garden tours, scour garden catalogs and magazines, and talk with other gardeners to get new ideas. You may want to start a section in your garden journal listing the flower combinations that work, new plants you want to try, and those to avoid. If you don't have a garden journal, now is a good time to start one.

Next, gather your family or other gardening partners together. Find out what everyone wants from the garden. You may want to include flowers for cutting, drying, or crafts. And don't forget about wildlife. Annuals are great lures for birds and butterflies, which add motion and color to your garden and may help get nongardeners interested in the landscape.

Think about creative combinations when you make your choices. Try mixing herbs like 'Purple Ruffles' basil and decorative vegetables like 'Bright Lights' Swiss chard in with annuals. Their color and texture, not to mention their culinary value, make them great additions to the annual garden.

Many magazines, websites, and growers provide container recipes and suggest plant combinations to help make garden design easier for you. Check out www.provenwinners.com and www.simplybeautifulgardens.com for a few ideas for designing with annuals.

As you look through the catalogs and garden centers, note the All-America Selections (AAS) logo. AAS winners have performed well in test gardens across the country. The plants were selected for their superior performance by independent AAS judges. We are lucky to have several test gardens and many display gardens in the Midwest. Visit the AAS website (www.all-americaselections.org) to find a garden near you.

Select plants suited to the growing conditions. Evaluate the sun and shade patterns where you will be growing annuals. Then take a closer look at the soil. If the soil is like modeling clay or is as porous as a sandy beach, invest some time and money to improve it before you plant. And match your plants to the moisture conditions and your ability to irrigate during dry periods. See the book's introduction, page 11 for tips on amending your soil.

THINK ABOUT DESIGN

Select plants that serve the desired function and tolerate, or preferably thrive in, the growing conditions. Note the height and width of each plant and then make a sketch of your flower garden. Place tall plants in the center of island beds or at the back of flower borders. Shorter plants should be planted near the edge, and everything else can go toward the middle. Plant in rows for a more formal look and, in masses or drifts for a more informal feel.

Don't limit your use of annuals to flower beds. Try them in containers, as a splash of color along the edge of a shrub bed, or intermingled with vegetables and perennials. Help pull your garden and landscape design together with some simple garden design strategies.

Select colors that help create the feel and look you want for your landscape. Warm colors of red, orange, and yellow make large areas appear smaller, add a feeling of warmth, and attract attention. Cool colors of blue, green, and violet make small areas appear larger and give a cool peaceful feeling to the area. Use contrasting colors to create a focal point and similar or analogous colors for continuity and blending. And remember it takes more cool-color flowers to offset a few bright orange, red, or yellow blossoms.

Repeat colors throughout the landscape through color echoing. For example, a red flower in one area can be echoed by the red foliage of a plant in another section and the red brick on the home. Color echoing increases the impact of the plants while creating a sense of unity throughout the yard.

Texture is another element that can help unify the garden or add contrast for greater impact. Fine-textured plants like 'Diamond Frost' euphorbia have small, dissected or grass-like foliage and airy or spike-like flowers. Bold textured plants have broad leaves with round flowers like sunflowers. Repeat textures throughout the landscape to tie the garden or parts of the landscape together. Mix a few bold-textured plants in with the fine-textured plants to give the garden some punch.

GETTING STARTED

Annuals can be started from seeds or purchased as transplants. Some annuals, like zinnias and marigolds, can be planted directly outside in the garden. Others, like geraniums, take a long time to mature and blossom. These should be started as seeds indoors for best results. Starting your own plants from seeds takes extra work but gives you a greater selection of new and different plant varieties—and a real sense of satisfaction.

Many gardeners prefer to buy transplants from their local garden center, greenhouse, or nursery. The extra expense provides the advantage of ready-to-plant and soon-to-bloom annuals. Select transplants with full-sized green leaves and stout stems. Avoid insect- and disease-infected plants. And this is a case where bigger isn't necessarily better. Smaller plants that aren't rootbound will suffer less transplant shock than larger-blooming, rootbound transplants.

PLANTING

Prepare your plants for the garden before you put them in the ground. Plants moving from the shelter of the greenhouse or your home need a little help preparing for the great outdoors. This process is called hardening off. Move the plants outdoors into partial shade. Gradually allow the soil to go drier between waterings and stop fertilizing. At the same time, gradually increase the amount of light the plants receive each day. In two weeks, the plants will be ready to move to their permanent location. Many garden centers do this job for us; ask if you're not sure.

Once the transplants are hardened-off you are ready to plant. Carefully slide the plants out of the container. Gently massage the roots before planting, to encourage them to grow out of the rootball and into the surrounding soil. Place the plant in the ground at the same level it was growing in the container.

Remove flowers and cut back leggy annuals at the time of planting. This encourages root development, branching, and better looking, healthier plants in the long run. Or remove the flowers on every other plant or every other row at planting. Remove the remaining flowers the following week. Then it will not seem so long before the new flowers appear.

WATERING AND FERTILIZING

Water new plantings thoroughly, moistening the top 6 inches of soil. This will encourage deep, more drought-tolerant roots. Check new plantings several times per week. The small rootball growing in the soilless mix will dry out quickly. Once established, plants need about 1 inch of water each week.

Water thoroughly whenever the top few inches of soil are moist but crumbly. During dry periods, you will usually provide the needed water once a week to plants growing in clay soil and half the weekly rate twice a week to plants in sandy soil. You may need to water more often during hot weather and less frequently when temperatures are cool.

Mulch once the soil warms to conserve moisture and decrease watering. Simply spread a thin layer of shredded leaves, evergreen needles, or other organic matter over the soil surface.

Fertilize according to soil test recommendations. If this is not available, three pounds or less per one hundred square feet of a low-nitrogen fertilizer per season is sufficient for most annuals. Consider incorporating a low-nitrogen slow-release fertilizer, such as Milorganite®, into the soil prior to planting. Or you can make three applications of a fast-release fertilizer once a month at a rate of one pound per one hundred square feet or according to the label directions. See page 14 for more tips on fertilization.

OVERWINTERING

Some gardeners extend their growing season and plant life by moving a few plants indoors for winter. Simply take cuttings in late August or early September for best results, though you can still clip a few stems before the first killing frost. Root 4-inch cuttings in moist vermiculite or perlite. Plant the rooted cuttings in any well-drained potting mix and grow them as a houseplant.

You can also bring the whole plant indoors and raise it like your other houseplants. Monitor and control pests as needed. Grow the overwintering annual in a bright, sunny window or under artificial lights and keep the soil moist. Don't be alarmed if the plant drops most of its leaves. It will soon send out new leaves more suited for its indoor location.

A common, but less successful, method for geraniums is dormant storage. Most basements are too warm for this method to work. But that doesn't stop a determined gardener. Place plants in a cool dark location for the winter. Some gardeners knock the soil off the roots and hang the plants from the ceiling or place them in a brown paper bag. Others leave the plants in their containers. In mid-March, pot up the plants if needed, and place them in a warm, sunny location. Prune back to 4 inches, water, and wait to fertilize until new growth appears. With some luck, you will have your favorite geranium to put out in the garden.

Now let's look at planting, growing, and caring for annuals throughout the year.

AGERATUM
Ageratum houstonianum

Why It's Special—The long bloom, butterfly appeal, and low maintenance make this an ideal plant for new and experienced gardeners. The compact types form tight mounds making them great edging and bedding plants. The taller varieties are looser, more open, and great for cutting or use as a filler in perennial gardens.

How to Plant & Grow—Purchase transplants or grow from seeds indoors. Start seeds indoors in mid-March. Follow label directions. Transplant hardened-off plants outdoors after all danger of frost is past. Space compact plants 6 inches apart and taller cultivars 9 inches apart.

Care & Problems—If placed properly, ageratums require little maintenance. Water thoroughly whenever the top few inches of soil are slightly dry. Occasional deadheading keeps the plants blooming and improves the appearance. Cut back leggy plants halfway to encourage more attractive growth. Reduce the risk of powdery mildew by growing plants in a sunny area and properly spacing them.

Bloom Color—Blue, lavender, white, and pink

Peak Season—Spring through frost

Mature Size (H x W)—6 to 15 in. x 12 in.

Water Needs—Overwatering can lead to root rot.

ALYSSUM
Lobularia maritima

Why It's Special—The lovely fragrance makes alyssum a nice addition to any landscape. I like to mix it with my perennials or use it as an edger where I can enjoy the fragrance and the butterflies they attract. And watch for seedlings that may sprout the following year, as long as you don't weed them out.

How to Plant & Grow—Purchase alyssum as a transplant or grow from seeds. Seeds should be started indoors in mid-March or directly outdoors after the last hard frost for later bloom. Hardened-off transplants can be planted outdoors after all danger of frost is past. Plant alyssum transplants 6 to 8 inches apart for a complete and quick cover.

Care & Problems—Extreme heat may cause the plants, especially purple ones, to stop flowering. Clip back leggy plants, water as needed, but don't fertilize. Plants will begin flowering as soon as temperatures cool.

Bloom Color—White, pink, lavender, and apricot

Peak Season—Spring through frost

Mature Size (H x W)—4 to 8 in. x 10 to 15 in.

Water Needs—Alyssum needs evenly moist soil.

ANGELONIA
Angelonia augustifolia

Why It's Special—The delicate looks are misleading as these beauties are heat and drought tolerant once established. Include angelonia, also known as summer snapdragon, in your containers, annual gardens, and a few in with your perennials. Enjoy its fragrance and beauty in flower arrangements.

How to Plant & Grow—Sow seeds indoors in late March according to packet directions. Or, purchase plants at the garden centers. Move hardened-off transplants into the garden once the soil has warmed and danger of frost has passed. Space plants 9 to 12 inches apart in full sun location with moist well-drained soil.

Care & Problems—Once established, water thoroughly and only when the top few inches of soil are crumbling and starting to dry. No deadheading is needed and the compact varieties do not pinching or pruning. You can cut taller varieties back midseason if you need and want to encourage more compact growth. Flowers will return in about two weeks.

Bloom Color—White, pink, blue, and bicolor

Peak Season—Spring through frost

Mature Size (H x W)—12 to 24 in. x 9 to 18 in.

Water Needs—Keep angelonia evenly moist.

BEGONIA
Begonia semperflorens

Why It's Special—This durable choice provides attractive foliage and a season of bloom with minimal care. Wax begonia leaves are glossy and come in green or bronze and are covered with masses of small flowers. The 'Dragon Wing' begonias are taller, have larger leaves, season-long bloom, are heat tolerant, and grow well in sun and shade.

How to Plant & Grow—Most gardeners buy transplants since the tiny seeds (2 million per ounce) take more than four months to develop into flowering plants. Plant hardened-off transplants outside after all danger of frost is past. Space small cultivars about 6 to 8 inches apart. Larger cultivars can be planted 8 to 12 inches apart.

Care & Problems—Avoid excess nitrogen and overhead watering, and remove diseased plant parts as they appear to help minimize disease problems. Wax begonias occasionally suffer from powdery mildew, botrytis blight, leaf spots, and stem rots. Regular deadheading in wet weather reduces these problems.

Bloom Color—White, red, rose, and pink

Peak Season—Summer to frost

Mature Size (H x W)—6 to 12 in. x 6 to 12 in.

Water Needs—Keep soil evenly moist.

CALENDULA
Calendula officinalis

Why It's Special—Also known as pot marigold, this annual provides color and edibility to plantings. Include these in container, flower, and herb gardens. Add a few to your garden bouquet and pluck a few petals to brighten a salad or flavor a soup.

How to Plant & Grow—Purchase plants or start seeds indoors six to eight weeks before the last spring frost. Or sow seeds directly in the garden in early summer for a fall display. Move hardened-off transplants into the garden after the last spring frost. Grow in moist, well-drained soils and space plants 8 inches apart.

Care & Problems—Calendula tends to stop flowering in hot dry weather. Look for more heat-resistant cultivars. Mulch the soil to keep roots cool and moist. Water thoroughly as needed and wait for cooler temperatures. These plants are fairly pest free. Watch for cabbage worms, leaf spot, mildew, rots, and aster yellows.

Bloom Color—Yellowish white, yellow, and orange

Peak Season—Spring and fall

Mature Size (H x W)—12 to 18 in. x 12 to 18 in.

Water Needs—Keep soil evenly moist.

CLEOME
Cleome hasslerana

Why It's Special—This unique large annual attracts butterflies and hummingbirds and the newer smaller cultivars allow even those with small spaces to enjoy their beauty. They make great cut flowers with an interesting, often described as musky or skunk-like, fragrance on warm nights.

How to Plant & Grow—Start seeds indoors about six weeks before the last frost. Cleome transplants are available at garden centers. Purchased or homegrown transplants should be hardened off and then planted outdoors after all danger of frost is past. They grow in a variety of soils and full sun to part shade. Remember, these are big plants that need lots of space; allow at least 2 feet between plants. Cleomes often reseed themselves in the garden.

Care & Problems—Although heat and drought, they will also benefit from ample moisture. These large plants are self-supporting (no staking required), but they do tend to slouch with age.

Bloom Color—White, pink, rose, or purple

Peak Season—Summer through fall

Mature Size (H x W)—Up to 6 ft. x 1 to 2 ft.

Water Needs—This plant is drought tolerant once established.

COCKSCOMB
Celosia species

Why It's Special—Cockscomb is a good choice for hot dry areas. It adds bright bold color to outdoor gardens and flower arrangements. The flowers can be crested like a rooster's comb (Cristata group) or plumed (Plumosa group) like a feather, or short, narrow and barley-like (Spicata group).

How to Plant & Grow—Start cockscomb seeds indoors eight weeks prior to the last spring frost or directly in the garden after danger of frost. Move transplants into the garden once the soil and air are warm. Space small cultivars 6 to 8 inches apart and larger ones 12 to 15 inches apart.

Care & Problems—Poorly drained and wet weather can lead to root rot and leaf spot. Spray mite infested plants with a strong blast of water or insecticidal soap if needed. Occasionally deadhead for season-long bloom.

Bloom Color—Red, yellow, gold, orange, and pink

Peak Season—Summer through fall blooms

Mature Size (H x W)—6 to 30 in. x 6 to 18 in.

Water Needs—Drought tolerant once established.

COLEUS
Solenostemon scutellarioides

Why It's Special—This easy-to-grow annual provides season-long color in sun and shade gardens. It is grown for its colorful foliage in various shapes, sizes, and variegated patterns, not its flowers. Select minimal flowering and self-branching types for easier maintenance. The new warmer colors and sun-loving cultivars add to its appeal.

How to Plant and Grow—Purchase coleus as transplants or start from seeds and cuttings. Coleus is very frost sensitive, so wait until all danger of frost is passed to move hardened-off transplants outdoors. Coleus prefers moist soil with lots of organic matter. Space plants 10 to 12 inches apart.

Care and Problems—Mulch to keep the roots cool and moist. Remove flowers as soon as they appear to encourage fuller compact growth. And watch for slugs!

Bloom Color—Foliage combinations of green, chartreuse, yellow, buff, salmon, orange, red, purple, and brown

Peak Season—Season-long foliage

Mature Size (H x W)—6 to 24 in. x 12 in.

Water Needs—Maintain an evenly moist soil.

COSMOS

Cosmos species

Why It's Special—Drought tolerance, butterfly appeal, and suitability as cut flowers make cosmos popular. *Cosmos sulphureus* produces single and double yellow, orange, or orange-red flowers throughout summer. *Cosmos bipinnatus* are taller plants with finer-textured leaves and large single flowers of pink, white, red, or purple. Watch for volunteer seedlings. Enjoy where they sprout or transplant to a desired location.

How to Plant & Grow—Start seeds indoors four weeks before the last spring frost or directly outside. Plant seeds or hardened-off transplants in the garden after the last spring frost. Cosmos tolerate hot, dry conditions once established. Space plants 12 inches apart.

Care & Problems—Avoid overfertilizing, which can cause tall, leafy plants to fall over. Pinch back tall cultivars early in the season to promote fuller, sturdier plants. Watch for aphids, Japanese beetles, wilt, and aster yellows. Remove aster yellows-infected plants to reduce spread of this disease.

Bloom Color—Yellow, orange, red, white, pink, rose, and purple

Peak Season—Summer until frost

Mature Size (H x W)—12 to 72 in. x 12 to 24 in.

Water Needs—Cosmos is drought tolerant once established.

DUSTY MILLER

Senecio cineraria

Why It's Special—The silvery gray foliage of dusty miller provides a nice contrast in the flower garden and brightens the nighttime landscape. The leaves can be slightly lobed or deeply divided and lacy, depending on the cultivar. Use as an edging plant or foil for dark colored flowers.

How to Plant & Grow—Seeds should be started indoors about ten weeks before the last spring frost. Place hardened-off transplants outdoors after all danger of a hard frost has passed. Dusty miller prefers well-drained soil. It will tolerate light shade but not wet feet. Space the plants 8 to 10 inches apart.

Care & Problems—Trim back unruly plants to keep them full and compact. Clip off any flowering stems that form to keep the plant neat and tidy or leave them for the butterflies to enjoy. Allow frost-tolerant plants to stand and brighten the fall landscape. Some gardeners have managed to overwinter plants.

Bloom Color—Silvery white foliage

Peak Season—Season-long foliage

Mature Size (H x W)—6 to 15 in. x 6 to 15 in.

Water Needs—Drought tolerant once established.

FAN FLOWER

Scaevola aemula

Why It's Special—The uniquely shaped flowers and low-maintenance qualities have quickly increased the popularity of this annual. Allow this trailing beauty to spill over and soften the edge of a container or raised bed. Or use it as an annual groundcover weaving around and under other plants.

How to Plant & Grow—Fan flowers are sold as seed or as bedding plants. Start seeds indoors six to eight weeks before the last spring frost. Place hardened-off transplants in the garden after the danger of frost has passed. Grow in full to part sun and moist, well-drained soils. Use several plants in a container, or space 20 to 24 inches apart in the garden.

Care & Problems—Established fan flowers are heat, drought, and salt tolerant. These plants are basically pest free. Avoid poorly drained soils and overwatering that can lead to root rot and death.

Bloom Color—Blue, violet, white, or mauve

Peak Season—Summer long blooms

Mature Size (H x W)—Up to 8 in. x 36 in.

Water Needs—Drought tolerant once established.

FLOWERING TOBACCO
Nicotiana alata

Why It's Special—Include free-flowering nicotiana in containers and gardens for a season-long floral display. The star-shaped flowers with long throats are perfect blooms for attracting hummingbirds and butterflies. Many are fragrant in the evening. Flowering tobacco plants will reseed themselves in your garden.

How to Plant & Grow—Start seeds indoors about eight weeks before the last spring frost. Flowering tobacco transplants are also available. Move hardened-off transplants outdoors after all danger of frost is past. They prefer moist, well-drained soil but will tolerate an occasional dry spell. Space transplants 8 to 12 inches apart, depending on the cultivar.

Care & Problems—Once it is established, it can tolerate dry periods, but may appear wilted in the hot afternoon sun. An occasional deadheading will help keep the display fresh and full. Watch for Colorado potato beetles; handpicking is usually sufficient control.

Bloom Color—White, red, pink, lavender, green, and yellow

Peak Season—Summer until frost

Mature Size (H x W)—10 in. to 5 ft. x 6 to 24 in.

Water Needs—Keep soil evenly moist to slightly dry.

FUCHSIA
Fuchsia hybrid

Why It's Special—Fuchsias put on quite the show on a patio, porch, or shepherd's crook in that shady spot in the landscape. Mix with other shade plants and use the upright types for vertical interest in containers and the garden. Place one of these beauties near your hummingbird feeder to help attract these colorful flyers.

How to Plant & Grow—Purchase hanging baskets, planters, or small individual plants. Fuchsia can be started from cuttings and seeds. Move hardened-off plants outdoors after all danger of frost is past. Grow fuchsias in shady locations with moist soil. Avoid hot sun and windy locations. Spacing varies with variety.

Care & Problems—Remove faded flowers to keep the plants blooming all summer long. Fuchsias will stop flowering during hot weather and resume once the weather cools. Fuchsias can be overwintered indoors. They have no serious pests, but watch for and control aphids during hot, dry weather.

Bloom Color—Pink, red, purple, and white

Peak Season—Summer until frost

Mature Size (H x W)—8 to 36 in. x 12 to 24 in.

Water Needs—Keep soil evenly moist.

GERANIUM
Pelargonium x hortorum

Why It's Special—Showy appearance and easy care make geraniums a good choice for containers, flower beds, and mixed borders. The trailing geranium used in hanging baskets and window boxes is the ivy geranium (*Pelargonium peltatum*). This plant performs best in full sun and cool conditions.

How to Plant & Grow—Sow seeds twelve to sixteen weeks prior to the last spring frost. Or purchase plants from the garden center. Plant hardened-off transplants outdoors after all danger of frost is past. Geraniums prefer full sun with moist, well-drained soil. Space the plants 8 to 12 inches apart.

Care & Problems—Mulch the soil to keep roots cool and moist and the plants at peak performance. Deadhead to keep the plants blooming and looking their best. Watch for bacterial leaf spot, stem rot, and botrytis blight. Avoid these problems by purchasing disease-free plants and providing proper care.

Bloom Color—Red, pink, rose, violet, salmon, and white

Peak Season—Summer until frost

Mature Size (H x W)—12 to 20 in. x 12 in.

Water Needs—Keep soil evenly moist.

HELIOTROPE
Heliotropium arborescens

Why It's Special—The wonderful fragrance, and bold flowers, as well as the hummingbird and butterfly appeal, will make you want to add a few heliotrope to your containers or flower gardens. Place it near the patio, window, or entryway where its fragrance, beauty, and the colorful visitors it attracts can be enjoyed.

How to Plant & Grow—Start seeds indoors ten to twelve weeks before the last spring frost. Be patient; it takes three weeks for the seeds to germinate. Or buy plants from your local garden center. Move hardened-off transplants outdoors after the danger of frost. Grow in full to part sun in moist, well-drained soil. Space plants 12 inches apart in the garden.

Care & Problems—Mulch the soil to conserve moisture and suppress weeds. Heliotropes are fairly pest free. Monitor plants for mealybugs, spider mites, aphids, and whiteflies, and control as needed.

Bloom Color—Violet-blue, light blue, and white

Peak Season—Summer until frost

Mature Size (H x W)—12 to 18 in. x 12 to 15 in.

Water Needs—Soil should be kept evenly moist.

IMPATIENS
Impatiens walleriana

Why It's Special—Made for the shade, these easy-care annuals are free flowering and won't need deadheading. Use them in containers or for a sea of color in shady gardens. And try the new SunPatiens® types for sunny locations.

How to Plant & Grow—Purchase plants or start impatiens from seeds twelve weeks before the last spring frost. Move hardened-off transplants outdoors after danger of frost has passed and the soil and air have warmed. Grow in moist, organic soil spaced 8 to 12 inches apart.

Care & Problems—Mulch the soil to keep the roots cool and moist. The more water and fertilizer you provide, the bigger the plants grow. Leggy or tired plants can be pinched back. They are very sensitive to frost. Downy mildew has become a major problem. Do *not* plant impatiens in beds infested with this disease. Or, plant the mildew-resistant New Guinea impatiens.

Bloom Color—White, red, pink, orange, and purple

Peak Season—Summer until frost

Mature Size (H x W)—6 to 18 in. x 12 to 24 in.

Water Needs—Keep soil evenly moist.

JOSEPH'S COAT
Alternanthera species

Why It's Special—Add color to containers and flower beds with this annual. The colorful, sometimes variegated, foliage can be used as a focal point in containers, accent in the garden or *en masse* for greater impact.

How to Plant & Grow—Purchase plants at the garden center or order seeds from a garden or seed catalog. Start seeds indoors eight to ten weeks before the last spring frost. Move hardened-off transplants outdoors after the danger of frost has passed. Grow in full sun for best color or in light shade in hotter locations. Space plants 6 to 12 inches depending on cultivar size.

Care & Problems—It has no serious insect or disease problems. Pinch back leggy plants to encourage dense, compact growth. Plants can be sheared for a more formal look. Take cuttings in late summer to start new plants to enjoy indoors over winter.

Bloom Color—Solid or variegated foliage with green, purple, pink, yellow, orange, red, and brown

Peak Season—Spring through fall

Mature Size (H x W)—6 to 12 in. x 6 to 18 in.

Water Needs—Maintain evenly moist soil.

LANTANA
Lantana camara

Why It's Special—These heat- and drought-tolerant flowers add color to your flower beds and containers with their flowers and the hummingbirds and butterflies they attract. Enthusiastic gardeners can train individual plants into small trees. Use tree forms as a focal point or to dress up the patio, deck, or balcony.

How to Plant & Grow—Purchase lantana transplants from your local garden center. Plant hardened-off transplants outdoors when the soil is warm and danger of frost has passed. Grow lantana in full sun in well-drained soils. Space transplants 12 to 15 inches apart in the garden.

Care & Problems—Water new plantings often enough to keep the soil moist. Gradually lengthen the time between waterings. Once established, plants are very heat and drought tolerant. Overwatering and poorly drained soils can lead to root rot. Deadhead and remove any berries that form for better bloom.

Bloom Color—Red, peach, purple, pink, orange, white, yellow, and often bicolored

Peak Season—Summer to frost

Mature Size (H x W)—12 to 20 in. x 12 to 15 in.

Water Needs—This plant is drought tolerant once established.

LICORICE VINE
Helichrysum petiolare

Why It's Special—Include this vine in your container plantings, hanging baskets, or as a groundcover mixed with colorful annuals. The silvery foliage is a nice foil for dark flowers and provides contrast to the glossy green leaves of neighboring plants.

How to Plant & Grow—Seeds of certain cultivars are available and can be started indoors twelve to fourteen weeks before the last spring frost. Or purchase plants. Hardened-off transplants can be moved outdoors after the danger of frost has passed. Grow in full to part sun and well-drained soils. Place one or two plants in mixed containers and space those growing in-ground 12 inches apart.

Care & Problems—Established plants are heat and drought tolerant. Avoid overwatering and excess fertilization, which can lead to leggy growth and increase the risk of disease. An occasional caterpillar may feed on the leaves. But try to tolerate the damage—the adult butterfly is a real beauty you'll want in the garden.

Bloom Color—Silver, chartreuse. or variegated foliage

Peak Season—Season-long interest

Mature Size (H x W)—Up to 2 feet long

Water Needs—Drought tolerant once established.

LISIANTHUS
Eustoma grandiflorum

Why It's Special—Lisianthus is a delicate beauty that is both heat and drought tolerant. Add it to your containers, borders, and flower arrangements. Tuck a few in the perennial garden to fill in voids. The cut flowers last up to ten days in a vase.

How to Plant & Grow—Start seeds indoors in late December or early January. Or purchase transplants. Grow in full sun to partial shade in moist, well-drained soils. Space smaller cultivars 6 inches apart and larger cultivars 9 to 12 inches apart.

Care & Problems—Avoid overwatering, which can lead to root rot, and overhead watering, which can lead to leaf spot and botrytis blight. Stake tall varieties or plant with sturdy neighbors for needed support. Deadhead during wet weather to reduce the risk of botrytis blight.

Bloom Color—Bicolor flowers of white, pink, red, lavender to blue, and yellow

Peak Season—Summer until frost

Mature Size (H x W)—6 to 30 in. x 6 to 12 in.

Water Needs—Drought tolerant once established.

LOBELIA
Lobelia erinus

Why It's Special—Lobelia's delicate texture makes both the mounded and trailing types easy to blend with perennials and other annuals. Use it as an edger, in containers, or cascading over boulders and garden walls. Select heat-tolerant cultivars to extend their peak blooming power.

How to Plant & Grow—Buy transplants or start from seed ten to twelve weeks prior to the last spring frost. Plant hardened-off transplants outdoors after all danger of frost has passed. Lobelia prefers full sun, cool temperatures, and moist, well-drained soil. An east-facing location provides just that. Space plants about 6 inches apart.

Care & Problems—Lobelias often stop growing and flowering in hot weather. Continue to water as needed but stop fertilizing when plants heat stall. Lightly prune lobelias after the first flush of flowers to encourage new leaf and flower growth. Leggy plants can be pruned back halfway.

Bloom Color—White, blue, rose, and purple

Peak Season—Spring and fall

Mature Size (H x W)—4 to 8 in. x 6 to 18 in.

Water Needs—Keep soil evenly moist.

MADAGASCAR PERIWINKLE
Catharanthus roseus

Why It's Special—Madagascar periwinkle has the same neat, tidy, and mounded appearance as impatiens but thrives and flowers in much more difficult growing conditions. Plants continue to bloom despite heat, drought, dry shade, and pollution. The glossy green leaves provide an attractive background for the colorful flowers. Use as a flowering annual groundcover or container plant.

How to Plant & Grow—Purchase transplants or start seeds ten to twelve weeks prior to the last spring frost. Move hardened-off transplants outdoors after the last spring frost. Plants prefer moist well-drained soil but established plants can tolerate heat and drought—but not wet soils. Space plants 8 to 12 inches apart.

Care & Problems—Madagascar periwinkles require very little care to maintain their appearance. Plants will rot in poorly drained or waterlogged soils. Leaf spot disease and slugs may be problems during wet weather.

Bloom Color—White, pink, rose, red, and rose-purple

Peak Season—Summer to fall

Mature Size (H x W)—8 to 18 in. x 8 to 17 in.

Water Needs—Drought tolerant once established.

MARIGOLD
Tagetes species

Why It's Special—With very little care, marigolds will reward you with season-long blooms. The French marigold, *Tagetes patula* (6 to 18 inches tall) has single or double flowers up to 2 inches across. The heat-tolerant African marigold, *Tagetes erecta* (10 to 36 inches tall), has 2- to 5-inch flowers.

How to Plant & Grow—Purchase transplants or start seeds indoors about four weeks before the last spring frost. Plant hardened-off transplants outdoors or sow seeds directly in the garden after all danger of frost is past. Space 6 to 18 inches apart.

Care & Problems—Mulch the soil and avoid excess fertilization that can prevent flowering. Deadhead to encourage branching and continual blooms. French marigolds will stop flowering during hot weather (heat stall). Protect plants from rabbits and woodchucks. And watch for occasional problems with slugs, spider mites, aphids, and aster yellows disease.

Bloom Color—Yellow, orange, gold, bronze, and creamy white

Peak Season—Summer through fall

Mature Size (H x W)—6 to 36 in. x 6 to 15 in.

Water Needs—Marigolds are drought tolerant once established.

MONEYWORT
Lysimachia nummularia

Why It's Special—This plant is sometimes sold as a perennial, but it's best to grow it as an annual in containers to keep it from becoming invasive. Allow the round, bright green or chartreuse leaves to cascade over the edge of containers. Avoid using this as a groundcover in landscapes near natural wetlands and springs. The plants appear to spread by cuttings rather than seed to limit their invasive nature.

How to Plant & Grow—Plant seeds in early spring, purchase plants, or dig and use divisions from in-ground plantings for your containers. Moneywort prefers shade with moist to wet organic soil. It will tolerate sun to shade and wet well-drained soil. Space plants 15 to 18 inches apart.

Care & Problems—Check containers daily and water as needed. Minimal fertilization is needed. Moneywort sawfly can devour lots of the leaves in early summer. Handpick these worm-like insects when they're found or let healthy plants fend for themselves.

Bloom Color—Yellow

Peak Season—June blooms; foliage all season

Mature Size (H x W)—2 to 4 in. x spreading

Water Needs—Keep soil evenly moist.

MOSS ROSE
Portulaca grandiflora

Why It's Special—Moss rose (also called rose moss) is a great choice for hot, dry locations and busy gardeners. Use moss rose in containers, rock gardens, and flower beds that can be enjoyed during the day when the flowers are open.

How to Plant & Grow—Start moss rose seeds indoors six weeks before the last frost. Plant hardened-off transplants outdoors or sow seeds directly in the garden after the danger of frost is past. Plant moss rose in areas with full sun and well-drained soil. Space transplants 6 to 12 inches apart.

Care & Problems—Keep the roots of young transplants slightly moist. Once established, allow the top few inches of soil to dry slightly before watering. Avoid overwatering, which leads to root and stem rot problems. Minimal fertilization is needed. Once you have grown moss rose, you will be rewarded with seedlings the following season. These can be dug and moved to the preferred planting location.

Bloom Color—White, yellow, orange, red, rose, and lavender

Peak Season—Summer through fall blooms

Mature Size (H x W)—4 to 8 in. x 6 in.

Water Needs—Moss rose is drought tolerant once established.

NASTURTIUM
Tropaeolum majus

Why It's Special—Edible and beautiful, with hummingbird and butterfly appeal, this makes a nice addition to container plantings and gardens. Spice up salads and other dishes with nasturtium's leaves, flowers, and seeds. Plants can be mounded, semi-vining, or climbers.

How to Plant & Grow—Purchase plants or start seeds indoors four to six weeks before the last spring frost. Consider using biodegradable pots to reduce transplant shock. Move transplants outdoors or sow seeds directly in the garden after the last spring frost. Grow nasturtiums in full sun in a well-drained location. Plant nasturtiums 8 to 12 inches apart.

Care & Problems—The old saying, "be nasty to your nasturtiums," is true. Excess nitrogen results in lots of large leaves and no flowers, and overwatering can lead to disease problems. Plants may fail to flower in extreme heat. Watch for aphids, mites, cabbage worms, and thrips. Use organic controls if you plan on eating your nasturtiums.

Bloom Color—Yellow, orange, red, and white

Peak Season—Summer to frost

Mature Size (H x W)—12 in. x 12 to 14 in.

Water Needs—Keep soil slightly dry.

PANSY
Viola x wittrockiana

Why It's Special—Extend the growing season and your garden's butterfly appeal with spring and fall pansies. Plant cold-hardy cultivars in fall for added fall and spring enjoyment. Use them as a groundcover around spring-flowering bulbs to double your flower display and mask fading bulb foliage. Add a few of these edible flowers to salads and desserts.

How to Plant & Grow—Buy plants or start seeds indoors in January. Or plant seeds outdoors in summer for a fall display. Plant hardened-off transplants outdoors in spring or fall. Grow in a cool sunny location for best results. Space plants 6 inches apart.

Care & Problems—Select heat-tolerant varieties and mulch when trying to grow pansies through our hot summers. Though they're free flowering, deadheading pansies will maximum their blooms. Slugs and fungal leaf spots may be problems in wet weather.

Bloom Color—White, blue, purple, yellow, dark red, rose, apricot

Peak Season—Spring to early summer and fall

Mature Size (H x W)—4 to 8 in. x 9 to 12 in.

Water Needs—Keep soil evenly moist.

PENTAS
Pentas lanceolata

Why It's Special—Pentas are a favorite of hummingbirds, butterflies, and the gardeners that have grown them. Include these long-blooming annuals in containers, mix a couple in with your perennials, and add a few to your garden bouquets. Place a few within view so you can enjoy their winged visitors.

How to Plant & Grow—Purchase plants or order seeds from garden catalogs and start your own. Sow seeds indoors about eight to ten weeks before the last spring frost. Grow pentas in full sun with moist, well-drained soils for best results. Space plants 10 to 12 inches apart.

Care & Problems—Keep the soil around new transplants slightly moist. Check containers daily, and water thoroughly as needed. These annuals will flower all summer long with little or no deadheading. Though generally pest free, you may have problems with mites and aphids during hot dry seasons.

Bloom Color—White, pink, rose, or lilac flowers

Peak Season—Summer until frost

Mature Size (H x W)—Up to 18 in. x up to 18 in.

Water Needs—Evenly moist soil is best.

PETUNIA
Petunia hybrids

Why It's Special—Include petunias for added color and fragrance as well as hummingbird and butterfly appeal. Select cultivars that require minimal deadheading and maximum beauty. And try the closely related *Calibrachoa*. It is compact, free flowering, and mixes well with other annuals.

How to Plant & Grow—Purchase plants or start petunias from seeds indoors ten weeks prior to the last spring frost. Place hardened-off transplants outdoors after the danger of frost is past. Grow petunias in well-drained soil. Plant 6 to 24 inches apart based upon their growth habit.

Care & Problems—Remove faded flowers and clip back leggy stems as needed for the cultivar you selected. Avoid overhead watering that increases the risk of botrytis blight and other diseases. Remove infested flowers and leaves as they appear. Avoid overwatering and waterlogged soils to prevent stem rot.

Bloom Color—Pink, red, violet, lavender, yellow, salmon, and white

Peak Season—Spring through fall

Mature Size (H x W)—6 to 18 in. x 6 to 36 in.

Water Needs—Evenly moist to slightly dry is ideal.

SALVIA
Salvia splendens

Why It's Special—Intense colors and large flower spikes make salvia a standout in the landscape. Both hummingbirds and butterflies feed on the nectar in the flowers and goldfinches enjoy the seeds. Its close relative mealycup sage, *Salvia farinacea*, has narrower flower spikes that are long-lasting and require little deadheading.

How to Plant & Grow—Purchase plants or start salvia from seeds indoors about six to eight weeks before the last spring frost. Plant hardened-off transplants outdoors after all danger of frost is past. Light shade and cooler temperatures intensifies the flower color without compromising the vigor. Space 8 to 12 inches apart.

Care & Problems—Mulch the soil around salvias to keep the roots cool and moist. Deadhead to encourage branching and continual blooming. Plant in full sun and properly space to reduce the risk of downy and powdery mildews. Avoid overhead watering and remove infected plant parts to reduce the spread of these diseases.

Bloom Color—Red, salmon, pink, blue, lavender, and white

Peak Season—Summer until frost

Mature Size (H x W)—8 to 30 in. x 8 to 12 in.

Water Needs—Evenly moist soil is best.

SNAPDRAGON
Antirrhinum majus

Why It's Special—Snapdragons are great additions to spring and fall gardens. These stately plants are topped with spikes of colorful flowers. Snapdragons are impressive outdoors in the garden or inside in a flower vase. Select heat-tolerant varieties for reliable summer bloom.

How to Plant & Grow—Purchase plants or start snapdragons from seeds indoors about ten weeks before the last spring frost. Or, direct-seed outdoors in the spring as soon as the soil is workable. Hardened-off transplants will tolerate light frost but should be protected from hard freezes. Space 6 to 12 inches apart.

Care & Problems—Mulch to help keep the roots cool and moist and encourage summer bloom. Plants may stop blooming in hot weather. Deadhead regularly and stake taller cultivars. Watch for volunteer seedlings and plants that survive the winter. Aphids, mites, and rust may cause problems.

Bloom Color—White, yellow, bronze, purple, pink, and red

Peak Season—Spring and fall

Mature Size (H x W)—6 to 48 in. x 6 to 24 in.

Water Needs—Keep soil evenly moist.

SPIKE
Cordyline species

Why It's Special—Spike plants have long been used as the "thriller" (vertical accent) in container gardens. And if you are tired of spike, select one of the many new colorful cultivars for variety. Enthusiastic gardeners can overwinter plants as houseplants indoors.

How to Plant & Grow—Plant spikes outdoors after all danger of frost is past. Container gardens can be moved indoors when frost threatens. Spikes prefer full to partial sun and moist, well-drained soil. Avoid wet soil and heavy shade where the plants are more likely to develop root rot and leaf spot disease. Space spikes 12 to 15 inches apart when planted in the garden.

Care & Problems—Spikes are very low-maintenance plants and fairly pestfree. They will tolerate temperatures in the 40s. Avoid excess moisture that can lead to root rot and leaf spot. Brown leaf tips occur in very dry soil and from the fluoride in the water. Keep soil slightly moist to correct the problem.

Bloom Color—Green or variegated foliage

Peak Season—Spring until frost

Mature Size (H x W)—24 in. x 15 in.

Water Needs—Evenly moist soil is best.

SWEET POTATO VINE
Ipomoea batatas cultivars

Why It's Special—Their heart-shaped or lobed foliage makes a nice trailing plant for containers and groundcovers in the annual garden. These vigorous growers are a cultivar of the edible sweet potato and a cousin to the morning glory.

How to Plant & Grow—Purchase plants, harden-off, and move them into the garden after the danger of frost has past. Grow sweet potato vines in full or part sun with moist, well-drained soil. One sweet potato vine per container is usually enough. Space plants 24 inches apart when grown in the garden.

Care & Problems—Check planters daily and water thoroughly whenever the top few inches of soil starts to dry. Sweet potato vines are low maintenance and relatively pest free. Some gardeners overwinter the plants as cuttings or by storing the tuberous root in a cool dark location.

Bloom Color—Lime green, purple, or variegated green, cream, and pink foliage

Peak Season—Colorful foliage all season

Mature Size (H x W)—Up to 3 ft. in length

Water Needs—Evenly moist soil is best.

SUNFLOWER
Helianthus annuus

Why It's Special—The large flowers add color to the garden, and the seeds attract hungry birds, squirrels, and children. Add a bit of variety with some of the newer introductions. You'll find sunflowers of various flower sizes, colors, and plant heights.

How to Plant & Grow—Start sunflowers from seeds outside after all danger of frost is past. Plant the seeds 6 inches apart and ½ inch deep. Thin seedlings to 18 to 24 inches between plants. Sunflowers can also be started indoors four to six weeks before the last spring frost. Grow sunflowers in well-drained soil spaced at least 24 inches apart.

Care & Problems—Proper spacing will help reduce problems with leaf spot and powdery mildew. Mask the problem by growing slightly shorter plants in front of diseased leaves. Aphids may cause minor damage. Cover seedheads with cheesecloth or netting to protect the harvest from squirrels and birds.

Bloom Color—Yellow, white, and bronze with a yellow, brown, purple, or crimson center

Peak Season—Midsummer to frost

Mature Size (H x W)—15 in. to 15 ft. x 12 to 24 in.

Water Needs—Drought tolerant once established.

VERBENA
Verbena hybrids

Why It's Special—With all the cultivars and related species available, there is bound to be a verbena that is right for your garden. There are upright and spreading types. The flowers come in a variety of colors and are quite showy. There are several related annual, biennial, and perennial verbenas.

How to Plant & Grow—Buy plants or start verbena seeds indoors twelve weeks prior to the last spring frost. Chill the seeds for seven days before seeding. Plant hardened-off transplants outdoors after the last spring frost. Grow verbena in well-drained soil. Space 12 to 18 inches apart.

Care & Problems—Some cultivars will stop blooming during hot, dry spells. Mulch the soil to keep the roots cool and moist. Remove faded flowers to encourage branching and continual blooms. Proper spacing and a full sun location will help reduce the risk of powdery mildew.

Bloom Color—White, lavender, purple, blue, pink, red, and apricot

Peak Season—Summer till frost

Mature Size (H x W)—Up to 15 in. x up to 20 in.

Water Needs—Verbena needs evenly moist to slightly dry soil.

ZINNIA
Zinnia elegans

Why It's Special—This eye-catching annual, in the garden or flower vase, is easy to start from seed indoors or right in the garden. Their heat and drought tolerance and hummingbird and butterfly appeal add to their value.

How to Plant & Grow—Buy plants or start zinnias from seeds indoors about six weeks before the last spring frost. Direct seed zinnias or plant hardened-off transplants in the garden after the last spring frost. Grow in well-drained soil. Space small cultivars 6 to 12 inches apart.

Care & Problems—Select leaf spot- and mildew-resistant cultivars whenever possible. Proper plant selection, siting, and spacing are critical to the health and appearance of zinnias. Avoid overhead watering to minimize the risk of disease and excess nitrogen fertilizer that can inhibit flowering. Remove faded flowers to encourage branching and continual blooms.

Bloom Color—White, yellow, green, red, orange, apricot, rose, red, and violet

Peak Season—Summer to frost

Mature Size (H x W)—6 to 36 in. x 18 to 24 in.

Water Needs—Zinnia is drought tolerant once established.

PLANTING SEEDS INDOORS

Seeds can be started in one of two ways. Sow them in a flat and then transplant young seedlings into individual containers. Or, sow one to two seeds directly into the individual pots. To start seeds:

1. Fill flats or containers with a sterile starter mix. Moisten the mixture prior to seeding. Sprinkle fine seeds on the soil surface and water them in. Larger seeds need to be planted a little deeper. Use a chopstick, pencil, or similar item to dig a shallow furrow or punch a planting hole into the mix. Plant seeds at a depth that is about twice their diameter.

2. Sprinkle seeds in the furrow or drop one or two in each hole. Cover with soil and water in with a fine mist. Avoid a strong stream of water that can dislodge the seeds.

3. Keep the soil warm and moist to ensure germination. Use commercially available heating cables or place the flats in a warm location (on top of refrigerators, heating ducts, or other warm places). Cover the containers with a sheet of plastic to help conserve moisture. Check daily and water often enough to keep the soil surface moist, but not wet.

4. Remove the plastic and move the container into the light as soon as the seedlings appear. Place lights 6 inches above the plants and keep them on for 16 hours a day. Lighting them longer will not help the plants, but will needlessly increase your electric bill.

5. Transplant seedlings growing in flats as soon as they form two sets of leaves (seed leaves and true leaves). The seed leaves are nondescript, while the true leaves look like the particular plant's leaves.

OVERWINTERING HIBISCUS, BOUGAINVILLEA, OLEANDER, AND OTHER TROPICALS INDOORS

1. Start by bringing the tropicals into the garage, screened-in porch, or indoor room away from your houseplants. Keep them isolated for several weeks. Check for insects and use insecticidal soap to treat any mites and aphids you discover. Handpick and destroy larger caterpillars, slugs, earwigs, and beetles.

2. Move the plants indoors to a warm, sunny location. A south-facing window, Florida room, or atrium would work fine. Or add an artificial light to improve the light conditions found in most of our homes.

3. Continue to water thoroughly whenever the top few inches of soil start to dry. Do not fertilize until the plant adjusts to its new location and shows signs of growth.

4. Prune only enough to fit the plant into its winter location. Do not worry about the falling leaves. The plant will replace the fallen leaves as soon as it adjusts to its new location.

5. Continue to watch for pests and water as needed. Enjoy the added greenery and occasional flowers.

6. Prune overgrown plants in late February to avoid delaying summer flowering.

JANUARY

- The catalogs are pouring in and the wish list keeps growing. Develop a plan for this season's garden before placing your order. Review your garden journal and pictures of last year's landscape. Plan to expand or reduce planting space based on last year's experience.

- Create a seeding chart for recording plant names, starting dates, and other important information. Use your garden journal or other notebook to record and save this valuable information for next year.

- Start pansies this month to have large transplants ready for your early spring garden. Check the back of the seed packet for best date to start seeds in your location.

- Adjust your watering schedule to match the needs of coleus, geraniums, fuchsias, and other annuals overwintered as houseplants. The shorter days, less intense sunlight, and low humidity of winter changes the plants' needs. Water the soil thoroughly, and wait until the soil is slightly dry before watering again.

FEBRUARY

- Check the planting dates on the seed packets and in catalogs. Sow seeds according to the label directions. February is the time to start many of the spring-blooming and long-season annuals.

- Use pelleted (coated) petunia and begonia seeds to make the planting of these small seeds easier. Or mix these and other small seeds with sand. This helps you spread the seeds more evenly over the soil surface.

- Check seedlings every day. Water thoroughly and often enough to keep the soil slightly moist. Fertilize seedlings every other week with a dilute solution of any complete water-soluble fertilizer. Adjust lights over seedlings so they are about 6 inches above the tops of the young plants.

- Monitor seedlings for sudden wilting and rotted stems caused by damping off. This fungus disease causes young seedlings to collapse. Remove infected plants as soon as they are discovered. Drench the soil with a fungicide labeled for this use. Prevent this disease by using a sterile starter mix and clean containers.

MARCH

- Pinch back indoor plantings to keep them compact. Remove the stem tip or a portion of the stem just above a healthy leaf. Start new plants from stem and leaf pieces that are 4 to 6 inches long. Remove the lowest set of leaves and place cuttings in moist vermiculite, perlite, or a well-drained potting mix. Roots should form in one to two weeks. Transplant rooted cuttings into a small container of potting mix.

- Start fertilizing recently potted annuals when new growth appears. Use a dilute solution of any flowering houseplant fertilizer on these and other annual plants.

- Get a jump on the growing season by using cold frames and row covers. Both trap heat around the plants. The row cover fabrics are loosely draped over the plants, anchored around the edges, and allow air, water, and light through to the plants. Both methods allow you to move plants outdoors earlier in spring. Use them to harden off indoor-grown seedlings or to start annuals from seed.

APRIL

- The changeable weather is hard on gardens and anxious gardeners. Make sure both the air and soil are warm before planting. Only the seeds of hardy plants can tolerate the cold soil.

- Prepare annual gardens for planting when the soil is moist but not too wet. Grab a handful of soil and gently squeeze it into a ball. Lightly tap the soil ball. If it breaks into smaller pieces, it is ready to work. If it stays in a wet ball, the soil is too wet to work. Wait a few days and try again.

- Plant hardened-off hardy annuals, such as pansies, dusty miller, and snapdragons, outdoors as the weather and soil temperatures allow. Keep mulch or row covers handy to protect transplants from unexpected drops in temperature.

- Remove weeds as soon as they appear. Pull or lightly hoe annual weeds. Consider treating badly infested gardens with a total vegetation killer prior to planting. Be sure to read and follow all label directions carefully.

MAY

- Continue planting hardy annuals. Plant half-hardy annuals in the garden after the danger of a hard frost has passed. Wait until both the air and the soil are warm to plant tender annuals.

- Thin or transplant annuals directly seeded into the garden. Leave the healthiest seedlings properly spaced in their permanent garden location. Move extra transplants to other planting beds and gardens with extra planting space.

- Place stakes next to tall annuals that need staking. Early stake placement prevents root and plant damage caused by staking established annuals that are already flopping over.

- Protect new plantings from cutworm damage. These insects chew through the stems of young transplants. They are most common in planting beds recently converted from lawn. Use cutworm collars made of cardboard or plastic. Recycle paper towel and toilet paper holders, plastic margarine tubs, or yogurt containers. Remove the bottom of the plastic containers and cut the paper rolls into 3- to 4-inch lengths. Slice the containers down the sides. Place collars around the new transplants and sink the bottoms several inches into the soil.

- Protect hanging baskets from birds and chipmunks. Cover baskets with bird netting. Secure the netting above and below the container. Do this at the first signs of a problem. Quick action will encourage the birds and animals to go elsewhere. Remove netting once wildlife is no longer a threat.

JUNE

- Mulch gardens with pine needles, shredded leaves, or other organic material. A thin layer (1 to 2 inches) of mulch helps conserve moisture, moderate soil temperature, and reduce weeds.

- Finish staking tall annuals that need a little added support. Stake early in the season to reduce the risk of damaging taller, more established plants.

- Remove flowers—deadhead—as they fade. Pinch or cut the flowering stem back to the first set of leaves or flower buds. Deadhead begonia and ageraturm during wet weather to reduce the risk of disease. Remove coleus flowers as they form. Ageratums, cleomes, gomphrenas, impatiens, narrow-leaf zinnias, New Guinea impatiens, wax begonias, and pentas are self-cleaning. These drop their dead blooms and do not need deadheading.

JULY

- There is still time to plant. Stop by your favorite garden center. Many offer late-season transplants for replacements or late additions. You might even find a bargain or two worth adding to the garden.

- Harvest flowers for fresh indoor enjoyment. Cut the flowers early in the morning for the best quality. Recut the stems just prior to placing the flowers in the vase. Wait until midday to harvest flowers for drying. Pick flowers at their peak. Bundle and hang in a dry, dark location to dry.

- Watch for Japanese beetles. These small, shiny beetles eat holes in plant leaves. Lacy leaves are often the first clue that the beetles are present. Remove and destroy the beetles. Insecticides can be used, but they are harmful to other beneficial insects. Do not use commercially available traps. These tend to bring more Japanese beetles into your garden.

- Check plantings for signs of leafhoppers. These wedge-shaped insects hop off the plant when disturbed. Their feeding can cause stunting and tip burn on the leaves. These insects also carry the aster yellow disease that causes a sudden wilting, yellowing, and death of susceptible plants. Prevent the spread of this disease by controlling the leafhoppers.

- Watch for heat stall in the garden. Purple alyssum, lobelia, snapdragons, garden pinks, and French marigolds are a few annuals that stop flowering during extremely hot weather. Continue to water as needed and do not fertilize. These plants will start flowering once the weather cools. If this is a yearly problem, find a cooler location for these plants. Next year, replace them with zinnia, gazania, moss rose, and other more heat-tolerant plants.

AUGUST

- The heat usually continues and often peaks this month. Watch for and manage heat stall as described in July. Cut back lobelia and heat-stressed alyssum. Cut plants back halfway, continue to water, and wait for the weather to cool.

- Check for powdery mildew. This fungal disease looks as if someone has sprinkled baby powder on the leaves. Make a note in your journal to use mildew-resistant plants and to correct growing conditions next year. Proper spacing for improved air circulation and sufficient sunlight will help reduce the risk of this disease.

- Continue pulling weeds before they set seed. One plant can leave behind hundreds of seeds for next season. Spend a little time pulling weeds now and save yourself a lot of time next year.

- It is never too soon to start preparing for winter. Start taking cuttings from annuals you want to overwinter indoors. Your garden plants are healthier and will root faster now than they will later in the season. See March for details.

IMPATIENS

SEPTEMBER

- Replace weatherworn annuals with fall bedding plants. Purchase pansies, flowering kale, and other cool-weather annuals to spruce up the garden for fall. You may have to wait until late August or early September when transplants are available.

- Try planting Icicle, Sub-Zero, Cool Wave, and other cold-hardy pansies. Plant them now for two seasons of enjoyment. These will bloom in fall, survive the winter, and provide another floral display in spring. Plant them in bulb gardens as groundcover around tulips, daffodils, and hyacinths. Their colorful flowers make a nice addition to blooming bulbs and help mask the declining foliage.

- Get out the row covers, blankets, and other frost protection. Protect the plants from the first frosty days of fall, and then you often have an additional week or two of warm weather. Those few extra days of flowers mean a lot when the snow begins to fall.

- Move hibiscus, other tropicals, and annuals overwintering inside to their indoor locations. These plants need bright light for the winter. Place them in a south-facing window or under artificial light for best results. Water thoroughly as needed.

- Remove all diseased and insect-infested plant material during fall cleanup. This reduces the potential for problems next season.

OCTOBER

- Take one last look at the garden. Make your final evaluations, being sure to include both successes and failures. Note frost tolerant plants to include next year and frost sensitive plants that leave a void in the garden after the first frost. Write down all those new plants and great ideas you want to try next season.

- Nature is busy planting your garden for next year. Flowering tobacco, cosmos, alyssum, snapdragons, and cleome are a few of the annuals that may reseed in the garden. Most are lost to fall cleanup and soil preparation. Pull out plants, but do not cultivate the soil. Sprinkle any remaining seeds over the soil surface. Next spring, wait for the surprise. You may want to turn only a few small spaces over to nature and save the rest of your seeds for spring planting.

- Shred fallen leaves with your mower and work them into the top 6 to 12 inches of garden soil. The leaf pieces decompose over the winter, improving the drainage of heavy clay soils and the water-holding capacity of sandy soils.

- Check on geraniums and other annuals in dormant storage. Move plants to a cooler, darker location if they begin to grow. If growth continues, pot them up and move them to a sunny window or under artificial lights.

NOVEMBER

- Store leftover seeds in their original packets. These contain all the plant and planting information you need. Store these in an airtight container in the refrigerator. The consistent storage conditions help preserve the seeds' viability.

- Indoor plants, including annuals grown indoors, need very little fertilizer. Use a dilute solution of flowering houseplant fertilizer if plants are actively growing and showing signs of nutrient deficiency. Otherwise, wait until plants adjust to their new location and begin to grow.

- Monitor and manage whiteflies, aphids, mites, and any other insects that may have moved indoors on the plants. These pests suck out plant juices, causing the leaves to yellow and eventually brown.

DECEMBER

- Garden planning often gets lost in the chaos of the holiday preparations. Take advantage of the coming holidays to extend your garden season and share it with others. Frame your best garden and flower photos and give them as gifts to friends and relatives. Use dried flowers from your garden to decorate gift packages and cards. A bouquet of dried flowers makes a great gift for any housebound person—gardener or not.

- Plants are still struggling to adjust to their indoor location. The poor light and low humidity result in poor growth. Wait until plants start to grow before adding any fertilizer. Apply a dilute solution of any flowering houseplant fertilizer to plants that are actively growing and showing signs of nutrient deficiencies.

- Fungus gnats are small insects that are often found flitting across the room. They often move in with overwintering plants or arrive on holiday plants. They do not hurt the plants; they just annoy us. These insects feed on the organic matter in the soil, such as dead plant roots and peat moss. Keep the soil slightly drier than normal to reduce their populations.

PANSIES

BULBS
for the Midwest

After surviving the cold and snow of a Midwest winter, the gardening season never seems long enough. Extend your garden's bloom time by incorporating spring-flowering bulbs into your landscape. But don't stop there. Try including some of the hardy and nonhardy summer- and fall-blooming bulbs. They can add color and interest to your annual, perennial, and container gardens.

Jumpstart your spring garden with a few of the very early blooming minor bulbs. Snowdrops (*Galanthus nivalis*) and winter aconite (*Eranthis hyemalis*) are shade tolerant and naturalize readily. The winter aconite is first to bloom. It is 3 to 4 inches tall with yellow, cup-shaped flowers. The snowdrops appear next with their pure white flowers on 6-inch plants. Glory-of-the-snow (*Chionodoxa luciliae*) will appear right before Siberian squill. The star-shaped flowers are bright blue with a white center. These early bloomers can tolerate the cold temperatures we seem to get each spring after our early spring plants start blooming. Though small in stature, these little beauties bring great hope of warmer weather to come.

For the purposes of this book, I am using the term "bulb" to include plants grown from true bulbs, rhizomes, corms, tubers, and tuberous roots. They may be hardy or nonhardy. Hardy bulbs can be left in the ground year-round. Nonhardy, sometimes called tropical, bulbs are planted outdoors each spring. You can remove them from the ground and store them indoors over the winter. The trick is finding storage areas cool enough to keep the bulbs dormant.

SELECTING AND PLANTING BULBS

Most of us think about adding bulbs to the garden with the first big daffodil display in the spring. Unfortunately, we usually forget about planting them until the next spring when the daffodils are again in bloom. Luckily, many mail-order companies have started sending out their bulb catalogs in the spring. It's an easy way to order the bulbs, while you are inspired by the spring bloom, and have them delivered in the fall in time for planting. Watch for other bulb catalogs later in the season and stop by the garden centers as soon as the bulbs go on display for the greatest selection. Select firm, blemish-free bulbs. Avoid those with nicks, cuts, or soft areas. Store bulbs in a cool, dark place until it is time to plant. Bulbs should be stored in perforated plastic or mesh bags. Do not store them in closed plastic bags where they can rot.

PLANTING AND CARE

Hardy Bulbs: Most bulbs prefer moist, well-drained soil during their growing season and a bit drier soil when dormant in summer. Work several inches of peat moss, compost, or other organic matter into the top 12 inches of soil before planting. Organic matter helps improve the drainage in heavy clay soil and increases the water-holding capacity of sandy soil. Fertilize bulb plantings according to soil test recommendations. In general, bulbs receive enough nutrients from your regular garden fertilization program. Most garden soils do not need phosphorus, so skip the bonemeal and super phosphate. Plus bonemeal tends to attract rodents that like to feast on our bulbs. Instead, use a bulb fertilizer or a low-nitrogen slow-release fertilizer at the time of planting if nutrients are needed. These provide enough nutrients for several years.

Plant most hardy bulbs in the fall when day and night temperatures start to be consistently cool and soil temperatures drop below 60 degrees. You can plant bulbs until the ground freezes. Though this is not the best practice but many procrastinators and busy gardeners have had to chip through the frozen soil to plant a few remaining bulbs. One gardener coined the manhole cover planting technique. He would outline the planting hole by picking through the frozen soil surface. Then, he'd pry the frozen soil off just like lifting a manhole cover. He planted the bulbs in the unfrozen soil below. Next he watered them in and then put the lid back on. He found the squirrels and chipmunks didn't bother them. Not your best option—but it is a good back-up plan.

In general, bulbs should be planted at a depth two or three times the vertical height of the bulb. Space them at least three to four times the width of the bulb apart. Water the newly planted bulbs. Avoid planting bulbs near your home's foundation, especially the south side, near a dryer vent, or close to other artificial heat sources. Bulbs planted in these spots tend to sprout early and are subject to cold damage.

Most Midwest gardeners have experienced the problem of a "premature spring." Every January or February, we get a week of warm weather, and bulbs start peeking through the ground just in time for the next cold wave. Prevent this by using winter mulch. Cover the ground with evergreen branches, weed-free straw, or marsh hay after the soil lightly freezes. Branches from discarded Christmas trees work great.

Remove the mulch when the air temperature hovers just above freezing or bulb growth appears. You can add, if needed, a low-nitrogen fertilizer to established bulb gardens in the early spring as the leaves appear. Don't forget to water if we have a dry spring. Remove faded flowers but

Roots will grow out of the basal plate at the bottom of bulbs. Make sure this basal plate is down when you plant the bulb or corm.

leave the leaves intact so they can produce the needed energy for the plants to return and flower next year. If you need to move existing bulbs, mark their location for a fall transplant. The next best time is as the leaves start to fade, though every gardener has broken the rules and still had some success. I have moved daffodils in full bloom and they survived and flowered the next year.

Nonhardy Bulbs: Tuberous begonias, cannas, and other nonhardy bulbs require a bit different care. These tender beauties cannot survive our cold winters, and our growing season is often too short to get the maximum bloom time. Garden centers carry a few of these bulbs in early spring. Check out bulb catalogs for a wider selection. Start most of these bulbs indoors in mid-March for earlier bloom outdoors. Gladiolas are the exception— plant these directly outdoors. Start the others indoors in a flat filled with half peat moss mixed with half vermiculite or perlite. Keep the planting mix warm, usually around 70 degrees Fahrenheit, and moist. Move to a sunny location or under artificial lights as soon as the bulbs begin to sprout. Once they have a few leaves, move the plants to a larger container or hanging basket. Water thoroughly and often enough to keep the soil slightly moist, about the consistency of a damp sponge. Fertilize with a diluted solution of a flowering plant fertilizer.

Start hardening off transplants about two weeks before moving the plants outdoors. Stop fertilizing, allow the soil to go a bit drier, and gradually expose them to the sunlight. Move hardened-off plants to their outdoor growing location after the danger of frost has past.

Treat these nonhardy plants more like annuals by keeping the soil slightly moist and fertilizing with a slow-release fertilizer at planting. This way every time you water you are fertilizing. No mixing or mess, and it doesn't get continually get put off to a future watering. Or use a fast release fertilizer as directed throughout the first half of the season. Dig the bulbs after a light frost kills the tops. Carefully lift the bulbs, remove the loose soil and allow them to dry (cure). Gently brush, don't scrub, off remaining soil, cut back foliage, and move them into storage. Pack bulbs in sand, peat moss, or vermiculite in a flat, box, or other container. See specific recommendations under the individual bulbs. Be sure to label the bulb, cultivar, and its color. This will make planting much easier and less of a surprise next season.

Move bulbs to a cool dark place for the winter. Look for a corner far from the furnace, a root cellar if you are lucky, or other location where the temperatures stay close to 50 degrees Fahrenheit. Many gardeners use a spare refrigerator to store their nonhardy bulbs. Set the thermostat to the desired temperature. Check stored bulbs monthly. Remove any that are showing sign of rot. Move sprouted bulbs to a cooler location. If growth continues, pot them up, move to a sunny window or under artificial light, and grow as a houseplant until they can be moved outdoors.

Caladiums and tuberous begonias can be brought indoors and grown like houseplants. Bring them indoors before the first fall frost. Isolate them from your houseplants for several weeks. Monitor and control any insects you find before adding them to your indoor garden. Harden off in spring before moving them back outdoors.

MANAGING ANIMAL PESTS

Each fall it seems like the squirrels and chipmunks dig bulbs faster than you can plant. Come spring the rabbits and deer eat the flowers on whatever the other animals left behind. Don't give up. The battle won't be easy, but the beauty these bulbs provide to the landscape make the battle worth the effort. Chicago Botanic Garden recommends mixing small pieces of lava rock with bulbs at planting. They find this helps discourage squirrels and other rodents. Or sprinkle cayenne pepper on the bulbs at planting. Some gardeners swear by these repellents while others have not had success.

Another option is to cover bulb plantings with chicken wire. Dig the planting hole to the proper depth. Cover the bulbs with soil. Then lay chicken wire over the bulbs bending it down around the sides of the planting. Finish covering the bulbs. The chicken wire creates a barrier that discourages the rodents from digging. In spring, the bulbs sprout and grow through the chicken wire.

Once the bulbs sprout (come on—be positive!), you can try commercial and homemade repellents, scare tactics, and barriers to protect your bulbs. The key to success with repellents is to apply it before the animals start feeding and reapply throughout the blooming season. A variety of scare tactics such as clanging pans, motion sensitive sprinklers, and white balloons may also keep these critters under control. If you live in the city your wildlife pests will not easily be scared by human smell and sounds.

Fencing is probably the most effective but usually least desirable method. Most gardeners do not want to view their garden through rabbit or deer fence. But that may be better than having no flowers to see at all. Circle the garden with a four-foot fence stretched tight to the ground to keep out rabbits. A five-foot deer fence around small gardens has been found to keep deer at bay.

If all this sounds like too much work, select bulbs that animals do not eat. Hyacinths, daffodils, allium, fritillaria, snowflake (*Leucojum*), camassia, and Spanish bluebells (*Hyacinthoides*) are larger bulbs that the animals seem to ignore. Include some animal-resistant minor bulbs such as grape hyacinths, squills, winter aconite (*Eranthis*), snowdrop (*Galanthus*), autumn crocus (*Colchicum*), glory-of-the-snow (*Chionodoxa*), and *Crocus tommasinianus*, which is squirrel resistant. Not a bad list and the many newer, more unique cultivars will allow you to add plenty of variety to your garden when using these.

Now, select a few hardy and tender bulbs to help you increase your garden's season-long beauty.

ALLIUM
Allium species

Why It's Special—Create season-long beauty with this group of bulbs. Whether large or small, allium's round flowers are great additions to the garden and fresh or dried flower arrangements. Alliums help bring in the birds, bees, and butterflies, but are usually passed over by the rabbits and deer.

How to Plant & Grow—Plant allium bulbs in fall. Most prefer full sun to light shade and well-drained soil. Many are drought tolerant. Plant the bulbs at a depth of 2 to 3 times their diameter, but no deeper than 6 inches in heavy soils. Spacing varies with the species.

Care & Problems—Winter mulching will help more tender alliums make it through northern winters and reduce the risk of early sprouting. Mask frost-damaged foliage common on early bloomers with other plants. Bulb rot is a common problem in cool, damp soil.

Hardiness—Varies with species

Bloom Color—White, purple, blue, pink, or yellow

Peak Season—Early, mid-, or late summer

Mature Size (H x W)—6 to 60 in. x 6 to 15 in.

Water Needs—Evenly moist to slightly dry soil is best.

CALADIUM
Caladium bicolor

Why It's Special—The colorful leaves of caladium can add life to shade and indoor gardens. The fancy-leaved caladiums have large colorful leaves and are the most popular. The narrow lance-leaved types are usually dwarf and more sun tolerant.

How to Plant & Grow—Caladiums can be started from tubers indoors in mid-March for an earlier display in the garden. Plant the caladium tuber knobby side up directly in the garden. Or, move hardened-off transplants outdoors once soil has warmed and all danger of frost has passed.

Care & Problems—Caladiums are basically pest-free. Keep the soil moist and mulch to reduce the risk of scorch when growing in full sun or hot weather. Move plants indoors and grow as a houseplant. Or dig them up after the first light frost, cure (dry), and store.

Hardiness—Overwinter indoors

Bloom Color—Red, pink, white, and green foliage

Peak Season—Spring until frost

Mature Size (H x W)—1 to 2 ft. x 12 to 24 in.

Water Needs—Keep soil evenly moist.

CALLA LILY
Zantedeschia aethiopica

Why It's Special— Calla lilies are a favorite cut flower and garden plant. The bright flowers and often spotted foliage brighten shady locations. Grow callas in a container, flower garden, or in and near water.

How to Plant & Grow—Plant rhizomes indoors in mid-March for an earlier outdoor flower display. In the garden, plant rhizomes 4 inches deep and 18 inches apart once the soil has warmed. Move hardened-off transplants outdoors after the danger of frost has passed. Calla lilies prefer moist, organic soil and will tolerate sun if the soil is kept moist.

Care & Problems—Remove faded flowers for a tidier appearance. Leaf spot fungal disease may be a problem in wet years. Remove infected leaves to control this problem. Dig up calla rhizomes in the fall after the first light frost, cure, and store.

Hardiness—Overwinter indoors

Bloom Color—White, yellow, orange, and red

Peak Season—Late spring through early summer

Mature Size (H x W)—2 to 3 ft. x 2 ft.

Water Needs—Evenly moist soil is best.

CANNA
Canna x generalis

Why It's Special—These bold beauties provide beauty and function in any size landscape. Use them as a vertical accent in containers and flower beds, to screen bad views, or to create a tropical summer retreat. Or include a few in your water gardens.

How to Plant & Grow—Plant rhizomes directly outdoors in the garden after the last spring frost. Set them 3 to 4 inches deep and 1 to 2 feet apart. Start canna rhizomes indoors in mid-March for earlier outdoor bloom, or purchase transplants. Move hardened-off transplants outdoors in well-drained soil after all danger of frost is past.

Care & Problems—Cannas are low-maintenance plants except for the Japanese beetles, aster yellows, and rot. Remove faded flowers to maintain a neat appearance and encourage continuous blooming. Dig up rhizomes in the fall after a light frost, cure (dry), and store. Divide rhizomes in the spring before planting.

Hardiness—Zone 7; otherwise overwinter indoors

Bloom Color—Orange, yellow, white, red, and pink

Peak Season—Midsummer through frost

Mature Size (H x W)—1 to 6 ft. x 18 to 24 in.

Water Needs—Maintain evenly moist soil.

COLCHICUM
Colchicum species

Why It's Special—Add a bit of surprise to your fall garden with colchicum, which is often called autumn crocus. The plant produces leaves in early spring, which die back to the ground in six to eight weeks. In fall, you will be pleasantly surprised when the flowers appear without leaves.

How to Plant & Grow—Order bulbs from garden catalogs or reliable online sites. Plant these corms by late August or as soon as they are available. Plant 3 to 5 inches deep and 4 to 6 inches apart. Mix with groundcovers and perennials to mask declining leaves in spring and double your flower display.

Care & Problems—Bulbs can remain in the same location for years. Fertilize to encourage bulbs to more quickly increase the planting's size. Mark the colchicum's location or mix with perennial plants to avoid accidentally disturbing the bulbs in summer.

Hardiness—Zones 4 through 7

Bloom Color—White, pink, and purple

Peak Season—Fall

Mature Size (H x W)—4 to 12 in. x 4 in.

Water Needs—Provide evenly moist soil when it's actively growing and blooming.

CROCUS
Crocus vernus

Why It's Special—Crocus is one of the first flowers to greet you in the spring. They make an impressive display when planted *en masse* under trees, naturalized in the lawn, or throughout perennial and rock gardens.

How to Plant & Grow—Plant crocus corms in the fall. They prefer well-drained soil but seem to tolerate all types of our soils. Place corms 3 inches deep and 4 inches apart. Plant them in groups of at least 15 to 20 for an eye-catching display. Crocus flowers will close on cloudy days or in heavy shade.

Care & Problems—Avoid overwatering that can lead to root rot. Crocuses are low-maintenance plants except for animal pests. Try repellents, scare tactics, and barriers, or better yet plant the squirrel-resistant species *Crocus tommasinianus*. Corm rot is a problem in poorly drained soil.

Hardiness—Hardy throughout the Midwest

Bloom Color—White, purple, striped, and yellow

Peak Season—Early spring

Mature Size (H x W)—4 to 6 in. x 4 to 6 in.

Water Needs—Maintain soil as evenly moist when plants are actively growing.

CROWN IMPERIAL
Fritillaria imperialis

Why It's Special—A stately appearance in the mid-spring garden and shade tolerance makes this a nice addition to both formal and informal gardens. Mix it with perennials to cover the fading foliage in late spring.

How to Plant & Grow—Plant this scaly bulb in fall after the temperatures are consistently cool and before the ground freezes. Moist, well-drained soil is a must for winter survival. Many gardeners plant the bulbs on their sides to avoid water collecting in the center leading to bulb rot. Plant the bulbs 6 inches deep and 8 to 12 inches apart.

Care & Problems—Fritillarias benefit from shade in hotter regions. Winter survival is the biggest challenge in northern regions. Cover plantings with a layer of weed-free straw, marsh hay, or evergreen boughs after the soil surface freezes.

Hardiness—Zones 4 to 8

Bloom Color—Orange or yellow flowers

Peak Season—Mid-spring

Mature Size (H x W)—3 to 4 ft. x 1 ft.

Water Needs—Keep soil evenly moist when growing, but drier when plants are dormant.

DAFFODIL
Narcissus species and hybrids

Why It's Special—Daffodils are guaranteed to brighten up any spring landscape. These animal-resistant bulbs are easy to grow. Include several different cultivars for variety and extended bloom. And consider forcing a few for your indoor enjoyment.

How to Plant and Grow—Plant daffodil bulbs in the fall. They tolerate clay soil but perform best in areas with well-drained soil. Plant the bulbs 5 to 6 inches deep and 6 to 12 inches apart.

Care and Problems—High temperatures during flowering can prevent bloom or shorten the floral display. Remove faded flowers for a tidier look but leave the foliage on the plant until it yellows or at least six weeks after flowering. Bulb rot can be a problem in poorly drained soil. Poor flowering can be caused by excess shade, overcrowding, overfertilizing, and cold-temperature injury to the buds.

Hardiness—Throughout the Midwest

Bloom Color—Yellow, white, orange, pink, and green

Peak Season—Early to mid-spring

Mature Size (H x W)—6 to 24 in. x 6 to 12 in.

Water Needs—Soil should be evenly moist when plants are growing and drier when they're dormant.

DAHLIA
Dahlia hybrids

Why It's Special—Grow show-worthy dahlias that you, the hummingbirds, and butterflies will enjoy. The wide range of flower sizes, types, and colors make it easy to find one or more you'll enjoy in the garden or a vase.

How to Plant & Grow—Start tuberous roots indoors in mid-March for earlier bloom. Each section must have at least one eye. Or plant tuberous roots directly in the garden after the last spring frost. Plant 4 inches deep on its side with the eye pointing up. Or purchase plants. Place hardened-off plants in the garden after the danger of frost has passed. Grow in moist, well-drained soil. Stake tall cultivars.

Care & Problems—Mulch to keep the soil cool and moist. Move dahlias into storage after the first light frost. Disbud to control growth, flower size, and number of blooms. Watch for and control mites, aphids, leafhoppers, and thrips as needed.

Hardiness—Overwinter indoors

Bloom Color—White, pink, red, orange, and yellow

Peak Season—Midsummer to frost blooms

Mature Size (H x W)—1 to 5 ft. x 12 to 24 in.

Water Needs—Evenly moist soil is important.

ELEPHANT EARS
Colocasia species

Why It's Special—Add drama or a focal point to containers, flower beds, and water gardens with elephant ears. Their large foliage, sometimes variegated or heavily veined, provides a tropical feel to our Midwestern landscapes. *Alocasia*, *Colocasia*, and *Xanthosoma* look similar and share the common name, elephant ears.

How to Plant & Grow—Purchase as large corms or plants. Start corms (pointed side up) indoors in mid-March for an earlier display in the garden. Hardened-off transplants can be moved outdoors once the soil has warmed and all danger of frost has passed.

Care & Problems—Remove older faded leaves for a tidier look. Prevent scorch and leaf browning by growing in moist soil and partial to full shade. Overwinter those that form large corms as a houseplant or store like cannas and other nonhardy bulbs. Most of the dwarf varieties do best when overwintered as houseplants.

Hardiness—Overwinter indoors

Bloom Color—Green, chartreuse, bronze, and purple foliage

Peak Season—Spring until frost

Mature Size (H x W)—Up to 5 ft. x up to 3 ft.

Water Needs—Keep soil evenly moist.

GLADIOLA
Gladiolus hortulanus

Why It's Special—Gladioli add vertical interest to the garden, attract hummingbirds and make great additions to flower arrangements. Stagger planting every two weeks through the end of June to extend your bloom and cutting time throughout the season.

How to Plant & Grow—Purchase and store only pest-free corms. Start planting outdoors in the garden when soil is workable. Gladiola will bloom in 60 to 120 days, depending on the cultivar. Plant corms 3 to 6 inches deep and 3 to 6 inches apart.

Care & Problems—Thrips, virus, and aster yellows can be problems. Discard infected plants and corms. Stake tall varieties. Dig up the corms in the fall after the leaves have turned brown. Dry corms (cure) at 80 degrees Fahrenheit for up to four weeks. Discard old or shriveled corms and store the remaining ones uncovered in a cool, well-ventilated location at 40 degrees Fahrenheit.

Hardiness—Overwinter corms indoors

Bloom Color—White, yellow, pink, red, orange, purple, blue, and green

Peak Season—Summer

Mature Size (H x W)—1 to 5 ft. x 6 to 8 in.

Water Needs—Moist (but well-drained) soil is needed.

GRAPE HYACINTH
Muscari botryoides

Why It's Special—Though small in size, the grape hyacinth can create great interest in the landscape. This easy-to-grow bulb is resistant to animals and multiplies quickly. Mix it with other, taller bulbs such as daffodils and tulips to double your bloom. The flowers are nice additions to forced bulb containers and miniature cut-flower arrangements.

How to Plant & Grow—Plant grape hyacinth bulbs in the fall 3 inches deep and 4 inches apart. Place in groups of at least 15 to 20 for the biggest impact.

Care & Problems—Grape hyacinths are low-maintenance plants. The leaves will persist and continue to grow most of the season. They usually die back in late summer and reappear in fall. They benefit from dividing every four or five years in the late summer or fall.

Hardiness—Hardy throughout the Midwest

Bloom Color—Blue and white

Peak Season—Early to mid-spring

Mature Size (H x W)—6 to 9 in. x 4 to 6 in.

Water Needs—Keep soil evenly moist when bulbs are growing, drier when they're dormant.

HYACINTH
Hyacinthus orientalis

Why It's Special—Hyacinths are sure to brighten up a landscape or room with their large flowers and sweet fragrance. Many gardeners and landscapers are using these animal-resistant bulbs in place of tulips and other deer and rabbit favorites. Use this plant outdoors in the garden or force it indoors. Mix with daffodils, tulips, or winter hardy pansies for added beauty.

How to Plant & Grow—Plant hyacinth bulbs in the fall in areas with full sun and moist, well-drained soil. Plant the bulbs 6 inches deep and 6 to 9 inches apart.

Care & Problems—Hyacinths are basically pest free but generally short lived in our area. Remove faded flowers to increase blooming potential for the following season. Hyacinths are subject to bulb rot. Plant them in well-drained locations and add organic matter to heavy clay soil to avoid this problem.

Hardiness—Hardy throughout the Midwest

Bloom Color—Blue, violet, white, rose, pink, yellow, salmon, and apricot

Peak Season—Early to mid-spring

Mature Size (H x W)—6 to 10 in. x 6 in.

Water Needs—Soil should be evenly moist when it's growing and flowering.

IRIS
Iris hybrids

Why It's Special—The stately beauty of the iris can fill in the blooming void between spring-flowering bulbs and early-summer perennials. The wide range of heights and colors, butterfly and hummingbird appeal, and beauty in a vase makes this plant well worth growing.

How to Plant & Grow—Plant iris rhizomes late summer through early fall, preferably by September 1, especially in the north, so the plants can develop roots before winter. Mulch late plantings after the ground lightly freezes. Plant iris rhizomes in well-drained soil, just below the soil surface with the leaf fan facing outward.

Care & Problems—Stake tall cultivars. Poor flowering can result from excess fertilizer, low light, overcrowding, late spring frost, and recent transplanting. Remove spent flowers. Divide overcrowded iris at least eight weeks after flowering. Watch for and control iris borer by removing leaf litter in fall. Remove leaf spot-infested leaves when found.

Hardiness—Hardy throughout the Midwest

Bloom Color—A wide range of colors

Peak Season—Late spring to early summer

Mature Size (H x W)—4 to 48 in. x 6 to 12 in.

Water Needs—Keep soil evenly moist.

LILY
Lilium species

Why It's Special—The classic lily is as at home both in formal and informal gardens. Though more challenging to grow than daffodils and crocuses, the flowers will convince you they are worth the effort. Use these often fragrant beauties in flower arrangements or to attract hummingbirds and butterflies to the garden.

How to Plant & Grow—Plant lily bulbs in the fall. Or purchase and plant pre-cooled lily bulbs as soon as the soil is workable in the spring. Lily plants are also available. Grow lilies in moist, well-drained soil. Plant lily bulbs at a depth two to three times their height and at least three times their width apart.

Care & Problems—Lilies are subject to bulb rot in poorly drained soils. Deer, rabbits, and groundhogs will eat the plants down to ground level. Watch for and remove lily beetles as found.

Hardiness—Hardy throughout Midwest

Bloom Color—White, yellow, orange, red, and pink

Peak Season—Early to midsummer

Mature Size (H x W)—12 to 6 ft. x 8 to 12 in.

Water Needs—Evenly moist soil is ideal.

SQUILL
Scilla siberica

Why It's Special—Its true blue color is hard to beat in the early spring garden. Naturalize squills in lawn areas and wooded landscapes, include them in rock gardens, or plant large drifts around trees and shrubs. Mix with groundcovers or with daffodils, tulips, and hyacinths for added color.

How to Plant & Grow—Plant bulbs in the fall 3 inches deep and 4 to 6 inches apart. Place in groups of at least fifteen to twenty for good impact.

Care & Problems—Squills are low-maintenance and basically pest-free plants. Crown rot can cause plants to wilt, yellow, and die. Most gardeners have too much success—complaining that their squills have taken over the garden and moved into the lawn! Try to plant where its invasive tendencies will not be a problem. Overcrowded poor flowering bulbs can be lifted and divided every four to five years.

Hardiness—Hardy throughout the Midwest

Bloom Color—Blue and white

Peak Season—Early spring

Mature Size (H x W)—6 in. x 4 to 6 in.

Water Needs—Keep an evenly moist soil when it's growing, drier when dormant.

TUBEROUS BEGONIA
Begonia tuberhybrida

Why It's Special—Bold, beautiful, and made for the shade, tuberous begonias can add a lot of color and texture to container and shade gardens. Extend the season by moving these begonias indoors before the first fall frost and growing them as houseplants for the winter.

How to Plant & Grow—Plant tubers indoors in mid-March. Place tubers rounded-side down (indented side up) in a soilless mix. Plant hardened-off transplants outdoors after all danger of frost is past. Space 6 inches apart or use three plants to fill a hanging basket.

Care & Problems—Avoid windy locations where the stems may break. Powdery mildew, botrytis blight, and downy mildew can be problems. Botrytis blight and downy mildew are common problems in wet seasons. Plants will scorch (brown leaf margins) when grown in full sun. After the first light frost, dig, dry, and store the tubers in peat moss at 45 to 50 degrees Fahrenheit.

Hardiness—Overwinter indoors

Bloom Color—Orange, red, yellow, and pink

Peak Season—Summer until light frost

Mature Size (H x W)—10 to 24 in. x 8 to 12 in.

Water Needs—Evenly moist soil is best.

TULIP
Tulipa species and hybrids

Why It's Special—Tulips provide a long season of color and variety with early, mid-, or late spring bloomers of various flower types. Watch for the hummingbirds and butterflies feasting on the blooms' nectar.

How to Plant & Grow—Plant tulip bulbs in the fall, 5 to 6 inches deep and 6 to 9 inches apart. Those with sandy or well-drained soils can plant tulips 8 inches deep. Plant tulips as late as possible to avoid fall sprouting. Mix them with pansies or smaller bulbs for a double layer of spring flowers.

Care & Problems—Include some of the longer-lived species tulips or replace the short-lived hybrids every few years. Leave the foliage in place for at least six to eight weeks after the tulips bloom. Tulips are subject to several rot diseases in poorly drained soil. Animals are major pests eating flowers, trampling plants, and digging up bulbs.

Hardiness—Hardy throughout the Midwest

Bloom Color—A wide range of colors

Peak Season—Early through late spring

Mature Size (H x W)—4 to 36 in. x 6 to 8 in.

Water Needs—Keep soil evenly moist.

FORCING AND STORING BULBS

Force spring-flowering bulbs for a touch of spring indoors. Daffodils, tulips, and hyacinths are often used for forcing. Select shorter cultivars or those specifically recommended for forcing. Plant several bulbs in a 4- to 6-inch container filled with a well-drained potting mix. Water thoroughly and move to a cold location (35 to 45 degrees Fahrenheit) for thirteen to fifteen weeks. For cold treatment:

- Store potted bulbs in a spare refrigerator. A colleague once told me, "Every gardener should have a spare refrigerator. Not for beer and soda, but for storing bulbs." Do not store fruit with the bulbs, and make sure the family knows this is not some new cooking trend.

- Store bulbs in a root cellar, attic, or other area where the temperatures stay cold but above freezing.

- Bury the potted bulbs in a vacant garden area outdoors. Dig a trench the same depth as the containers. Place the containers in the trench and fill with soil. Cover the area with evergreen branches or straw once the ground begins to freeze.

- One gardener gets double duty from his pond. Once the pond is drained for winter, he fills it with potted bulbs. He covers the pots with dry leaves and the pond with a piece of plywood.

- A Master Gardener bought one of the Styrofoam cut-flower containers from a wholesale florist. He fills it with potted bulbs and stores it in his unheated garage for winter. The unheated garage gives the bulbs the cold they need and the insulated container prevents them from freezing in extremely cold weather.

TULIP BULBS

EASTER LILY

EASTER (LILY) IN JULY

Do not compost that Easter lily. Move it outdoors and start your own Easter-in-July garden. Both the traditional and hardy lilies forced for Easter can be planted outdoors for years of added beauty. Northern gardeners may have limited success with the traditional Easter lily and may want to consider one of the hardier species now being sold by florists.

1. Continue to care for your lily after the flowers fade.

2. Remove faded flowers and fertilize with a dilute solution of any flowering houseplant fertilizer.

3. Prepare a planting site in full sun with well-drained soils. Plan on using these tall plants as backdrops or vertical accents.

4. Move the bulbs outdoors in late May or early June. Transplant slightly deeper so that the bulb is about 6 inches deep. Leave the leaves intact and water as needed.

5. Be patient. The bulbs may not bloom until the second summer (mid- to late-July) after transplanting.

GLADIOLAS

BULBS IN FLORAL ARRANGEMENTS

Spring and summer-flowering bulbs make great additions to any flower arrangement. Their beauty and fragrance (some, not all) extend your garden enjoyment to the indoors. Increase the vase life of cut flowers by:

- Using a sharp knife or cutting scissors, cut the base of the stem on an angle.

- Place flowers in water right after cutting. Take a bucket of water along with you to the garden. This is better for the flowers and makes it easier for you to manage all those blooms.

- Harvest most flowers as the buds are just beginning to open. Harvest gladiola when the flowers on the bottom one-third just start to open, the middle one-third are swollen, and the top one-third are tight buds.

- Place freshly harvested gladiolus in a bucket of warm water in a cool location to harden. This should keep the flower stems straight.

- Give daffodils a vase of their own. They excrete a gummy substance from the cut stems. This substance blocks the stems of other cut flowers, shortening their vase life.

ADD A BIT OF SURPRISE

Autumn crocus (*Colchicum*) and surprise lilies (*Lycoris*) can add the "ah factor" to your garden. I like to design little surprises into my gardens to make people stop, take a second look, and say "Ah, what a great idea!" Seeing crocus blooming in September can do just that.

Part of the surprise is how these plants grow. They produce leaves in early spring. The leaves persist for about six to eight weeks and then die back for the season. Then suddenly, in late August or September, the flowers (no leaves) appear. It truly was a surprise in my garden. A friend gave me a surprise lily. I planted it in an area where the leaves would not be noticed, and they were not, in spring. That fall, I was pleasantly surprised—I had already forgotten.

Here are some tips for growing success:

- Mix these bulbs with perennials and groundcovers. Autumn crocus planted in vinca groundcover (periwinkle) doubles your bloom time. The vinca produces attractive flowers in spring followed by the leafless autumn crocus blooming in fall.

- Select a planting location where the early spring foliage will be hidden or a nice addition, not a distraction, in the garden.

- Plan and plant these fall-blooming beauties June through late August or early September when they are available.

- Dig and divide them (when necessary) as soon as the leaves die in spring. Plant divisions in other garden areas or share with friends.

AUTUMN CROCUS
COLCHICUM SPECIOSUM

JANUARY

- Fight winter blues by forcing some paper-white narcissus.

   1. Fill a shallow container with sterile pea gravel, pebbles, or marbles. Add enough water to reach the top of the gravel. Place the bulbs on the gravel and cover with just enough gravel to hold them in place.

   2. Or plant them in a container of any well-drained potting mix. Leave the tops of the bulbs exposed. Keep the planting mix moist, but not wet.

   3. Move the potted bulbs to a cool (45 to 60 degrees Fahrenheit) location for rooting.

   4. Place them in a bright location as soon as the leaves start to grow. It takes just a few weeks to get flowers.

- You may have received an amaryllis as a gift or have one stored in the basement. Now is the time to pot it up and get it growing. See page 62 for details.

- Start bringing forced bulbs planted in October out of cold storage. Stagger forcing times to extend your indoor bloom. Move bulbs to a cool, bright location. Water thoroughly as the soil below the surface just begins to feel dry and wait for a glorious display. Remove spent flowers, continue to water, and fertilize with a diluted solution of any flowering houseplant fertilizer.

FEBRUARY

- Monitor your outdoor plantings. Note any areas with standing water or ice. These conditions can lead to bulb rot and even death. Note the location of any bulbs that sprout during one of our winter thaws. Plan on moving them this year or mulching them next fall after the ground freezes.

- Watch for premature sprouting of bulbs during winter thaws. Fortunately bulbs are tough. The exposed leaves may be damaged by the subsequent cold, but as long as the flower buds are still buried in the soil, you'll have a great spring display. Make a note to winter mulch or move bulbs from problem areas next fall.

- Fungus gnats are often mistaken for fruit flies. They can be seen flitting across a room, usually in front of a guest. These gnats feed on the organic matter in the soil and are not harmful, just annoying. Remove spent blooms and drying leaves on forced bulbs.

MARCH

- Start planting tender bulbs indoors in mid- to late March through early April. Cannas, dahlias, tuberous begonias, and caladiums started indoors will bloom earlier in the garden. If indoor growing space is limited, wait and plant them directly outdoors in late spring. See the plant profiles for planting tips.

- Check for frost heaving. Unmulched gardens or those with inconsistent snow cover are subject to freezing and thawing temperatures. The fluctuating temperatures cause the soil to shift, pushing bulbs and other plants right out of the soil. Gently tamp heaved plants back in place.

- Remove the mulch only if the bulbs start to grow and temperatures are hovering near freezing. Keep some mulch handy to cover bulbs during extreme cold snaps. Fortunately, bulbs are tough and can tolerate pretty cold temperatures and even a blanket of snow.

- Disappearing bulbs can be caused by several problems. Poor drainage leading to root rot, removing bulb foliage right after bloom and animals digging or eating the bulbs.

APRIL

- Remove winter mulch as the bulbs begin to grow and the weather consistently hovers near freezing. Northern gardeners may want to keep a little mulch handy in case of sudden and extreme drops in temperature.

- Outdoor bulb plantings may need to be watered in a dry spring. Water when the bulbs show signs of wilting. Water thoroughly with 1 inch or enough water to moisten the top 6 to 8 inches of soil.

- Frost can damage daffodil buds and prevent them from fully developing. Bud blast results in brown, dry, and failed daffodil flower buds. It appears to be more common on late-blooming and double-flowering cultivars. Extreme temperature fluctuations, inadequate water, and wet fall seasons have been blamed for this disorder. Adjust care and replace varieties that continually suffer from this disorder.

- Leave bulb foliage intact. The green leaves produce energy that is needed for the plants to grow and flower next year. Deadhead the flowers for aesthetic reasons and to help lengthen tulip and daffdodil's lifespan.

- Prevent iris borer with proper sanitation in the fall. If this wasn't done, and borers have been a problem, you may decide to use an insecticide. Apply an insecticide, labeled for use on iris borers, when the leaves are 4 to 6 inches tall. Or go online and order beneficial nematodes. Purchase those known to control iris borer and follow label directions.

MAY

- As bulbs fade, plan to deal with the fading foliage. Mask the declining foliage by planting annuals or perennials between the bulbs. Tying and braiding the bulbs is not the best option, but it's better than removing the leaves. Or treat the bulbs like annuals and replace each fall.

- Plant gladiolus corms every two weeks once the soil warms through June. This will extend the bloom time throughout the summer. Plant full-sized, healthy corms 4 inches deep and 9 inches apart.

- Cut canna, dahlia, begonia, and caladium "bulbs" and hardened-off transplants outdoors after danger of frost has passed. Check the plant profiles for details.

- Deadhead faded flowers of tulips and hyacinths to promote more vigorous growth. Deadhead other bulbs for aesthetic reasons. You may want to remove the whole flower stem for a cleaner look.

JUNE

- Stake tall bearded iris, dahlias, and glads for a more attractive display. Be careful not to spear the rhizomes, tuberous roots, and corms in the process.

- Dig and divide spring-flowering bulbs after the leaves fade. The plants have already stored their energy for the next season and the faded leaves make them easy to locate. Otherwise, mark the spot and move them in fall while you are planting your other bulbs.

- Don't worry if you accidentally dig up hardy bulbs while planting perennials and annuals. Just pop them back in the ground. If you divided them with the shovel, consider it propagated. Replant both halves. You may be lucky and get two bulbs from one.

- Pinch out the tips of dahlias when they reach 15 inches. This encourages branching and results in more flowers on each plant. You can also pinch back leggy begonias at this time.

A mass planting of spring bulbs like these irises provides an elegant border to a pathway.

JULY

- Check limp and pale irises for borers. Dig up rhizomes, cut off soft and borer-infested portions of the rhizome, and replant. Make a note on your garden calendar to cut back and clean up iris foliage in fall.

- Earwigs, aphids, and mites are common pests found on a variety of plants, including bulbs. Earwigs often feed on flower petals. They can be trapped and killed or treated with an insecticide. Just be aware these chemicals also harm beneficial insects. Aphids and mites can be controlled with insecticidal soap.

- Thrips cause a scratched appearance on the leaves and distorted flowers on gladiola and occasionally on dahlias. Repeated applications of insecticides can help minimize the damage. Badly infested gladiolus corms should be treated or discarded prior to storage.

- Powdery mildew, leaf spot, botrytis, and anthracnose are often seen in wet summers. These cause leaves to be spotted or discolored. Remove infected leaves and faded flowers to reduce botrytis blight, leaf spot, and anthracnose disease. Sanitation and improved weather are usually sufficient control.

- Lilies are a favorite of rabbits and deer. Start applying homemade or commercial repellents early, vary the products used, and repeat applications after heavy rains. Scare tactics may be effective.

- Disbud dahlias for fewer but larger flowers. Remove at least two pairs of side buds that develop below the terminal (tip) bud. Remove three pairs of buds if you want giant dahlias.

AUGUST

- Start digging and dividing iris about six to eight weeks after bloom. Cut leaves in a fan shape back to 6 inches. This makes them easier to handle, reduces water loss, and improves their appearance. Dig rhizomes and check for borers. Kill borers and remove old and damaged rhizomes. Plant the healthy rhizomes back to back with growing points facing out or 5 inches apart in a properly prepared location. The rhizomes should be just below the soil surface with the leaves and buds facing upward.

- Stop fertilizing in-ground plantings and reduce fertilization of container plantings. Late season fertilization encourages late season growth that will not prepare the plant for winter.

STORAGE REQUIREMENTS FOR TENDER BULBS

BULB	CURE TIME	STORAGE	TEMP.
Tuberous Begonias	Several days	Dry peat	50°F
Caladium	Several days	Dry peat	50°F
Calla	1-2 days	Peat moss or perlite	50°F
Canna	Overnight	Peat moss	45-50°F
Dahlia	Several hours	Dry peat or sawdust	45°F
Gladiolus	2 weeks	Dry/uncovered	40°F

- Virus and aster yellows can cause poor flowering and distorted flower spikes on gladiola. There are no chemical cures for these diseases. Remove infected plants as soon as they are found. This helps reduce the risk to nearby healthy plants. Control aphids and leafhoppers feeding on the plants. These insects carry the diseases from sick to healthy plants. Controlling the insects reduces the spread of these diseases. Discard corms of any diseased gladiola.

SEPTEMBER

- Visit your favorite garden center and purchase your spring-flowering bulbs. Buy some extra bulbs for forcing. Store bulbs in a cool, dark place until it is time to plant. The basement, spare refrigerator, or similar location will work. Avoid storing bulbs in a refrigerator that contains ripening fruit (this interferes with flower development) or can be accessed by children who might accidentally eat the bulbs.

- Wait until air temperatures are consistently cool and soil temperatures are below 60 degrees to plant spring-flowering bulbs. Bulbs planted early are more likely to sprout during a warm fall. You have plenty of time—until the ground freezes—to get these bulbs into the ground.

- Caladiums, calla lilies, and tuberous begonias can be grown indoors for the winter. Move container plants inside prior to the first killing frost. Dig up inground plants, pot up, and move indoors. Care for them as you would your other houseplants.

- Yellowing foliage or the first fall frost means it is time to get busy. Dig, cure, and store tender bulbs for winter. See October for details.

- Prevent iris borer by removing old iris leaves and debris. Fall sanitation eliminates the sites for iris borer adults to lay their eggs. Without eggs, there will be no borers next season.

OCTOBER

- This month is peak time for bulb planting throughout much of the Midwest. Start planting daffodils, tulips, crocus, and other spring-flowering bulbs. These are generally planted at a depth of two to three times the vertical diameter. Plant two to three times the diameter apart, or per label directions. Water thoroughly and as needed throughout fall.

- Plant bulbs in pots for forcing. Water thoroughly and store them in a cold, 35- to 45-degrees Fahrenheit storage area for thirteen to fifteen weeks. Plant bulbs by early October for January flowers and by mid-October for February flowers.

- Dig, cure, and store tender bulbs after a light frost.

  1. Carefully dig up tender bulbs. Allow plenty of digging room for the additional bulbs that have formed over summer.

  2. Prepare (cure) bulbs for storage. Set them in a warm, dry place out of direct light. See the Storage Chart (opposite page) for specific recommendations.

  3. Gently brush off (do *not* scrub) excess soil and trim off dried foliage and stems.

  4. Place cured bulbs in a box or flat filled with peat moss, sawdust, or other storage material. Gladioli prefer to be stored dry (uncovered).

  5. Label the type and color of the bulb.

  6. Move to a cool, dark location for the winter.

NOVEMBER

- So you bought too many bulbs or overestimated your planting space. Here are some possible planting solutions: Heel in bulbs in a vacant or annual garden area; force bulbs for indoor enjoyment or gifts; scatter bulbs of daffodils, crocus, grape hyacinths, snow-drops, or squills and plant them where they fall; plant bulbs along the woodland or shade garden's edge; or plant squills, grape hyacinths, or crocus in the lawn. Just make sure you want them in the lawn as they are difficult to remove.

- Plant bulbs in pots for forcing. Store them in a cold, 35- to 45-degree-Fahrenheit storage area for thirteen to fifteen weeks. Plant bulbs in early to mid-November for March and April flowers.

- Mulch after the ground freezes to prevent early sprouting. This is usually after a week of freezing temperatures. A layer of evergreen branches, straw, or hay works fine. Do not worry if it snows before you get the mulch in place. Snow is the best mulch available and it is free.

DECEMBER

- Try paperwhites for indoor bloom. These bulbs do not need a cold treatment and are readily available at most garden centers. See January for tips on forcing paperwhites (*Narcissus*).

- Plant and enjoy or give the gift of an amaryllis:

  1. Plant the amaryllis in a pot slightly larger than the bulb.

  2. Place the bulb so that the pointed half is above the soil.

  3. Fill the pot with any sterile, well-drained potting mix.

  4. Water and move the pot to a cool, bright location, such as a sunny window in a cool room with temperatures around 60 to 65 degrees Fahrenheit. Keep the soil moist, but not wet. Soon new growth will appear; if you're lucky, it will be a flowering stem.

  5. Remove the flower stem when the plant has finished blooming to direct the energy to rejuvenating the bulb, not producing seeds.

  6. Move the plant to a sunny window, continue to water and fertilize with any dilute solution of a flowering house-plant fertilizer.

  7. Harden off the plant and move it outdoors after the danger of frost. Water and fertilize as needed. Bring it back indoors, before the first fall frost, for winter and a chance to rebloom. Allow the plants to go dormant. Store in a cool location and do not water for eight to ten weeks. Then topdress or repot. It will take four to eight weeks to rebloom. Or keep your amaryllis plant growing year round. Leave it in the container. Move it outdoors for summer and indoors in a well-lit location for winter.

GROUNDCOVERS
& VINES
for the Midwest

Groundcovers and vines are the carpets and wall coverings for your outdoor living space. They serve both functional and aesthetic purposes in the landscape. Use vines and groundcovers to soften hard surfaces and structures, block bad views, and decrease maintenance.

Grow vines on trellises to create privacy, screen a bad view, or cover an ugly fence. Use them in both large areas and narrow spaces where most shrubs outgrow.

Cover an arbor or trellis with vines to create shade. A decorative arbor covered with vines can create shade for outdoor patios and decks. Or create your own shade for shade-loving plants, such as hostas and ferns.

Use groundcovers under trees and shrubs to improve growing conditions. A perennial groundcover will help keep tree and shrub roots cool and moist throughout the growing season. It also keeps harmful mowers and weed whips away from trunks, stems, and surface roots.

Create groundcover beds around trees and shrubs to reduce mowing and hand trimming. Mow around one large bed of groundcover, trees, and shrubs instead of individual plants.

Add texture and seasonal interest to vertical and horizontal spaces. Vines and groundcovers allow you to expand planting options.

PLANNING

Select the right plant for the available sunlight, soil type, and moisture. Matching a plant to the climate, growing conditions, and available space will reduce pest problems, minimize maintenance, and give you the most attractive plant possible.

Avoid aggressive plants that can take over the landscape. These vines and groundcovers will require a lot of work to keep them inbounds. Several, such as crown vetch and oriental bittersweet, have become invasive and should not be planted.

Select vines that are best suited to climb the wall, trellis, or support selected. Or select the support structure best suited to the vine you want to grow. Use twining type vines, such as honeysuckle, clematis, and American bittersweet, for chain-link fences, trellises, and arbors. Cover walls and stones with wires and netting to train twining vines over these types of structures.

Consider using clinging vines, such as euonymus and climbing hydrangea, on stone and brick structures. These vines use rootlike structures to hold them to the surfaces they climb. Do not train clinging vines directly on wooden buildings. Their roots can damage the wood and the excess foliage can trap moisture, causing the wood to deteriorate.

Try letting a few vines run wild. Use them as groundcovers or let them crawl over stones, onto shrubs, and up tree trunks. Use nonaggressive plants that will not suffocate their neighbors or strangle the stems and trunks. Climbing hydrangea can be allowed to climb tree trunks for added

interest. Do not use twining vines, such as bittersweet, that can girdle the tree and potentially kill it.

Use groundcovers and vines in mass or mixed with other plants. Select companion plants that are equally aggressive and require the same growing conditions. Mix plants with plain, variegated, or colorful foliage and various flowering times to extend the season-long interest. Initially plant annual and perennial vines together. The annuals will provide quick cover and flowers while the perennial vines are getting established.

SOIL PREPARATION FOR GROUNDCOVERS AND PLANTING BEDS

Soil preparation varies with the location, existing conditions, and plants you are growing.

Do minimal digging around established trees and shrubs. Extensive, deep tilling can damage tree roots and kill the very plant that you are trying to enhance. Modifying the planting hole, but not the surrounding area, can limit plant root growth beyond the planting hole. Select the soil preparation method that best fits your growing conditions.

Start with a soil test. This will help you determine what if any fertilizer and amendments you will need. Add organic matter to new garden areas. Use organic matter as a mulch to slowly improve soil under established trees and shrubs.

Outline the new bed using a hose or rope. Avoid tight angles and narrow paths that will be hard to mow around. Edge the bed using a sharp shovel. Remove or kill the existing grass and weeds for new planting beds. Use a sod cutter to remove existing grass. Compost, green side down, or use quality pieces to patch bare spots in the lawn. Or kill the existing grass and weeds with a total vegetation killer. Wait the required time (check the label) to till up and rake off the dead grass. Or use the cardboard or newspapers and mulch method described below.

Add the recommended fertilizer and several inches of organic matter to the top 6 to 12 inches of soil. Follow soil test results, or use 2 to 4

pounds of a low-nitrogen (first of the three numbers on the bag) fertilizer per 100 square feet. Use fertilizers with little or no phosphorus (the middle number on the bag) or potassium (last of the three numbers) since our soils tend to have excess amounts of these.

Take special precautions when planting around established trees or where erosion is a concern. Do not cover the roots with soil or till deeply. Cultivation damages the tree's fine feeder roots located in the top 12 inches of soil.

Outline and edge the planting bed. Kill the existing weeds and turf with a total vegetation killer. Leave the dead layer intact to serve as mulch. Cover the dead layer with woodchips, shredded bark, or other organic mulch. The double layer of mulch helps suppress weeds, prevent erosion on slopes, and adds organic matter to the soil.

Or cut the existing grass and weeds very short. Cover with cardboard or several layers of newspaper and woodchips. Plant the groundcovers through the mulch. With either of the above methods, waiting a few months for the dead grass and paper mulch to breakdown makes planting much easier.

Add Seasonal Color with annuals while minimizing root disturbance under established trees. Sink old nursery pots in the soil so that the upper lip is even with the soil surface. Each year, set a smaller container filled with colorful annuals inside the buried pot. Replace them each season without disturbing the tree roots.

Or set aboveground containers among groundcovers. They add height, structure, and color without damaging the tree roots or stressing your back muscles.

PLANTING

Start planting once the site is prepared. Set groundcovers at their proper spacing on the soil surface. Review your plant layout and adjust as needed.

Dig a hole at least two to three times wider but no deeper than the container. Use a trowel or shovel to roughen up the sides of the planting hole.

This eliminates a glazed surface that prevents roots from penetrating the surrounding soil.

Gently push on the container sides to loosen the roots. Slide the plant out of the pot. Do not pull it out by the stem. Place the plant in the hole so that the rootball is even with the soil surface.

Or cut away the pot on delicate, poorly rooted, or potbound plants. Remove the bottom of the container. Place the plant in the hole (with rest of the container still attached) so that the rootball is even with the soil surface. Once in place, slice through the side of the pot and peel it away from the rootball.

Next fill the hole with the existing soil. Water to settle the soil and eliminate air pockets. Mulch the plants with woodchips, shredded bark, or other organic matter.

WATER

Check new plantings several times per week. Water whenever the top few inches just begin to dry. After several weeks, water thoroughly but less frequently. Wait until the top few inches just start to dry. Then water enough to moisten the top 6 to 8 inches.

Continue to check groundcovers growing under trees. Dense canopies of maples, oaks, and spruce not only shade plants but often prevent rainfall from reaching the groundcover below.

Water established plants on an as-needed rather than calendar basis. Thoroughly water, wetting the top 6 inches of soil. Water again whenever the top 4 inches start to dry.

FERTILIZING

Test your soil before adding fertilizer, sulfur, or lime. A soil test will tell you how much, if any, of these amendments you need to add. Contact your local university Extension service for soil testing information.

Or use 1 pound of actual nitrogen per 1000 square feet. This is equal to 4 pounds of ammonium sulfate (21-0-0), or 16 pounds of Milorganite® (5-2-0). Select a fertilizer (such as those mentioned) with little or no phosphorus, since our soils tend to be high to excessive in this nutrient.

PRUNING

Prune vines and groundcovers with a purpose in mind. Cut back rampant growers to control their size, remove diseased or insect infested stems to reduce pest problems, and cut out wayward branches to direct growth.

Remove diseased and damaged branches as soon as they appear. Disinfect tools between cuts with a solution of one part bleach to nine parts water.

Time other pruning based on plant growth and flowering. Prune spring-flowering plants such as five-leaf akebia and barrenwort after they bloom. Trim summer and fall bloomers such as sweet autumn clematis and honeysuckle anytime during the dormant season. Late winter pruning allows you to combine winter repair with routine pruning. See Pruning Guidelines for selected vines and groundcovers on page 83.

PESTS

Avoid problems by placing the right plant in the most suitable location. Always select the most pest-resistant vines and groundcovers available.

Check plants throughout the growing season. Remove spotted leaves and small insect populations as soon as they appear. This is usually sufficient for controlling most insects and disease.

Properly identify any problem before reaching for a chemical control. It is important for the health of your plant, the safety of the environment, and the effectiveness of the control that you use the right product at the proper time and rate.

Some popular vines and groundcovers have become invaders in our natural areas. These are not included in the profile and tips on eradicating them are covered in the monthly tips. Consider replacing these or struggling groundcovers and vines with one of these better suited plants.

AMERICAN BITTERSWEET
Celastrus scandens

Why It's Special—American bittersweet will quickly cover a fence or trellis and mask a bad view. This ornamental native can add year-round interest with yellow fall color and the decorative fruit the birds will enjoy and you can use in dried arrangements. Do not plant the invasive Oriental bittersweet, *Celastrus orbiculatus*.

How to Plant & Grow—Plant bare-root plants in early spring before growth begins and potted plants anytime during the growing season. Bittersweet thrives and fruits best in full sun and well-drained soil. You will need at least one male for every five female plants to have fruit (gender is on the label).

Care & Problems—Provide established plants with benign neglect for more controlled growth. The more water and fertilizer provided the more aggressive the plant and fewer fruit. Prune in the late winter or early spring before growth begins.

Hardiness—Throughout the Midwest

Seasonal Color—Yellow-white blooms; yellow fall foliage; orange fruit

Peak Season—May-June blooms; fall foliage & colorful fruit

Mature Size (H x W)—20 to 30 ft. long

Water Needs—Drought tolerant once established.

ARCTIC BEAUTY KIWI
Actinidia kolomikta 'Arctic Beauty'

Why It's Special—This hardy and ornamental relative of the edible kiwi makes a nice seasonal screen, vertical accent, or backdrop for other plants. The leaves start out purple, turn green with a white and pink blotch for summer, and change to yellow in fall.

How to Plant & Grow—Plant container plants anytime during the growing season. You'll have the best foliage color in partially shaded locations. Plant at least one male for every five female plants for fruit (gender is on the label).

Care & Problems—Avoid excess nitrogen fertilizer that will inhibit flowering, fruiting, and good foliage color. Hardiness is its biggest problem for those on the northern limits of hardiness. Prune established plants in early spring before growth begins.

Hardiness—Zones 4 to 8

Seasonal Color—White blooms, colorful foliage

Peak Season—Mid-May through June blooms; colorful foliage all season; yellow fall color

Mature Size (H x W)—15 to 20 ft. long

Water Needs—Soil should be evenly moist.

BARRENWORT
Epimedium x rubrum

Why It's Special—Barrenwort's changing character provides year-round interest in your landscape. Use them in small groupings, mixed with other shade lovers and in rock gardens. Or grow these dry shade-tolerant groundcovers under trees where grass won't grow. And enjoy a few as cut flowers.

How to Plant & Grow—Plant barrenwort in the spring for best results. You can divide existing plantings in the spring or early summer after the new leaves reach full size. Barrenwort prefers moist, well-drained soil. Space plants 9 to 12 inches apart.

Care & Problems—Give these slow growers, and those competing with tree roots, a boost of low-nitrogen slow-release fertilizer as needed. Cut back old foliage in late winter or early spring before new growth begins to better enjoy the flowers. Some daring Zone 3 gardeners have had success growing barrenwort.

Hardiness—Zones 4 to 8

Seasonal Color—Red, yellow, or white blooms

Peak Season—Spring blooms; red-tinged spring and red fall foliage

Mature Size (H x W)—8 to 12 in. x 8 to 12 in.

Water Needs—Drought tolerant once established.

BEARBERRY
Arctostaphylos uva-ursi

Why It's Special—Include this beautiful native groundcover for multiple seasons of color in your landscape. Watch for bees and other beneficial insects that visit the flowers and birds that will feast on the berries adding color and motion to your garden.

How to Plant & Grow—Bearberry is adaptable but must have good drainage to thrive. And even though it prefers acid soil it seems to adapt to alkaline soils. Plant 12 to 24 inches apart and be patient as it slowly spreads to 2 to 4 feet.

Care & Problems—Avoid overfertilization that not only stimulates growth of the bearberry but also the weeds that can quickly take over the planting. It's basically pest free though mildew, rust, and galls can be a problem. Minimal pruning is needed.

Hardiness—Zones 2 to 6

Seasonal Colors—White-tinged pink

Peak Season—Spring blooms; evergreen; red berries fall into winter

Mature Size (H x W)—6 to 12 in. x 2 to 4 ft.

Water Needs—Keep soil slightly dry.

BUGLEWEED
Ajuga reptans

Why It's Special—Bugleweed is a quick, mat-forming plant that works well under trees, in rock gardens, or as a groundcover in large beds. The spring flowers and beautiful evergreen foliage add year-round interest to the garden.

How to Plant & Grow—Grow in sun or shade but you'll have the best flowers in full sun with moist, well-drained soil. Avoid open or exposed areas where this plant may suffer winter kill in northern regions. Space plants 12 inches apart. Divide anytime with proper post-transplant care.

Care & Problems—One healthy plant can fill a 3-square-foot area in one season. Edge beds to keep this vigorous plant contained. Cut off or mow faded flowers to prevent reseeding and to keep the plants looking good. Lift and divide crowded plants to reduce the risk of crown rot.

Hardiness—Throughout the Midwest

Seasonal Color—Violet and blue-purple; colorful foliage

Peak Season—Late spring; foliage year-round

Mature Size (H x W)—6 to 9 in. x 24 to 36 in.

Water Needs—Evenly moist soil is best.

CINQUEFOIL
Potentilla species

Why It's Special—Cinquefoil tolerates hot and dry locations. A close relative of the summer-flowering potentilla, it is a good groundcover for those gardening in sandy soils and glacial till. The growth habit and dissected foliage is similar to barren strawberry. Some cinquefoils lose their leaves for the winter, while others are evergreen.

How to Plant & Grow—Plant cinquefoil throughout the summer. Dig and divide overgrown plantings in the spring. Grow in full sun or partially shaded locations. They need good drainage and tolerate infertile soils. Space plants and divisions 6 to 12 inches apart.

Care & Problems—Most species are drought tolerant once established. All benefit from supplemental watering during extended dry periods. Avoid excess fertilizer than can lead to poor growth and reduced flowering. Some species benefit from pruning whenever the plants appear unkempt. Root rot and winter dieback is common in heavy and poorly drained soils.

Hardiness—Hardy to Zone 3

Seasonal Color—White and bright yellow

Peak Season—Late spring to summer

Mature Size (H x W)—3 to 10 in. x 12 to 24 in.

Water Needs—Drought tolerant once established.

CLEMATIS
Clematis species

Why It's Special—This small plant provides lots of late spring, summer, or fall color, even in very small spaces. Use clematis to brighten up any vertical space by training the twining vines on trellises, mailboxes, and lampposts.

How to Plant & Grow—Plant dormant bare-root plants outdoors as soon as the soil is workable. Plant container-grown clematis in the spring and early summer. Grow clematis in a sunny location with the roots mulched or shaded by a groundcover.

Care & Problems—Clematis is fairly pest free. Blackened leaves and stems are the result of stem wilt. Avoid damaging it and remove infected stems to ground level. Most gardeners prune heavily each year to maintain a small flowering plant. Wait to prune early spring-blooming clematis until after flowering. Prune summer and fall bloomers during the dormant season above a set of healthy buds 6 to 12 inches above the soil.

Hardiness—Throughout the Midwest

Seasonal Color—White, purple, blue, pink, and red

Peak Season—Summer and fall blooms

Mature Size (H x W)—5 to 18 ft. long

Water Needs—Keep soil evenly moist.

CLIMBING HYDRANGEA
Hydrangea anomala petiolaris

Why It's Special—Climbing hydrangea is a great four-season vine. Its fragrant white flowers are followed by seedheads that persist all season. The leaves may turn yellow in fall or drop off green exposing the hydrangea's cinnamon brown peeling bark. Be patient as it takes several years to get established and start flowering.

How to Plant and Grow—Plant in spring as it is slow to recover from transplanting. Grow it in partial or shaded locations. It prefers moist, well-drained soil and may suffer from scorch (brown leaf edges) if grown in full sun or dry soil.

Care and Problems—Climbing hydrangeas start off slowly. Avoid high-nitrogen fertilizers that can inhibit bloom. Train on a brick or stone wall, a fence, or an arbor. Or allow it to creep over the ground. Established plants need minimal pruning.

Hardiness—Zones 4 to 7

Seasonal Color—White blooms; yellow fall color

Peak Season—June or early July blooms

Mature Size (H x W)—60 to 80 ft. long

Water Needs—Evenly moist soil is best.

DEADNETTLE
Lamium maculatum

Why It's Special—Deadnettle is such an ugly name for such a pretty plant! The green-and-white foliage brightens up shady locations all season long. Once established, it will grow well in the dry shade found under the dense canopy of many shade trees. Use it in large or small groundcover plantings and even containers.

How to Plant & Grow—Plant throughout the growing season. Divide plants in early spring for best results. It can be a little aggressive for some garden settings, so pick its neighbors carefully. Space plants 12 to 18 inches apart.

Care & Problems—Deadnettle prefers moist, well-drained soil and will become open and a bit leggy in dry conditions. Leaves may scorch when grown in full sun. Prune plants growing in dry shade to encourage fuller, more compact growth.

Hardiness—Hardy to Zone 4

Seasonal Color—Rose-purple, white, and red

Peak Season—May through midsummer; variegated foliage all season

Mature Size (H x W)—8 to 12 in. x 3 ft.

Water Needs—Evenly moist soil is best, but it will tolerate dry shade.

DUTCHMAN'S PIPE
Aristolochia macrophylla

Why It's Special—Dutchman's pipe has long been used to screen a porch or climb a trellis. The large heart-shaped leaves form a dense screen and shade. A look under the leaves in late May or early June will reveal small pipe-shaped flowers.

How to Plant & Grow—Grow in full sun to part shade and moist, well-drained soil. You can start plants from seed. Check the label on the seed packet for more specific directions. Divide in spring, layer, or take cuttings in midsummer.

Care & Problems—This twining vine is easy to grow and will quickly fill its support. Prune in late winter or early spring before growth begins to control its size. The pipevine swallowtail is a beautiful visitor in parts of the Midwest. The large amount of foliage they consume is not detrimental to the health of an established plant.

Hardiness—Zones 4 through 8

Seasonal Color—Known for subtle pipe-shaped blooms

Peak Season—Late May or early June

Mature Size (H x W)—15 to 30 feet long

Water Needs—Keep soil evenly moist.

FOAMFLOWER
Tiarella species

 ☀

Why It's Special—The shape, texture and variety of colorful foliage make this native a good choice for groundcover and perennial beds. Combine these with coralbells to create a tapestry of color and texture under a shade tree.

How to Plant & Grow—Grow this woodland native in partial to full shade and cool moist soil. Though tolerant of full sun with moist soil, you'll get the best results with the least effort if you grow these plants in partial shade. Space 12 to 18 inches apart.

Care & Problems—Mulch to keep the soil cool and moist and weeds under control. Water thoroughly and as needed to keep the soil moist but not wet. Drought stress can cause brown leaf edges (scorch) and overall decline of the plants. Monitor plantings for frost heaving in spring and reset plants at the proper depth and water as needed in spring.

Hardiness—Throughout the Midwest

Seasonal Color—White blooms; colorful foliage

Peak Season—Mid-spring blooms

Mature Size (H x W)—6 to 12 in. x 12 to 24 in.

Water Needs—Evenly moist soil is best.

GINGER
Asarum species

Why It's Special—Can't grow anything under that spruce tree? Try Canadian ginger. Both the evergreen European and deciduous Canadian ginger can take heavy shade and moist conditions that most plants won't tolerate. The glossy green leaves of European ginger reflect the light and help brighten shady locations.

How to Plant & Grow—Plant in spring, spaced 8 to 12 inches apart. Divide and plant in early spring before growth for best results. Grow in moist soil with lots of organic matter. Site European ginger in a protected location or winter mulch for best results. Canadian ginger is hardier and is a good choice for native woodland gardens.

Care & Problems—These are low-maintenance, pest-free plants. European ginger can be a bit more challenging for those in the north and less heat tolerant in the southern Midwest. Canadian ginger can be aggressive.

Hardiness—Throughout the Midwest

Seasonal Color—Greenish purple or brown under the leaves

Peak Season—Mid- to late spring blooms; European ginger foliage is evergreen

Mature Size (H x W)—6 to 12 in. x 12 in.

Water Needs—Soil should be evenly moist, but Canadian ginger is more drought tolerant.

HYACINTH BEAN
Lablab purpureus

Why It's Special—This low-maintenance twining vine provides lots of colorful flowers and fruit summer through frost. The dark green, heart-shaped leaves with purple veins are held on reddish stems. The fragrant, rosy purple flowers are followed by dark purple beans. It's a fancy relative of our garden beans.

How to Plant & Grow—Start seeds indoors four to six weeks before the last spring frost for early summer bloom. Or wait until the danger of frost has passed to plant hardened-off plants or sow seeds 1 inch deep directly outdoors.

Care & Problems—Grow hyacinth beans in full sun and moist, well-drained garden soil. Fertilize according to soil test recommendations or with a low-nitrogen slow-release fertilizer. Watch for volunteer seedlings in next year's garden. Tie young plants to a trellis, fence, or other support. Once it makes contact, it will climb up the structure with minimal guidance. Only remove ripe fruit if production slows.

Hardiness—Annual

Seasonal Color—Rosy purple flowers; purple fruit

Peak Season—Summer through fall

Mature Size (H x W)—10 to 20 feet long

Water Needs—Keep soil evenly moist.

HONEYSUCKLE VINE
Lonicera species

Why It's Special—Here's a vine suited to most gardens. Plant it in an area where you can enjoy the sometimes fragrant flowers and hummingbirds that come to visit. Avoid growing the invasive Japanese honeysuckle (*Lonicera japonica*).

How to Plant & Grow—Container-grown vines can be planted anytime during the growing season but they do best if planted in spring. Grow it in full sun and partial shade with moist, well-drained soils.

Care & Problems—Avoid excess nitrogen that encourages leaf growth and discourages flowering. Trumpet honeysuckle is a low-maintenance vine but may have problems with aphids and mildew. The plants will survive, but an infestation can ruin many of the blossoms. Woodbine honeysuckle (*Lonicera periclymenum*) tends to be more resistant to mildew. Prune overgrown plants to fit the available space in late winter or early spring before growth begins.

Hardiness—Throughout the Midwest

Seasonal Color—Orange, pink, or red blooms

Peak Season—June through October

Mature Size (H x W)—12 ft. long

Water Needs—Evenly moist to slightly dry soil is best.

LILYTURF
Liriope muscari

Why It's Special—The tufts of grass-like foliage make a nice edger, groundcover under trees, and addition to perennial gardens. Evergreen in southern portions of the Midwest, lilyturf turns brown over winter in other areas. Its late summer flowers resemble grape hyacinths, adding to its appeal. Plus, the deer and rabbits tend to leave it alone.

How to Plant & Grow—Plant in light shade and moist soil for best performance. Established plants tolerate a wide range of moisture and light. Divide in spring. Space plants 12 inches apart.

Care & Problems—Mow or cut back old foliage in spring before new growth begins. This plant is not reliably hardy in all parts of Zone 5. Creeping lilyturf is aggressive but has survived in some Zone 4 gardens.

Hardiness—Zones 5 to 10

Seasonal Color—Lavender and white

Peak Season—Midsummer flowers; foliage all season

Mature Size (H x W)—8 to 15 in. x 10 to 12 in.

Water Needs—Drought tolerant once established.

MANDEVEILLA
Mandeveilla splendens

Why It's Special—The nonstop bloom and low maintenance makes this annual vine an asset in the garden. Train this twining vine up a stake for vertical interest or allow it to fill and spill over a hanging basket. The glossy green leaves make a nice backdrop for the large long-lasting blooms.

How to Plant & Grow—Purchase mandeveilla as a hanging basket or large container ready for the patio, balcony, or deck. Or sink the pot in the ground and train it up an existing trellis. Purchase smaller plants where available to create your own container combinations. Use this plant on a small trellis as a thriller or allow it to spill over the edge of the pot.

Care & Problems—It's pest-free but not winter hardy. Move containers indoors to a sunny window, water as needed, and watch for mites and aphids. Gradually reintroduce it to the outdoors after the danger of frost has passed.

Hardiness—Annual

Seasonal Color—Pink, white, red, purple, and bicolor flowers

Peak Season—Summer until frost

Water Needs—Check containers daily; water thoroughly as needed.

MORNING GLORY
Ipomoea purpurea

Why It's Special—Morning glory is an old-fashioned favorite that is still popular in modern landscapes. This fast grower provides summer-long beauty with very little care and in very little space. Though each flower lasts only one day, it is replaced the next day by new blossoms.

How to Plant & Grow—Start morning glory vines from seeds indoors, four to six weeks prior to the last spring frost. Nick (scratch) the seed coat or soak it in warm water for twenty-four hours before planting. Plant hardened-off transplants or seeds directly outdoors after the last spring frost. Space transplants 12 inches apart.

Care & Problems—Excess water and fertilizer will result in lots of leaves, but no flowers. These often do not bloom until late in the season. New introductions such as 'Early Call' produce earlier blossoms. Morning glory will reseed; weed out unwanted seedlings. *All parts of morning glory are toxic.*

Hardiness—Annual

Seasonal Color—Purple, blue, pink, red, and white flowers

Peak Season—Summer to fall

Mature Size (H x W)—8 to 10 ft. long

Water Needs—Evenly moist soil is best.

MOTHER OF THYME
Thymus serpyllum

Why It's Special—Thyme has long been used for its fragrance and flavor. Its creeping growth habit makes it a good groundcover for sunny, dry locations. Add attractive leaves and a summer-long bloom, and you have a groundcover fit for most landscapes.

How to Plant & Grow—Start seeds indoors in early spring. Plant hardened-off thyme plants throughout the growing season. Lift and divide established plants in spring. Take cuttings of new growth to root and plant later in the summer. Grow thyme in full sun and well-drained soil. Space plants 6 to 18 inches apart.

Care & Problems—Avoid excess fertilizer that encourages tall, weak, and unattractive growth. Do not overwater as that can lead to root rot and winter dieback. Winter dieback can be a problem in extremely cold winters or poorly drained locations. Fortunately, stems will often root and survive even when the parent plant dies. Prune back plants in the spring after leaves begin to sprout but before flowering begins.

Hardiness—Throughout the Midwest

Seasonal Color—Purple flowers

Peak Season—Summer

Mature Size (H x W)—3 to 6 in. x 18 in.

Water Needs—Drought tolerant once established.

PACHYSANDRA
Pachysandra terminalis

Why It's Special—Pachysandra's glossy green leaves provide year-round interest, making it a popular groundcover. It is often used in mass plantings under trees and shrubs both in formal and informal gardens.

How to Plant & Grow—Plant anytime during the growing season. Plant divisions and rooted cuttings in the spring or early summer. Earlier plantings allow transplants to get established before winter. Pachysandra needs moist, well-drained soil to thrive. Space plants 12 inches apart.

Care & Problems—Plants will yellow when grown in full sun. Winter wind and sun can also cause yellowing. Leaf blight, root rot, and euonymus scale can be devastating problems. Proper soil preparation, placement, and care will help prevent these problems. Remove blight-infected leaves as soon as they appear. Treat euonymus scale when the young shell-less scales are active. This coincides with the beginning of Japanese tree lilac and catalpa bloom.

Hardiness—Zones 4 through 9

Seasonal Color—White flowers

Peak Season—Early spring; evergreen foliage

Mature Size (H x W)—6 to 8 in. x 12 to 18 in.

Water Needs—Evenly moist soil is best.

PASSION FLOWER
Passiflora incarnata

Why It's Special—One look at the unique flower will make you want to add this vine to your garden. The butterflies it attracts and the edible fruit add to its appeal.

How to Plant & Grow—Start from seeds indoors, following package directions. Start new plants from cuttings taken in June or try layering. Plant passion flowers early in the season to allow plants to establish before winter. Those in colder regions where the plant is not hardy can grow this in a container and overwinter it as a houseplant indoors.

Care & Problems—Those in the northern portion of its hardiness zone should plant in a sheltered location for the greatest chance of success. The plants will die to the ground but quickly grow to full size each season. These plants will send up runners. Remove unwanted runners with a sharp spade.

Hardiness—Zones 5 to 9

Seasonal Color—White and purple blooms

Peak Season—Midsummer to fall

Mature Size (H x W)—6 to 8 ft.

Water Needs—Keep soil evenly moist.

RUSSIAN CYPRESS
Microbiota decussata

Why It's Special—Russian cypress foliage looks like an arborvitae while its growth habit resembles that of a creeping juniper. This partially shade-tolerant groundcover looks good in rock gardens, shrub borders, and under trees.

How to Plant & Grow—Plant in a cool location with moist, well-drained soil for best results. Provide afternoon shade, especially in hotter regions of the Midwest. Space at least 3 to 4 feet apart.

Care & Problems—Heat, heavy soils, and root rot will kill this plant. It may suffer in the hot summers of Zone 7. Otherwise, there are no serious problems. Prune to control growth and remove stray branches in spring before new growth begins or summer after the first flush of growth. Don't panic when the foliage turns brownish purple; it's this plant's normal winter color.

Hardiness—Zones 3 to 7

Seasonal Color—Green in summer; brownish purple in winter

Peak Season—Year-round

Mature Size (H x W)—12 to 15 in. x up to 12 ft.

Water Needs—Keep soil evenly moist.

SWEET WOODRUFF
Galium odoratum

Why It's Special—Sweet woodruff's bright green, fragrant leaves will cover the ground from early spring through late fall. Add a little patch to your garden or put a large planting under some trees and shrubs. Allow this plant to wander through perennial gardens and mixed borders. Dry and use the leaves in potpourris.

How to Plant & Grow—Plant throughout the season. Dig, divide, and plant divisions in early spring for best results. Woodruff prefers shade and moist, well-drained soil but tolerates a wide range of conditions. It tends to burn out in full sun and dry locations. Space plants 12 inches apart.

Care & Problems—Woodruff is attractive throughout the summer. Clip it back several times during the season to create a more formal appearance. Poor flowering and a fungal leaf spot and crown rot may be a problem on rare occasions.

Hardiness—Zones 4 to 8

Seasonal Colors—White

Peak Season—Mid-spring

Mature Size (H x W)—6 to 8 in. x 12 to 15 in.

Water Needs—Keep soil evenly moist.

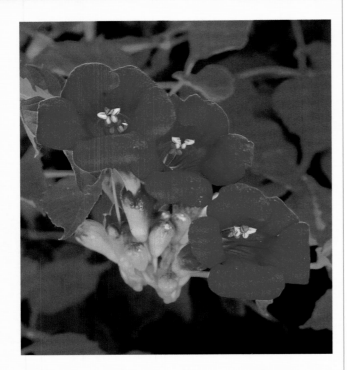

TRUMPET VINE

Campsis radicans

Why It's Special—Trumpet vine's tough nature, beautiful flowers, and its hummingbird appeal make it a good addition to any landscape with the space to accommodate. Train on a fence, over a structure, or into a tree. But keep the pruners handy, as these rampant growers will overtake anything in their path!

How to Plant & Grow—Plant bare-root trumpet vines in the early spring before growth begins. Plant container-grown plants anytime during the growing season.

Care & Problems—It may take several years for your plant to bloom. Excessive shade and nitrogen can prevent flowering. Avoid high-nitrogen fertilizers around or near trumpet vines. Trumpet vines are slow to leaf out and may suffer winter injury. This is not a problem since they grow so fast. They also spread underground, developing suckers near and even quite a distance from the parent plant. Use a sharp shovel to prune out the suckers at ground level.

Hardiness—Zones 4 to 10

Seasonal Color—Orange and yellow flowers

Peak Season—July

Mature Size (H x W)—40 ft. or more in length

Water Needs—Drought tolerant once established.

WISTERIA

Wisteria species

Why It's Special—Wisteria is the classic beauty of flowering vines. It can be espaliered on a wall, grown over a pergola, or trained into a tree form. The classic Japanese and Chinese wisteria vines are sold as hardy in Zones 4 or 5. The plants will survive but seldom flower in these zones. Kentucky wisteria, *Wisteria macrostachya*, is a better choice. It's not quite as dramatic, but it is more reliable and is still an impressive sight in bloom.

How to Plant & Grow—Plant container-grown wisteria in the spring. Grow it in full sun to light shade and in moist, well-drained soil.

Care & Problems—Wisteria may not bloom for the first seven years. Avoid overfertilizing wisteria as that can interfere with flowering. Pruning is the only real maintenance needed. Prune Kentucky wisteria in late winter before growth begins. Wait until after flowering to prune Chinese or Japanese wisterias.

Hardiness—Zones 4 to 9

Seasonal Color—Purple to violet and white flowers

Peak Season—Late spring or early summer

Mature Size (H x W)—30 ft. long

Water Needs—Keep soil evenly moist.

PRUNING SPECIFIC PLANT TYPES

For all, remove damaged leaves and stems. Prune following these guidelines:

- **Junipers:** Prune in early spring or early to mid-July. Remove dead branches and shape in spring. Make cuts back to a healthy stem deep in the plant to hide cuts. Lightly prune junipers to remove wayward branches back to shorter side branches if needed in mid-July. Disinfect tools with a solution of one part bleach to nine parts water when pruning diseased plants.

- **Bittersweet:** Prune in winter or early spring. After planting, prune to train young stems to climb the plant support. For established plants, trim to control size. Cut overly long shoots back to three to four buds from the main stem. Prune back large shoots to 12 to 16 inches above ground level. Do not over-prune.

- **Boston ivy and Virginia creeper:** Prune during the dormant season. After planting, train young stems to their support. For established plants, prune to control growth and keep them inbounds. Remove or shorten any stems that are growing away from their support. Renovate overgrown plants by pruning them back to 3 feet of the base. Wear a leather glove to rub the remaining dried pads off the support.

- **Clematis:** Prune clematis to control growth, encourage branching near the base of the plant, and improve flowering. The type of clematis you are growing will determine the time and type of pruning it requires. Spring-blooming clematis bloom on old wood. Prune after flowering. Some like 'Nellie Moser', 'Henry', 'The President', and 'Bees Jubilee' bloom on old and new growth. Prune dead and weak stems back to a healthy stem or ground level in late winter or early spring before growth begins. Prune the remaining stems back to a pair of strong buds after the first bloom for maximum flowering. The last group of clematis blooms on new growth. Prune these in late winter or early spring before growth begins. Remove dead stems back to ground level. Cut the remaining stems back to 6 to 12 inches.

- **Euonymus (vines):** Prune in mid- to late spring. For young plants, tip prune to encourage fuller growth. For established plants, remove old and dead wood.

- **Hardy kiwi:** Prune in late winter or early spring. After planting, cut back to strong buds about 12 to 16 inches above the ground. Train five to seven strong shoots on the support. Next spring, prune stout side shoots (laterals) by one-third and weak laterals back to one or two buds. For established plants, shorten growth by one-third to one-half to control its size. Occasionally remove an old stem to ground level.

- **Honeysuckle:** Prune in early spring. After planting, cut back young plants by two-thirds. Next year, select strong shoots to form a framework. Remove other shoots. For established plants, prune out the tips of shoots that have reached the desired height. Cut off overly long shoots to healthy buds. Renovate overgrown plants by pruning stems back to 2 feet above the ground. Thin the new growth as needed.

- **Trumpet vine:** Prune in late winter or early spring. After planting, prune all stems back to 6 inches above ground level. Remove all but two or three of the strongest shoots. Train these stems to the support. For established plants, prune yearly to control growth. Remove weak and damaged stems to the main framework. Cut the side shoots back to two or three buds from the main stems forming the framework. Prune out dead main branches to the base. Train the strongest shoot to replace it. Renovate by cutting all growth back to 12 inches above the ground.

- **Wisteria:** At planting, cut back the main stem (leader) to a strong bud about 30 to 36 inches above ground level. Train two strong side shoots (laterals) over the fence, trellis, or arbor. The following spring, prune the leader to 30 inches above the topmost lateral branch. Shorten the laterals by one-third of their total lengths. Select another pair of laterals to grow and help cover the trellis. Next winter, cut the leader back to 30 inches above the uppermost lateral. Then prune all the laterals back by one-third. Repeat each winter until the plant reaches full size. Prune established plants in early summer right after flowering. Cut offshoots (small branches) back to within five or six buds of a main branch.

JANUARY

- Take a walk through the landscape to see how the vines and groundcovers are surviving the winter. Note plants that are subject to snow loads and salt. Evaluate these plants in the spring. You may need to move sensitive plants or change snow management practices in the future.

- Evaluate the winter sun and winds. Both can be drying to evergreen groundcovers and vines. Recycle your Christmas tree to create a windbreak and shade for pachysandra and other sensitive plants. Make a note to move, shelter, or create a more permanent solution.

- Monitor the health of tropical vines overwintering indoors. Increase the light and humidity around failing plants. Move them in front of an unobstructed south-facing window. Add artificial light if needed. Hang fluorescent lights above or aim spotlight-type fluorescent lights up into the foliage.

FEBRUARY

- Check container plants overwintering outdoors and in the garage. Water whenever the soil is frost-free and dry. Apply enough water so that the excess runs out the bottom.

- Continue to check outdoor plants for animal damage. Look for tracks, droppings, and other signs of animal damage. Euonymus, junipers, and other groundcovers make great winter housing and food for rabbits and voles. Apply commercial or homemade repellents to high-risk plantings.

- Trim branches on outdoor plants that are dead and damaged. Wait until the worst of winter weather has passed for routine pruning.

MARCH

- Calculate the square footage of your new and existing groundcover beds. Then use the "Spacing Chart" to calculate the number of plants needed. Or do the math yourself. See page 136 for both.

- Check groundcovers that are shallow-rooted for frost heaving. These plants are often pushed out of the soil after a winter of freezing and thawing. Gently press them back into the soil and water in place.

- Edge planting beds with a sharp spade or edging machine. This will help keep the groundcovers in and the surrounding grass out of the planting beds.

- Time to start pruning vines and groundcovers. Remove dead and damaged stems and branches. See specific directions for some common vines on page 83.

APRIL

- Plant bare-root plants as soon as they arrive. Pack the roots in moist peat, and keep the plants in a cool, frost-free location until planted. Plant so that the crown (the point where stem joins the roots) is even with the soil.

- Start annual vines from seeds indoors. Starting them indoors results in earlier flowering for a longer bloom period. See "Annuals" chapter for tips.

- Remove damaged leaves on groundcovers. To make spring flowers more visible, cut off old leaves on barrenwort (*Epimedium*) before growth begins.

MAY

- Move tropical vines overwintered indoors, outside once the danger of frost has passed. Gradually introduce them to the outdoors. Follow the same procedures used for hardening off annuals.

- Dig and divide overcrowded, declining, and poorly flowering groundcovers. Use a shovel to lift plants. Remove dead centers and declining plants. Cut the remaining clump into several smaller pieces. Plant the divisions in properly prepared soils at the recommended spacing for that species.

- Monitor euonymus and wintercreeper vines for euonymus caterpillar. These wormlike insects spin a webbed nest in the plants. Remove and destroy. Or treat with *Bacillus thuringiensis*. Spray the webbed nests and surrounding foliage. This bacterial insecticide will kill the caterpillars, but it will not harm people, pets, wildlife, or other types of insects.

- Check junipers for phomopsis blight. This fungal disease causes individual stems to turn brown and die. Prune dead branches back to a healthy stem or the main trunk. Disinfect tools between cuts with rubbing alcohol or a solution of one part bleach to nine parts water.

- Cut back creeping phlox after the flowers fade. Prune plants back halfway to encourage fresh, new growth.

JUNE

- Apply a 2- to 3-inch layer of shredded leaves, evergreen needles, woodchips, or twice-shredded bark around groundcovers and vines. Mulch conserves moisture, reduce weeds, and improve the soil. Do not bury the crowns of the groundcovers or the base of the vines. This can lead to rot and decline.

- Renovate overgrown and weedy groundcovers. Dig out the healthy plants and remove them from the garden. Remove or use a total vegetation killer to kill all the weeds and unwanted plants. Amend and fertilize the soil. Divide the healthy plants into smaller pieces. Plant the divisions at the proper spacing, water thoroughly, and mulch.

- Treat euonymus scale found on wintercreeper and euonymus vines. These hard-shelled insects can be found on the stems and leaves. Spray the plants with an insecticidal soap or ultrafine oil when the Japanese tree lilacs are in bloom. This is about mid- to late June. Repeat at 10- to 12-day intervals for a total of three applications.

- Remove spotted leaves and stems on lily-of-the-valley and pachysandra. These fungal leaf spot and blight diseases can usually be controlled with sanitation. Remove infected leaves and stems as soon as they appear. In fall, rake fallen leaves off the plantings to reduce the conditions that increase the risk of this disease.

- Check clematis for wilt. Leaves wilt, and both the leaves and areas of the stem turn black. Prune infected stems back to healthy tissue or ground level. Disinfect tools between cuts. Use a solution of rubbing alcohol or one part bleach to nine parts water.

- Monitor bugleweed (*Ajuga*) for crown rot. Look for patches of dead and dying plants. Remove and discard sick plants. Improve soil drainage and avoid overhead watering to reduce future problems. Treat the infected area with a fungicide before replanting.

- Clip back or lightly mow bugleweed after it flowers. This will improve the appearance and prevent unwanted seedlings from taking over the garden.

JULY

- Pull weeds as soon as they appear. This is a big task when establishing a groundcover. Invest time now to eliminate the need to renovate a weed-infested planting. Try the milk-jug technique described on pages 110 and 136.

- Watch for scorch on groundcovers and vines growing in hot, sunny locations. Mulch the roots to reduce drought stress and scorch. Move plants that continually suffer from scorch to a shadier location.

- Monitor plants for Japanese beetles. These insects have made it to the Midwest and are causing damage throughout the area. These metallic, green-brown beetles eat the leaves of hundreds of different plants. Pick beetles off the plants and drop in a bucket of soapy water.

AUGUST

- Water established plantings during extended dry periods. Wet the top 6 to 8 inches when the soil is crumbly and moist.

- Do not fertilize in-ground plantings. Late-season fertilization can stimulate late-season growth that will not have time to harden off before winter.

- Capture and destroy slugs eating holes in the leaves of hostas and other shade lovers. Set out shallow tins, sunk into the ground, filled with beer, or use the natural products with iron phosphate as the active ingredient.

- Check honeysuckle vines for aphids. Dislodge the insects with a strong blast of water. Use several applications of insecticidal soap or Neem if populations reach damaging levels.

- Watch honeysuckle and other plants for powdery mildew. This fungus causes a white film on the leaves. Severe infestations block the sunlight, causing leaves to yellow. Increase sunlight and air circulation to reduce this problem. Try some of the new Neem-based fungicides to reduce further infection.

SEPTEMBER

- Move tropical vines indoors for winter as the temperatures cool, but before the first killing frost. Prune tropical vines back just enough to make them manageable for their indoor home. Control insect problems before moving them indoors with other houseplants.

- Decide how to manage any perennial vines that will need some winter protection. These can be planted in the ground, stored in an unheated garage, or given extra protection for the winter.

- Blow or rake fallen leaves off plants. Large leaves trap moisture, block sunlight, and lead to crown rot and other disease problems on groundcovers. Or cover plantings with netting to catch the falling leaves. Remove the leaf-covered netting. Drag it off or roll it up to keep the leaves on the netting until you clear the groundcover planting. Replace the netting and keep removing leaves until all of them have fallen to the ground.

OCTOBER

- Finish planting early in the month. This gives the plants time to start rooting into surrounding soil before the ground freezes. Wait until next spring to plant tender and borderline hardy plants. Give them as much time as possible to become established before winter.

- Overwinter hardy unplanted vines and groundcovers or container plantings for winter. Sink weatherproof pots into the ground to insulate the roots. Or move the potted vines into an unheated garage for winter and surround with bags of potting mix, packing peanuts or other insulating material. Water whenever the ground thaws and is dry. Or move the planters to a sheltered location. Pack bales of straw around the pot for added root insulation.

- Water new and established plantings thoroughly before the ground freezes.

NOVEMBER

- Remove the last of the fall leaves. Gently rake or blow leaves off groundcover plantings. Shred and compost or recycle the fallen leaves. Shredded leaves can be placed on the soil surface for mulch. They help insulate the roots, conserve moisture, reduce weeds, and add nutrients to the soil as they decompose.

- Protect plantings from voles and rabbits. Place a cylinder of hardware cloth around euonymus vines and other susceptible vines. Sink it several inches into the soil. Make sure it is at least 4 feet tall to discourage rabbits. Or spray susceptible vines and groundcovers, such as cranberry cotoneaster, with a homemade or commercial repellent.

- Remove dead and damaged branches whenever they are found. Disinfect tools between cuts on diseased plants. Use rubbing alcohol or a solution of one part bleach to nine parts water.

DECEMBER

- Check on vines stored in the garage or protected area for winter. Water whenever the soil thaws and the top 2 to 3 inches are dry. Add enough water to moisten all the soil.

- Adjust location or winter mulch if needed. Use evergreen boughs to protect European ginger and other tender plants from winter injury. Use your discarded holiday tree to create shade and windbreaks for tender vines. Evergreen vines, such as euonymus, often suffer leaf burn from winter winds.

- Shovel snow first and use de-icing salts only if needed. Consider spending a bit extra for plant friendly products to avoid damaging plants growing near walks and drives.

Annual flowers flank the perennial evergreen pachysandra groundcover for added seasonal color.

LAWNS
for the Midwest

Grass provides a unifying element in the landscape by connecting different gardens and creating a backdrop for other plants. It does not create a unified response when talking to gardeners. Some see lawns as a matter of pride, others a necessary evil, and some an environmental nightmare. Whether you view your lawn as a thing of beauty or as something to keep your feet from getting muddy when it rains, a healthy lawn will give you the results you want.

No matter what your perspective, you can minimize your efforts and maximize your results by matching mowing, fertilizing, and watering to the grass's needs, your quality goals, and the time available. Keep the grass healthy and you will reduce the time needed to rid it of insects, diseases, and weeds.

The amount of effort needed to manage your lawn depends somewhat on the level of quality desired and the amount of use your lawn receives. A golf course quality lawn will require more care than a lawn maintained at a lower quality level. A well-used lawn, with space for kids' play and sports, will also require more care than one merely viewed from the porch or only occasionally walked upon. Look at how you use your lawn and what quality level you desire to determine your yearly care schedule.

High-quality lawns with dense weed-free grass will receive the maximum number of fertilizations, three or four times per year, regular irrigation, and the most potential for pesticide (weedkillers, insecticides, and fungicides) use. Those interested in a nice looking, less-than-perfect lawn can get by with fewer fertilizer applications and less pesticide use. And we now have more eco-friendly options that also minimize your workload. No matter what quality level you desire, proper care and properly timed management are the keys to building a healthy and attractive lawn.

Kentucky bluegrass (*Poa pratensis*) is a good lawngrass choice for most of the midwest.

SELECTING THE RIGHT GRASS

Putting the right plant in the right location applies to lawns as well as to other garden plants. Cool-season grasses like Kentucky bluegrass, fine fescue, and perennial ryegrass are the best choices for the Midwest. These grasses provide some of the first and last glimpses of green in our cold northern climate. Those gardening south of the Missouri River can also grow warm-season grasses like zoysia. Those north of the Missouri River should not succumb to the zoysia ads that promise a dense, drought-tolerant, weed-free lawn. You will have this but you will also have a brown lawn for most of the year, including the cool months of spring and fall.

Those looking for lower maintenance lawns may want to consider the rhizomatous tall fescues (rtf). Tall fescues have long been used in the south for their heat and drought tolerance. The rtf varieties form a dense carpet like our more traditional lawns but are more heat and drought tolerant once established. The native buffalo grass is even more heat and drought tolerant, but can be slow to establish in the more northern parts of the Midwest.

And those looking for a lower maintenance and more ecological alternative to lawns should consider a no mow option. Mixes of various fine fescues provide a deep-rooted lawn in well-drained soils that require less fertilizations, watering, and mowing than traditional lawn grasses. They can be mowed monthly for a cropped appearance, just in fall when managing leaves, once in late spring when seedheads appear, or not at all. Check out Neil Diboll's No Mow Lawn factsheet at www.prairienursery.com for more details on selection, planting, and care.

No matter what type of grass you grow or management you select, a healthy lawn starts from the ground up. Investing time and effort before seeding or sodding your lawn will save you a lot of time and frustration managing problems in the future. Seeding a lawn takes more time to establish, but it saves you money and increases your selection of grass-seed mixtures. Sodded lawns give you instant beauty—at a price.

The best time to seed a lawn is late summer or early fall. The soil is warm and air is cool, perfect for our lawn grasses. Spring is next best time to seed a lawn. Sod can be laid anytime it is available for purchase and the soil can be prepared.

Start with a soil test to determine what nutrients and soil amendments should be added to the soil prior to planting. Contact your local Extension office or a state certified lab for details on taking and submitting a soil test. Allow several weeks for test results.

HOW TO SEED A LAWN

Kill the existing grass and weeds while you wait for the test results. Use a total vegetation killer such as Roundup® or Finale® for quickest results. Weedy areas may benefit from two applications made two weeks apart. Read and follow label directions exactly and wait the recommended time between treatment and tilling. Twice monthly cultivation for two years or solarization for six to eight weeks in summer are non-chemical options to killing vegetation.

Next, cultivate the top 6 inches to loosen compacted soil and turn under dead weeds and grass. This is your rough grade. But remember, only work the soil when it is moist but not wet to avoid compaction and clods. Working overly dry soil can destroy the soil structure.

Rake the area smooth, removing any rocks and debris. Allow the soil to settle. Time, rainfall, or a light sprinkling with water will help the soil to settle. Fill in any low spots. Slope the soil away from the house and make the final grade 1 inch lower than adjacent sidewalks and drives.

Till the recommended amount of fertilizer, organic matter and any other needed amendments into the top 6 inches of the soil. In general, new lawns need 1 pound of actual nitrogen per 1,000 square feet and several inches of organic matter such as compost. Many states have banned the use

A drop spreader is often used for fertilizing, but can also be used to apply seed. It ensures even grass seed coverage for a more uniform lawn.

Mulch newly seeded lawns to conserve moisture and reduce erosion. Use one of the cellulose based mulches, weed-free straw or hay, or floating row covers sold as GrassFast® or Reemay® for mulch. Cover the area with the row cover and anchor the edges with stones, boards, or wire anchors. Or spread the straw or hay over the soil surface. Apply a thin layer so some of the soil is still visible through the mulch. Thin layers of these materials can be left on the lawn to decompose naturally.

Water after seeding and frequently enough to keep the soil surface moist, but not soggy. You may need to water once or twice a day for several weeks. Once the grass begins to grow, you can reduce the watering frequency. Established seedlings should be watered thoroughly, but less frequently.

Start mowing once the grass is about 4 inches tall. Mow it to a height of 3 to 3½ inches for a healthier more drought- and pest-tolerant lawn. Continue mowing as needed.

HOW TO SOD A LAWN

Follow these steps for sodding. Prepare the soil as you would for seeding a lawn. Then calculate the amount of sod needed to cover the area. A roll of sod is usually 1½ feet wide by 6 feet long. It will cover 9 square feet.

Order sod to be delivered or plan on picking it up just prior to installation. Select freshly cut sod with a good green color free of weeds and pests. Use sod that has a blend of several grass varieties and is grown on a soil similar to yours. Store the sod, if needed, in a cool, shady place to prevent it from overheating and drying out. Lay it as soon as possible.

Use a driveway, sidewalk, or curb as your starting point. Lay the first row of sod next to the longest of these straight edges. Butt the sod ends together and make sure the roots contact the soil. Stagger the seams, as if you were laying bricks. Use a knife to trim the sod to fit. And lay the sod perpendicular to the slope on steep hills. Use wooden stakes to hold it in place.

of phosphorous fertilizers on lawns unless one is establishing a new lawn or a soil test indicates phosphorous is needed.

Rake the amended soil smooth and make any final adjustments to the final grade. Follow seeding rates on the back of the grass seed package. Using a drop-type or rotary spreader, sow half the seed in one direction and the remainder at right angles to the first.

Use a grass mix suitable for your light conditions. Lightly rake seeds into the top ¼ inch of soil. This is usually sufficient to ensure seed-to-soil contact. You can also use an empty lawn roller just to be sure. Always use rollers empty to avoid soil compaction.

Laying sod is the quickest and most satisfying (but also the most expensive) way to create an instant lawn.

Run an empty lawn roller over the sod if needed. Push it perpendicular to the direction that the sod was laid. Rolling removes air pockets and ensures good root-to-soil contact.

Water the sod immediately, moistening the sod and the top 3 to 4 inches of soil. Keep the sod and soil surface moist until the sod has rooted into the soil below. Continue watering thoroughly, but less frequently once this happens. Mow the sod once it is firmly rooted in place.

CARING FOR YOUR LAWN

Proper care is the best defense against weeds, disease, and insects. The three major practices include watering, fertilizing, and mowing. Manage these properly and you will be rewarded with a beautiful, healthy lawn.

WATER

Established lawns need about 1 inch of water per week from rain or irrigation. On clay soils, apply the needed water once a week. Sandy soils should receive ½ inch of water twice a week.

Improperly watered lawns suffer more problems than those that depend on rainfall as the sole source of water. Make the most of your efforts, if you decide to water your lawn by doing so properly.

Water lawns thoroughly when your footprints persist, the grass turns bluish gray, or the leaves start to roll. Water early in the day for best results. Watering early reduces disease problems and water lost to evaporation.

Monitor the amount of water you apply by setting several straight-sided cans under the area covered by a sprinkler. Once filled with the required amount of water, turn off the sprinkler and move it to the next location. Note the pressure used and the time it took to apply the needed water. Now you'll have an idea of how long you need to water.

If you allow your lawns to go dormant during hot dry weather, leave them dormant. Those lawns allowed to go in and out of dormancy suffer more than those left dormant. Minimize foot traffic and do not use high-nitrogen fertilizers or weedkillers on dormant lawns. Apply ¼ an inch of water to dormant lawns every 3 to 4 weeks during extended drought. This keeps the crown of the plant alive without breaking dormancy.

MOWING

Grow cool-season grasses 3 to 4 inches high. Taller grass produces deeper, more drought-tolerant roots and is better able to fight off insects, weeds, and disease. Mow frequently enough so that you remove no more than one-third (about 1 inch) of

A vertical mower (also called a power rake) makes quick work of the rigorious job of dethatching your lawn.

the total height. This is less stressful on the grass. Plus, you can leave these short clippings on the lawn. They break down quickly adding nutrients, moisture, and organic matter to the soil. They do not cause thatch. Use a mulching mower or run the mower over long clippings to cut them down in size. You can use long clippings as mulch or add them to the compost pile if the lawn has not been treated with a weed killer.

Sharpen the mower blades to make a clean cut that looks nicer and closes quickly, reducing moisture loss. You'll also use less gas and energy when mowing with sharp blades. And consider a reel type push or an electric mower where practical to reduce noise and air pollution when cutting the grass.

And sweep clippings off walks, drives, and other hard surfaces to keep this plant matter out of our waterways.

FERTILIZATION

Your soil test results will tell you what type and how much fertilizer the lawn grass you're growing will need. Most Midwest lawns are a blend of Kentucky bluegrass, fine fescues, and perennial ryegrass. These lawn areas need 1 to 3 pounds of nitrogen (N) per season. Most soils have high to excessive levels of phosphorus (P) and potassium (K) and need little or none of these nutrients. Plus, many states have banned the use of fertilizers containing phosphorous on established lawns. They can be used when establishing new lawns or if your soil test results show they are lacking.

Select the fertilizer recommended by your soil test and consider a low-nitrogen slow-release fertilizer. They feed the lawn over a long period of time, tend to be goof-proof, and will not burn the lawn in hot dry weather. Avoid midsummer fertilization on nonirrigated lawns as it can damage turf and encourage weed growth.

Start by calculating your lawn area by measuring the length and width of each section. Multiply the length times width to find the square footage of that portion of lawn. Approximate the area of irregularly shaped parcels.

Check the back of the fertilizer bags for details on application rates. They usually provide the square footage a bag will cover or rate of application per 1,000 square feet of lawn. Many also provide the recommended setting for various popular spreaders further making proper fertilizer application easier.

Apply half the needed fertilizer in one direction and the remaining half in the other direction. This will reduce the risk of striping and fertilizer burn. Be careful not to overlap or leave the spreader open when making your turns. And always sweep any fertilizer, grass clippings, or other chemicals off the drive, walks, or other hard surfaces. This prevents them from being washed into and polluting our waterways.

FERTILIZATION SCHEDULE

Apply the majority of fertilizer to cool-season grasses in fall. Make one fall application if you're going with a low-maintenance approach and three or four applications for moderate to highly managed lawns. Use the holiday schedule of Memorial Day, Labor Day as temperatures cool, and sometime between Halloween and Thanksgiving (but before the ground freezes). Use a low-nitrogen slow-release fertilizer for the spring application to avoid burn if the weather turns hot and dry. Those in the southern regions of the Midwest should skip the spring fertilization unless using a low-nitrogen slow-release fertilizer or irrigating throughout the summer. Only fertilize in midsummer if you are irrigating your lawn and going for "golf course" quality. Use a low-nitrogen slow-release fertilizer at this time to avoid burn.

Those growing warm-season grasses like zoysia should fertilize in May and mid-July (no later than August) and buffalograss in June.

AERATING AND DETHATCHING THE LAWN

Should you core aerate or dethatch your lawn this season? All the neighbors are doing it, so how about you? These practices have become a common part of the lawn care scene. Make sure you have a problem that these practices will solve before renting the equipment or hiring a professional. Core aeration can help reduce problems with compaction, and both dethatching and core aeration are useful to control thatch.

Thatch is a normal part of lawn culture. It is a layer of partially decomposed grass plants. It is not caused by short grass clippings left on the lawn to decompose. Leave a thin layer, ½ inch or less, of thatch to conserve moisture and reduce wear. Remove thick layers, greater than ½ inch, as these can prevent water and nutrients from reaching the grass roots.

Dethatching machines, called vertical mowers, are used to physically remove the layer of thatch. These machines cut through the thatch and pull it to the surface. This is stressful on the lawn and should only be done when the lawn is actively growing. Rake and compost the thatch removed during this process. This is also a good time to overseed thin lawns. Spread the seed over the recently dethatched lawn. The disturbed lawn provides a good surface for the seed to contact the soil and germinate.

Core aerators remove plugs of soil from the lawn. They open up the soil surface, allowing the thatch to decompose. Breaking up the cores and spreading the soil over the lawn surface helps speed up the process.

Aeration also reduces soil compaction. Compacted soils are poorly drained, limit root growth, and result in thin, unhealthy lawns. Lawns growing in clay soils or in high traffic areas are subject to compaction. Make sure the aerator cores through the thatch layer and several inches into the soil. This process opens up the soil, allowing air, water, and nutrients to reach the plant roots. Aeration is less stressful on the lawn than dethatching, but it is most effective when done in spring or fall when the lawn is actively growing. This is also a good time to overseed as the cores provide good seed-to-soil contact.

Prevent thatch from becoming a problem and eliminating the need to dethatch by adjusting your lawn care. Do not overwater or overfertilize the lawn and avoid excessive use of insecticides that may reduce earthworm populations. Earthworms are nature's aerating machines. And leave short clippings on the lawn to decompose. Mulch, or remove and compost long clippings that are free of pesticides.

PESTS

A healthy lawn is your best defense against weeds, insects, and diseases. Mow high, fertilize properly, and water during droughts to keep weeds and other pests under control. If a problem is discovered, find out why it has developed. Correcting the cause, not just killing the pest, will give you better long-term results.

BLUEGRASS
Poa pratensis

Why It's Special—The fine texture, medium to dark green color, and tolerance to mowing makes this a good choice for a manicured lawn in sunny areas. Use a mix of several varieties of bluegrass to create a more disease- and insect-resistant lawn.

How to Plant & Grow—Bluegrass grows best in full sun. It can be started from seed or sod. It thrives in cool temperatures and will go dormant and turn brown during hot weather and drought conditions. It usually recovers from normal droughts.

Care & Problems—Insect problems are more common during hot dry weather and diseases during moist seasons. Watch for Japanese beetles and other grubs as well as chinchbugs, sod webworms, and green aphids. Helminthosporium leaf spot, necrotic ring spot, snowmold, and summer patch are a few of its more common problems.

Hardiness—Throughout the Midwest but will turn brown during hot dry periods

Type—Cool-season

Texture—Fine

Mowing Height—3 to 4½ inches, removing no more than one-third total height

Water Needs—Water thoroughly whenever the top few inches of soil are crumbly and moist or footprints remain in lawn, usually 1 inch of water per week.

BUFFALOGRASS
Buchloe dactyloides

Why It's Special—This is the only native turfgrass. It is good for hot dry areas.

How to Plant & Grow—Lawns can be started from seed or plugs of sod. Start lawns in late spring for best results. Those with long warm falls can start new lawns in late summer. It's slow to establish in cooler parts of the Midwest and it may be hard to find. Avoid excess water and fertilizer that will increase weed problems. Fertilize in early June and early August with a low-nitrogen slow-release fertilizer.

Care & Problems—Once established and properly managed you will have few, if any, problems with buffalograss.

Hardiness—Throughout the Midwest

Type—Warm-season

Texture—Fine

Mowing Height—Mow weekly when grass is 3 inches high for a manicured lawn but only once every three to four weeks when the grass is 3 to 4 inches tall for a low-maintenance lawn. Remove no more than one-third total height.

Water Needs—Drought tolerant once established. This grass will go dormant but tolerates extended droughts. Only water during drought if you want to prevent the lawn from going dormant.

FINE FESCUE
Festuca species

Why It's Special—These are the main grasses for shadier and no mow lawns. They're often mixed with bluegrass in sun-shade mixes. Fescues tend to be more drought tolerant than bluegrass. Mow to achieve a manicured lawn weekly to 2½ to 3½ inches, and no-mow lawns every three to four weeks to 4 inches.

How to Plant & Grow—Start from seed. Fine fescues grow best in full sun to partial shade but will tolerate a bit more shade. It thrives in cool temperatures and will go dormant and turn brown during hot weather and drought conditions. It usually recovers from normal droughts.

Care & Problems—They generally have few problems. Japanese beetles and other grubs, sod webworms, and green aphid; as well as Helminthosporium leaf spot, necrotic ring spot, and rust are the main things to watch for.

Hardiness—Throughout the Midwest

Type—Cool-season

Texture—Depends on variety

Mowing Height—Depends on use. Mow at 2½ to 3½ inches, removing no more than one-third total height.

Water Needs—Water thoroughly whenever top few inches of soil are crumbly and moist or footprints remain in the lawn.

PERENNIAL RYEGRASS
Lolium perenne

Why It's Special—Turf-type perennial ryegrasses are now a major part of grass seed mixes. Their quick germination helps with lawn establishment and the finer texture and color of the turf-type varieties blend easily with bluegrass and fine fescues. Their pest resistance and durability make them suitable for high-traffic lawns and athletic fields.

How to Plant & Grow—Perennial ryegrass grows best in full sun but tolerates partial shade. It thrives in cool temperatures and will go dormant and turn brown during hot weather and drought conditions. It usually recovers from normal droughts.

Care & Problems—Perennial rye generally has few problems. Watch for Japanese beetles and other grubs as well as chinchbugs and sod webworm. Helminthosporium leaf spot, necrotic ring spot, and rust diseases may occur.

Hardiness—May suffer damage in extreme northern regions of the Midwest

Type—Cool-season

Texture—Fine

Mowing Height—Mow at 3½ to 4½ inches, removing no more than one-third total height.

Water Needs—Water 1 inch per week to keep it actively growing. Water thoroughly whenever top few inches of soil are crumbly and moist or footprints remain in the lawn.

TURF TYPE TALL FESCUE
Festuca arundinacea cultivars

Why It's Special—The turf type tall fescues create a more uniform lawn than the straight species with their more bunching type of growth habit. Use turf type tall fescues for lower maintenance lawns and highly used locations as it fills in damaged spots quickly. It's more drought tolerant than bluegrass, fescues, and ryegrass.

How to Plant & Grow—These grow best in full sun to partial shade but will tolerate a bit more shade. They are available as seed or sod. Prepare the soil and provide seed or sod the amount of moisture needed for establishment. Do not mix with other grasses as its lighter color and coarser texture is hard to blend with more traditional lawn grasses. Water turf-type tall fescue lawns thoroughly during drought if you want to prevent dormancy.

Care & Problems—These grasses generally have few problems. Grubs as well as Helminthosporium leaf spot, necrotic ring spot, and rust are the main ones.

Hardiness—Throughout the Midwest

Type—Cool-season

Texture—Coarse

Mowing Height—Mow at 3 to 4½ inches, removing no more than one-third total height.

Water Needs—Drought tolerant, requiring about 30 percent less water than traditional lawns and one of the last to go dormant in hot dry weather.

ZOYSIA
Zoysia species

Why It's Special—Zoysia is a great low-maintenance, dense, drought-tolerant turf for southern Midwest lawns. North of the Missouri River it may not survive winter or will be brown during cooler months of the growing season (spring and fall). Zentih and Meyer are more cold hardy and better suited to the climate in lower Midwest.

How to Plant & Grow—Available as seed, sprigs, plugs, and sod. Zoysia lawns need minimal fertilization. Make no more than two applications of a slow-release fertilizer starting in May and no later than early August. Overwatering and overfertilization can reduce the vigor of the zoysia and increase weed problems.

Care & Problems—Thatch is a problem. Monitor and remove when thatch is more than ½ inch thick. Zoysia generally has few insect and disease problems. Watch for grubs and billbugs and manage as needed.

Hardiness—Not hardy for areas north of the Missouri River

Type—Warm-season

Texture—Coarse

Mowing Height—Mow at 1½ to 2½ inches, removing no more than one-third the total height.

Water Needs—Drought tolerant once established. Zoysia needs about ½ inch of water per week to prevent dormancy.

SELECTING GRASS SEED

Select a seed mix suited to the growing conditions and intended use. Cool-season grass seed mixes should contain several varieties of each type (bluegrass, fescue, and ryegrass) of grass. This increases disease resistance and reduces the risk of losing your whole lawn to a pest infestation.

Purchase high quality seed. Check the date to make sure the seed is fresh. Select a grass seed with a high rate of germination. The higher the germination rate, the more viable (living) seeds the mix contains. The purity rate tells you what percentage of the mix is desirable grass seed. The remainder includes other grass seeds, weed seeds, dirt, and chaff. A high percent of purity means you are paying for seeds and not unwanted "other ingredients."

DEALING WITH SHADE

Nothing beats a nice stand of shade trees when it comes to beating the summer heat—unless you are trying to grow grass under those trees, that is! The lack of sunlight and competition for water make it difficult, if not impossible, to grow grass under some shade trees. But you do not have to sacrifice the shade or give up on the lawn. Here are some tips for getting both the shade and the lawn you want:

- Plant shade-tolerant grass seed mixes in these areas. They contain a high percentage of fine fescue grass. This shade- and drought-tolerant grass is the best choice for shady locations.

- Plant shade-tolerant groundcovers in heavily shaded areas. Hostas, barrenwort (*Epimedium*), pachysandra, deadnettle (*Lamium*), and Canadian ginger are just a few of the shade-tolerant groundcovers you can try. Start with just a few plants to make sure there is enough sunlight and moisture for the groundcovers.

- Mulch densely shaded areas. Spread 3 inches of woodchips under the tree. Keep the woodchips away from a tree's trunk. The woodchips improve the growing conditions, while keeping the lawn mower and weedwhip away from the trunk of a tree.

MANAGING MUSHROOMS AND MOSS IN THE LAWN

Mushrooms and moss can drive turf enthusiasts to distraction. There is no miracle cure for either. Like all weeds, once we find the cause of the problem, we have also found the cure.

- Mushrooms are the fruiting bodies of fungi. They typically appear after a period of cool, wet weather. The underground fungus feeds on decaying tree roots and wood in the soil. Once the food source is gone, the fungus disappears. Rake and break up the mushrooms to prevent kids and pets from eating them. Time is the only eco-friendly cure.

- Moss also thrives in moist conditions. It is commonly seen in shaded areas with compacted and poorly drained soils. Change the poor growing conditions, and you will eliminate the moss.

- Increase sunlight by having a certified arborist thin the tree canopies. Add organic matter to improve drainage and try shade-tolerant grass and groundcovers.

- If the moss returns, you may have to look for alternatives to grass. Try mulching the area with woodchips or shredded bark. Or better yet, add a few steppingstones and call it a moss garden!

GRASS LAWN CHOKED BY WEEDS AND MOSS

DOG URINE BURN

DOG URINE BURN

Dogs often cause brown spots of dead grass in the lawn. Their nitrogen-rich urine acts just like fertilizer burn. The treatment is the same. Thoroughly water the area to dilute the urine and wash it through the soil. It may not be practical, but it is effective. The surrounding grass will eventually fill in these brown areas. Nature and time do heal many landscape problems. I have had mixed reports on some of the new urine-neutralizing products. Several people have reported great success while others find the watering works just as well. Some gardeners train their dogs to go in a specific area. They may have several mulched areas for this purpose.

COMMON DISEASES

Monitor your lawns for disease problems. They are more common on stressed lawns and wet weather. Here are a few of the more common Midwest lawn diseases:

- Helminthosporium leaf spot and melting-out diseases cause irregular patches of brown and dying grass. A close look at nearby blades reveals brown to black spots on leaves. As the disease progresses, the patch gets larger and the grass begins to disintegrate and disappear (melt away). Overseed areas with resistant grass varieties.

- Snow mold is most evident in the spring as the snow and ice melt. Infected lawns have small to large patches of white or gray matted turf. The grass thins and is slow to recover in spring. Lightly rake the lawn in early spring, and avoid overuse of nitrogen in the spring.

- Powdery mildew looks as though someone has sprinkled baby powder on the leaves. It is most common during droughts and on shady lawns in the fall, but it can appear anytime during the growing season. Overseed shady areas with fine fescue, or increase the sunlight by thinning the crowns of trees.

- Rust-infected lawns have brown, orange, or yellow spots on the leaves. This is a common problem on drought-stressed and newly seeded lawns with a high percentage of ryegrass. As the percentage of bluegrass and fescue increases, rust usually becomes less of a problem. Proper care increases turf health and allows it to tolerate the damage. Treatment is usually not needed.

- Necrotic ring spot (formerly known as fusarium blight) appears as circles or irregular patches of dead grass with tufts of green grass in the center. All bluegrass and fescue varieties appear to be susceptible. Overseeding with perennial ryegrass may help mask symptoms. Proper care and time for the disease to run its course is usually the most successful treatment.

- Fairy ring is not life threatening, but it can cause aesthetic concerns. Infected lawns have rings of dark green, yellow, or dying turf. The rings appear for a short time, disappear, and then return—slightly larger in diameter—later or the next season. During wet periods, mushrooms will appear within the ring. No control is needed (or practical). Water fairy rings during drought to minimize the symptoms.

SNOW MOLD

MONITOR FOR INSECTS

Before reaching for the can of insecticide, make sure insects are really the problem with your lawn. Here are some easy tests you can conduct to determine if insects are damaging your lawn:

- Flotation Test: This test is used for chinch bugs. Remove both ends of a coffee can or similar container. Sink the can in the grass at the edge of the dead area. Fill the can with water and agitate the grass. Chinch bugs will float to the surface. Test several areas. Treatment is needed if you find two or three of these insects per test.

- Irritation Test: This test will detect sodwebworm larvae. Mix I tablespoon dishwashing detergent in I gallon of water. Sprinkle the soapy water over I square yard of lawn. Conduct the test in several areas, both damaged spots and areas adjacent to the damaged grass. Check the treated areas several times over the next ten minutes. Treat if one or more sodwebworm larvae are present.

- Turf Removal: This is done to confirm the presence of grubs. Cut out and remove I square foot of turf. Check the top 4 to 6 inches of soil for white grub larvae. Replace the sample and keep the soil moist until it re-roots. Treat if three or four grubs are found per I square foot of turf.

RENOVATING A LAWN

Fall is the best and spring is the next best time to renovate poor quality lawns. Renovation is the last step before replacement. Use this method on lawns that are thin, have lots of bare spots, or are full of weeds. Consider hiring a professional for large jobs. To renovate your lawn:

1. Cut the grass as short as possible. It will act as a living mulch. Rake off and compost clippings.

2. Remove the thatch layer if it is greater than ½ inch thick. Use a vertical mower to lift the thatch. Set the revolving blades to slice into the top ½ inch of soil. This will remove the thatch while creating grooves or slits in the soil surface. These slits make a good seedbed. Rake up and compost the debris.

3. Or core aerate compacted soil to improve drainage and seeding success. Core aerate in several directions.

4. Spread grass seed over the renovated area using a broadcast or drop-type spreader. Apply half the recommended amount in one direction and the remainder at right angles to the first. Rake for good seed-to-soil contact.

5. Fertilize renovated lawns the next month.

6. Raise the mower back to the recommended 3 or 3½ inch mowing height. Cut the grass once it reaches 4 inches tall.

JANUARY

- Shovel walks and driveways before using deicing salts to reduce damage to lawns and other valuable plants.

- Avoid walking on frozen grass that lacks the protective covering of snow.

- Watch for vole activity. These rodents scurry beneath the snow eating seeds, chewing on bark, and wearing trails in the lawn. Be prepared to do a little raking and overseeding in the spring.

FEBRUARY

- As the snow recedes lightly rake to fluff and dry grass to reduce the risk of snow mold disease.

- Once the snow has melted and soil has thawed (most of us will have to wait) water the grass along the driveway and sidewalks to leach (wash) the salts through the soil.

- This is a great time to take your lawn mower to the repair shop and beat the spring rush.

MARCH

- Get out the leaf rake as soon as the snow and ice melt. Lightly rake to dry the grass and reduce the risk of snow mold. Remove any leaves and debris that may have collected prior to the snowfall.

- In dry springs, water areas exposed to deicing salts to wash the salts through the soil and reduce damage caused. Water areas of the lawn that were seeded or sodded at the end of last season. This will reduce the stress on the young, developing root systems.

- Tamp down runways formed by vole activity over winter. Severely damaged areas may need to be reseeded. Fill in any holes dug by animals or created by winter activities.

APRIL

- Those in Missouri and Kansas can dethatch and aerate actively growing lawns and plant cool-season grasses, the rest of the Midwest needs to wait until end of this month or early May for the soil to warm.

- This is a good time to repair damaged areas in the lawn. You can purchase lawn repair kits. These contain the seed and mulch needed to repair problem areas. You can make your own lawn patch by mixing a handful of a quality grass-seed mix into a bucket of topsoil. Remove the dead turf, loosen and amend soil as needed, and then apply the patch. Mulch to conserve moisture.

- If your healthy lawn has not kept crabgrass under control you may want to use a crabgrass pre-emergent. Corn gluten makes a good pre-emergent for crabgrass and other plants.

Apply crabgrass pre-emergents to problem areas, about the time that the Vanhoutte spirea (bridal wreath) start to bloom or lilac buds swell. This is when soil temperature is about 50 degrees F and crabgrass starts to germinate. Do not use these products if you plan to seed or overseed the lawn this spring. Pre-emergents will kill the desirable grass seeds as well as the weed seeds.

MAY

- This is the second-best time to seed or overseed cool-season lawns in most of the Midwest (fall is the best time) and it's still a good time to lay sod.

- Mid-May is the best time to fertilize zoysia lawns in Missouri and Kansas.

- Late May to early June is the first time to fertilize your cool season lawn. Consider using a low-nitrogen slow-release fertilizer to reduce the risk of burn on nonirrigated lawns. Those in southern Missouri and Kansas may want to skip this application on non-irrigated lawns.

- Control creeping Charlie, also known as ground ivy, when in full bloom for best results. Spot treat with broadleaf weedkillers labeled for this as well as the organic broadleaf weedkiller containing the active ingredient Fehedta or hedta iron.

JUNE

- Continue watering new lawns. Water established lawns only as needed. If your footprints remain in the lawn, the color turns a dull bluish gray, or the leaves start to roll, it is time to water the lawn. Water thoroughly, but less frequently to encourage deep roots for drought tolerance.

- Turf-damaging grubs are the immature larvae of several different beetles. They feed on grass roots, causing the turf to be uniformly thin, droughty, or dead. Treat only if three or four grubs are found per every 1 square foot of turf sampled.

- Anthills may sporadically appear throughout the lawn. They generally do not harm anything, but just annoy some homeowners. If their activity is damaging the turf roots, or if you cannot abide their presence, you may chose to use an insecticide. Spot treat to avoid killing the good insects in the soil. Select an insecticide labeled for use on lawns to control the problem pest.

- The warm weather is perfect for most weeds. Do not use herbicides (weedkillers) in the summer. They can damage your lawn when applied in hot, dry weather. Dig up small numbers of weeds or those in bloom. Removing their flowers will help reduce future weed problems.

JULY

- Fertilize zoysia lawns if needed in mid-July but no later than early August.

- As the heat increases and the weather turns dry, you will need to decide how you will manage your lawn through droughts. Growing lawns need 1 inch of water per week. You may need to step in and give nature a hand during July and August. Or allow your lawn to go dormant. During an extended drought water dormant lawns ¼ inch every three or four weeks. This is enough water to prevent the plants from drying, while still keeping them dormant.

- Only irrigated and highly managed lawns can be fertilized this month. Use a low-nitrogen slow-release fertilizer to reduce the risk of burn. Do not fertilize dormant or non-irrigated lawns. This can damage and even kill the grass.

AUGUST

- Mid-August through mid-September, as temperatures cool, is the best time to repair, replace, or start a new lawn in the upper Midwest. Those in warmer areas should wait for cooler weather.

- Dormant lawns should be left dormant until the drought conditions pass. Give them ¼ inch of water during extended (three to four weeks) drought periods.

- Skunks, raccoons, and moles can damage lawns with their digging and tunneling. These critters are searching for big, fat, tasty grubs. Continual damage means they have found a food source and plan to stay. Get rid of the grubs and you will solve the problem. Squirrels can also dig in the lawn. They are storing nuts and seeds for future meals. The damage is irritating, but not a threat to the health of the lawn. Gently tamp down disturbed areas.

- Drought-stressed and newly seeded lawns are often infected with rust. You may notice an orange residue on grass leaves or your shoes after walking across the lawn. The symptoms will soon disappear and the grass will begin to recover on its own. Treatment is usually not needed.

SEPTEMBER

- Whether you are renovating an existing lawn, starting a new one, or just patching bare spots, early to mid-September is the best time to plant cool season grass seed. Those in southern areas of Midwest can continue seeding lawns into mid-October.

- Now is the time to correct compacted soils and thatch problems with core aeration. Dethatching can also be done and overseeding after both is beneficial for thin lawns.

- Make your Labor Day fertilizer application once the temperatures cool. The September fertilization helps lawns recover from the stresses of summer.

- Fall is the best time to control perennial weeds, such as dandelions and plantain. The chemicals are usually more effective, and the actively growing grass will quickly fill in the empty spaces.

- You can control violets in the lawn with a broadleaf weedkiller for difficult weeds. Make the first application in mid-September. Repeat in late October if weeds are still present.

- Grubs are starting to move deeper into the soil for winter. Complete all grub treatments by September 15 in upper Midwest and end of the month farther south. Only treat lawns that have been diagnosed with a problem that needs control.

OCTOBER

- Shred leaves with the mower the next time you cut the grass. You may need to make several passes with the mower during peak leaf drop. As long as you can see the grass blades, the lawn will be fine.

- Late October is the most important fertilizer application for your cool season lawn. Use a low-nitrogen slow-release fertilizer for best results.

- Keep cutting the grass as long as it keeps growing. No need to cut it short. Remove no more than one-third of the total height at each cutting.

- Apply a broadleaf herbicide (weedkiller) to creeping Charlie and other difficult to control weeds in mid- to late October after a hard frost. Make a second application to violets if needed.

NOVEMBER

- Dormant seeding is risky. Unseasonably warm weather coaxes the seed to germinate. A quick drop back to normal cold can kill the young seedlings. You might want to risk a little seed and some time on small areas, but think twice before seeding large areas or new lawns.

- Winterize your mower. Empty the gas tank, or fill it with a gas preservative. Clean off dirt and matted grass and check the owner's manual for specific information.

- Safely store fertilizers and pesticides. Always leave pesticides in their original containers, place in a locked area, away from pets and children. Store granular formulations in cool, dry locations and liquids out of direct sunlight and freezing temperatures.

DECEMBER

- Shovel first before applying deicing salt. This reduces the amount of salt needed to control ice on walks and drives. It also eliminates salt-laden snow from ending up on the lawn. And consider using plant-friendly deicing compounds.

- Apply deicing compounds down the middle of walks and drives, avoiding the grass.

- Note the areas most affected by deicing salts. Water these areas in spring to dilute the salts and wash them through the soil. Or consider redesigning the area to minimize damage. You may want to expand the walk and replace problem areas with pavers, mulch, annuals, or more salt-tolerant plants.

Lawns are fairly resilient. With a little time and elbow grease, you can turn your lawn to dense, deep green brilliance.

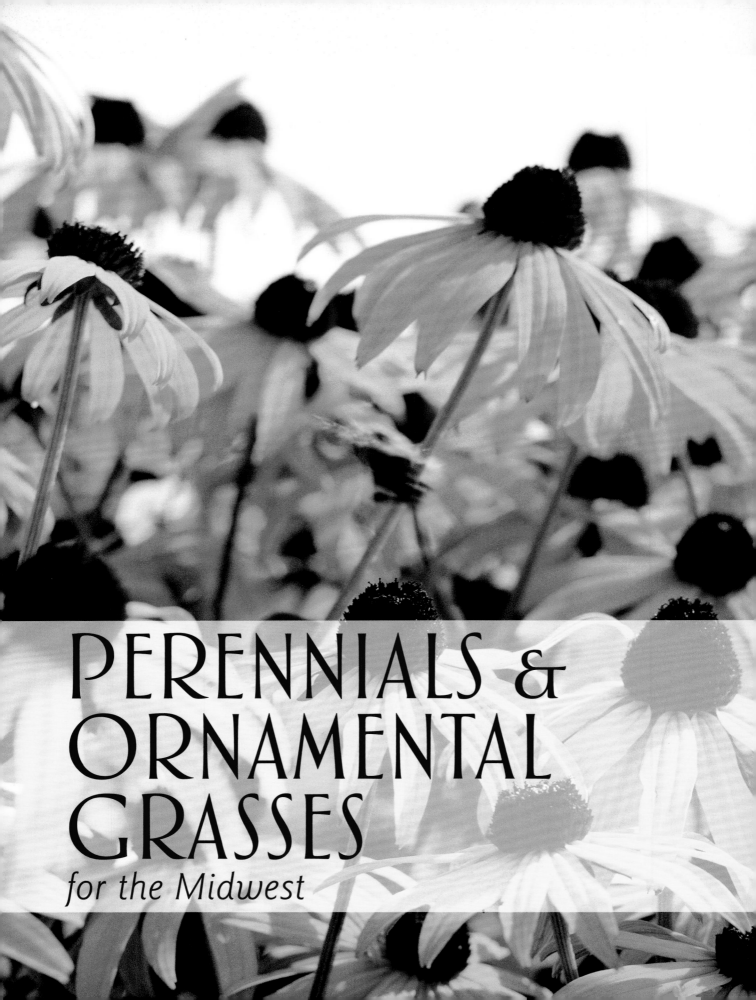

PERENNIALS & ORNAMENTAL GRASSES

for the Midwest

Perennials, including ornamental grasses, are an important part of Midwest landscapes. No longer relegated to a single garden in the back, they are now being used throughout the yard. Many people have eliminated their lawns and replaced them with perennial plantings. Others have ripped out the yews and junipers around the foundation and replaced them with perennials and other ornamental shrubs. Some gardeners have added just a few plants as groundcovers or specimens in their existing landscape. Whether you are adding a few or a few hundred perennials, proper selection, planting, and care are essential to gardening success.

Whether you're creating an English cottage garden or the New American Garden (style), everyone seems to want season-long blooms with no maintenance. While many perennials require less maintenance than other landscape plants, they do require some yearly care. You will need to prune back in the spring and divide occasionally. Some perennials need fertilizing, deadheading, and winter protection.

Very few perennials bloom from spring through fall. But a well-planned garden can provide year-round interest from the foliage, flowers, and seedpods. Some gardeners mix a few annuals in with their perennials. Annuals can fill in voids left by winter damage, empty spots between new plantings, and planning mistakes. Use tall cultivars of ageratums, linear-leafed zinnias, and other perennial-looking plants. Or use individual plants, rather than mass plantings, to help them blend into your perennial garden design.

Start looking through the plant profiles in this book, magazines, and botanical gardens to create a list of perennials and ornamental grasses you want to include. Always select perennials suited to the growing conditions. That includes soil, light, moisture, and, of course, hardiness. Look for low-maintenance plants if you are busy, have more garden than time, or just prefer to spend more time relaxing in, rather than working on your garden.

Consider the foliage, as well as the flowers, when planning your garden. Some plants, such as coralbells and the ornamental grasses, have attractive foliage all season long. Others, such as poppies and bleeding heart, fade away in midsummer. And do not forget about fall color. Many perennials, such as willow amsonia, evening primrose, and some sedums, have colorful fall foliage.

Include some perennials that provide winter interest and food for wildlife. Add ornamental grasses, rudbeckias, coneflowers, and other plants that have attractive seedpods.

DESIGN

Once you have a list of potential plants for the garden, check out their bloom period. You can design your landscape so something is always blooming in every part of the yard. Or you may prefer peak areas of interest that change throughout the season. You may have one garden or a section of a garden that looks great for a short period of time. As it fades, another area comes into full bloom and becomes the new focal point. Place the gardens in areas where you will get the most enjoyment when they are at their peak. Design your plantings to fit your lifestyle and needs.

Now look at your design realistically. Most people take on more than they can maintain. It seems everyone has bigger plans and more plants than time available. Beginning gardeners or those with limited time should start small. Design beds with easy access for planting and maintaining. Try using fewer types but more of each type of perennial in your garden. That design strategy will result in an easier to maintain garden that will provide a bigger overall effect. Don't forget to plan for some winter interest. Seedpods and evergreen leaves can add impact and attract birds during our longest season—winter.

SOIL PREPARATION

Take time to properly prepare the soil before planting. Investing the time and effort up front will minimize future maintenance and pest problems. See this book's introduction for ways to convert existing lawn and weed patches into beautiful garden beds.

Start with a soil test to find out how much if any additional nutrients are needed. Begin preparing soil when you have time, the soil is workable, and of course before you start planting. Grab a handful of soil, gently squeeze and then tap with your finger. If it breaks into smaller pieces, then the soil is ready to work.

Add 2 to 4 inches of compost, aged manure, or other organic matter into the top 12 inches of soil. Organic matter improves drainage in heavy clay soils and increases the water-holding ability of sandy and rocky soils.

Only add fertilizer if it is recommended by your soil test report. Research has found that a 1- to 2-inch layer of organic matter applied to the soil surface every other year provides sufficient nutrients for perennials. Excess fertilizer can cause poor flowering, leggy growth, and stunted root systems. Use no more than 1 pound of a 10 percent, or 2 pounds of a 5 percent nitrogen fertilizer per 100 square feet if your plants need a boost. A low-nitrogen slow-release fertilizer will provide small amounts of nutrients to your plants throughout the season. And they won't burn the plants in hot dry weather.

Once the organic matter and fertilizer are incorporated, level and rake the garden bed smooth. Lightly sprinkle with water or wait several days for the soil to settle.

PLANTING

Perennials are sold bare-root, container-grown, and field-potted. Bare-root perennials are plants sold without any growing media on the roots. Store them in a cool, but not freezing, location until you are ready to plant. Keep the roots moist and packed in peat moss, sawdust, or another similar material. Move dormant bare-root plants into the garden as soon as the soil is workable and ready for planting. Pot up bare-root plants that begin to grow in transport or storage. Grow in a sunny window indoors or outdoors in the protection of a coldframe. Move these plants into the garden after hardening off, and the danger of severe weather has passed.

Container-grown plants are grown and sold in pots. Some are grown outdoors and can be planted as soon as they are purchased. Others are grown in greenhouses and need to be hardened off, toughened to outdoor conditions, before planting. Store potted perennials in a shaded location until they can be planted in the garden. These small pots need to be watered daily. Water and allow the potted plants to drain prior to planting. Remove container-grown plants from the pot. Loosen potbound roots to encourage root development into the surrounding soil. Plant these at the same level they were growing in the container.

Field-potted plants are grown in the field and potted for delivery as they are dug. The freshly potted plants often lack a cohesive rootball. Minimize problems by digging the hole first. Cut off the bottom of the pot and set it into the planting hole. Adjust planting depth so the crown, the point where the stem joins the roots, is even with the soil surface. Slice down the side and peel away the pot. Backfill, gently tamp, and water to eliminate air pockets.

Check all new plantings for soil settling. Perennials often die when the soil settles and their roots are exposed. Fill in low spots and cover exposed roots as needed.

CARE

New plantings need extra attention. Check them every other day for the first few weeks. Water thoroughly and often enough to keep the soil slightly moist. Gradually increase the time between waterings. The goal is to encourage deep drought-tolerant and pest-resistant roots.

Most established perennials need about an inch of water per week. Water thoroughly, moistening the top 6 inches of soil. Once established, many perennials will only need supplemental watering during extended dry periods. Water whenever the top 4 inches of soil are crumbly and slightly moist. This is usually about once a week in clay soils and twice a week in sandy soil when the weather is dry.

Try to water early in the day and apply the water directly to the soil with soaker hoses or drip irrigation. You'll waste less water and avoid diseases caused by wet foliage.

Mulch perennials with a 1- to 2-inch layer of organic material such as twice-shredded bark, shredded leaves, or evergreen needles. It conserves moisture, reduces weed problems, and improves the soil as they decompose.

Deadheading and pruning can help control growth, increase flowering, and reduce pest problems. Some plants require a lot of work, and others perform fine on their own. Some cultivars require less maintenance and have fewer problems than the species. Select the perennial and its cultivars that best fit your growing conditions and maintenance schedule.

Control plant height, reduce floppiness, and delay flowering with proper pruning. Cut back sedum, coneflower, asters, and mums early in the season. This encourages shorter, stiffer branches. Stop pruning late June to early July to avoid delaying bloom until frost.

Pinch out the growing tips on small plants or prune back taller plants halfway down the stem. Prune above a set of healthy leaves. See plant profiles and monthly tips for more specifics.

Use garden scissors or hand pruners to make the cuts when pruning or deadheading. Remove the flower stem just above the first set of leaves or side shoots. Prune back further on the stem after the second flush of flowers. This encourages branching and new, more attractive foliage.

Divide perennials to improve their health and appearance or to start new plants. It's time to get busy when the perennials are too big for the location, flower poorly, flop over, or open in the center. In general, lift and divide spring-flowering plants in late summer and fall-flowering plants in the spring. Summer bloomers can be divided in spring or late summer. But you will soon discover that gardeners divide perennials when they have time. As long as you provide proper post-transplant care, the plants will be fine. See page 136 for step-by-step directions.

As you dig and divide take time to improve the soil in current and future location for the overgrown perennial and its divisions. Work a couple handfuls of compost into the soil before replanting.

Add life to tired beds. If the plants are few and far between and the weeds are many, it's time to start over. But if the perennials just need a bit of TLC and the weeds are few, try vertical mulching. Spread the 1- to 2-inch layer of compost over the soil surface. Use an auger bit (used for planting bulbs) on your cordless drill. Drill 6-inch deep holes throughout the garden. Fill the holes with additional compost if desired. You'll aerate the soil while moving the compost down to the root zone of the plants.

Winter-mulch new plantings and tender perennials. Cover the plants with evergreen branches, straw, or marsh hay after the ground lightly freezes. Remove the mulch in the spring as new growth begins. Winter-mulching keeps the soil temperature consistently cold. That eliminates frost heaving caused by the freezing and thawing of soil throughout the winter. Frost heaving damages plant roots and can even push perennials right out of the soil.

PESTS

Weeds are a major pest. They compete with perennials for water and nutrients and often harbor insects and diseases. Pull these invaders as soon as they appear. Healthy perennials growing in properly prepared soil will be able to crowd out most weeds by the second or third summer. You may need to enlist help controlling quackgrass, bindweed, and other hard-to-control perennial weeds. Spot treat with a total vegetation killer such as Roundup® or Finale®. These materials are absorbed by the leaves and move through the plant killing the roots and all. Protect nearby plants that can also be killed by these herbicides. Once the chemical touches the soil, it won't harm the plants.

Use a milk jug or soda bottle with the bottom removed to isolate the weeds when spraying. Set the milk jug over the weed. Spray the total vegetation killer through the top opening. Once it drips off the leaves and inside of the bottle you can move it to the next weed. Or, if you have more weeds than flowers, cover the flowers, and spray the surrounding weeds.

Help suppress weeds by covering the soil surface with a couple inches of shredded leaves, evergreen needles, or other organic mulch. These suppress weeds, conserve moisture, and help improve the soil as they decompose. And the seedlings that are able to make it through the mulch are much easier to pull.

Follow a Plant Health Care approach when managing insects and diseases. See page 16 for details on this method. And look at the individual plant profiles and monthly tips for more information on managing pests.

A great way to reduce future problems is to remove all disease- and insect-infested plant debris in the fall. But leave the seedheads and healthy foliage for winter interest, to attract birds and increase hardiness. Save major cleanup for late winter or early spring before new growth begins. You'll be ready to spend some time in your garden after our long winters and before the busy garden season gets underway.

Despite the long list of chores, perennial gardening can be relatively low maintenance and worth the effort. The best part, you'll find, is the seasonal change. It is so exciting to watch the first plants peek through the cold soil in the spring. The garden continues to grow and change through summer and fall. And in winter, the snow-covered seedheads, rustling foliage, and visiting birds will add a new dimension to the season.

Consider adding a few of the Perennial Plants of the Year. These plants were selected by members of the Perennial Plant Association for their low maintenance, ease of propagation, multi-season interest, and suitability to a wide range of climates. See www.perennialplant.org for more information. Past winners of the Perennial Plant of the Year include:

2014: Northwind Switchgrass (*Panicum virgatum* 'Northwind')

2013: Variegated Solomon's Seal (*Polygonatum odoratum* 'Variegatum')

2012: Jack Frost Siberian bugloss (*Brunnera* 'Jack Frost')

2011: Blue Star (*Amsonia hubrichtii*)

2010: Blue false indigo (*Baptisia australis*)

2009: Japanese Forest Grass (*Hakonachloa macra* 'Aureola')

2008: Rozanne cranesbill geranium (*Geranium* 'Rozanne')

2007: Walker's Low catmint (*Nepeta* 'Walker's Low)

2006: Firewitch cheddar pink (*Dianthus gratianopolitanus* 'Feuerhexe')

2005: Lenten rose (*Helleborus* x hybridus)

2004: Japanese painted fern (*Athyrium niponicum* 'Pictum')

2003: Becky shasta daisy (*Leucanthemum* 'Becky')

2002: Phlox 'David' (*Phlox* 'David')

2001: Karl Foerster feather reed grass (*Calamagrostis* x *acutiflora* 'Karl Foerster')

2000: Butterfly blue pincushion flower (*Scabiosa columbaria* 'Butterfly Blue')

1999: Goldsturm black-eyed Susan (*Rudbeckia fulgida* var. *sullivantii* 'Gold-sturm')

1998: Magnus purple coneflower (*Echinacea purpurea* 'Magnus')

1997: May Night salvia (*Salvia* 'May Night')

1996: Husker red beardstongue (*Penstemon digitalis* 'Husker Red')

1995: Russian sage (*Perovskia atriplicifolia*)

1994: Sprite astilbe (*Astilbe* 'Sprite')

1993: Sunny Border blue speedwell (*Veronica* 'Sunny Border Blue')

1992: Moonbeam coreopsis (*Coreopsis verticillata* 'Moonbeam')

1991: Palace purple alumroot (*Huechera micrantha* 'Palace Purple')

1990: Native creeping phlox (*Phlox stolonifera*)

AMSONIA
Amsonia hubrichtii

Why It's Special—Multiple seasons of interest was just one of many attributes that made this a Perennial Plant of the Year. Its airy fine foliage is a nice backdrop for the steel blue spring flowers. The narrow leaves turn a clear yellow in fall that glow in the garden.

How to Plant & Grow—Start plants from seeds indoors in spring. Plant dormant plants in spring when severe weather has passed and soil is workable. Plant hardened-off transplants in the garden after the danger of frost has passed. Dig and divide in spring or fall to propagate more plants. Space plants 3 feet apart.

Care & Problems—Avoid high-nitrogen fertilizers, excess fertilization, and heavy shade that can cause plants to flop open. After flowering, cut the plants back to 6 to 8 inches above the ground for denser growth. Or mix it with neighboring plants that can provide support.

Hardiness—Zones 4 to 9

Seasonal Color—Steel blue flowers; golden yellow fall foliage

Peak Season—May and June

Mature Size (H x W)—2 to 3 ft. x 2 to 3 ft.

Water Needs—Keep soil evenly moist.

ARTEMISIA
Artemisia species

Why It's Special—The fragrant, silver leaves of artemisia can brighten any garden all season long. Use these plants in hot dry locations as well as in cut and dried flower arrangements. This group of plants is commonly called wormwood for their past use as an ant- (in cupboards) and moth- (in clothing) repellent.

How to Plant & Grow—Plant hardened-off artemisia anytime during the growing season. Grow in well-drained infertile soils to avoid floppy growth. Space plants 15 to 24 inches apart.

Care & Problems—Avoid excess fertilization that leads to floppy open growth and overwatering that leads to root rot. Established artemisia will be able to crowd out most weeds by the second or third summer. Divide fast-growing artemisias every few years to control the spread and keep the plants healthy. Prune plantings once or twice a season before flowering to encourage shorter, stiffer growth and to prevent open centers on the low growing, mounded types.

Hardiness—Throughout the Midwest, varies by species

Seasonal Color—Silver foliage

Peak Season—Season-long

Mature Size (H x W)—1 to 3 ft. x 1 to 3 ft.

Water Needs—Drought tolerant once established.

ASTER
Symphytrichum species

Why It's Special— Asters can add a last flash of color to the landscape before the snow falls. Include asters in your garden to help attract butterflies, for use as cut flowers, and for a little winter interest.

How to Plant & Grow—Plant dormant asters in the spring after the danger of severe weather has passed. Plant hardened-off potted plants anytime during the growing season. Plant less hardy species and cultivars early in the season to give them time to establish before winter. Plant asters at least 2 feet apart.

Care & Problems—Avoid excess fertilization that can reduce flowering and increase floppy growth. Pinch back tall asters to 6 inches throughout June. Divide asters every three years to control the growth of taller plants and increase the vigor of less hardy species. Let the plants stand for winter to increase their hardiness and add a little winter interest. Asters are susceptible to wilt and powdery mildew. Remove wilt-infested plants.

Hardiness—Throughout the Midwest

Seasonal Color—Purple, white, and pink

Peak Season—Summer through fall

Mature Size (H x W)—2 to 5 ft. x 1 to 3 ft.

Water Needs—Evenly moist, well-drained soil is best.

ASTILBE
Astilbe species

Why It's Special—Astilbes can add color, attractive foliage, and texture to the shadier side of your landscape. Select a variety of astilbes with different bloom times to provide summer-long color. Leave the seedheads of late bloomers intact for winter interest. Use their flowers and foliage for cut flower arrangements.

How to Plant & Grow—Plant dormant plants in the spring after the danger of severe weather has passed. Plant hardened-off potted plants anytime during the growing season. Planting early in the season gives these slow-to-establish plants time to establish before winter. Space 12 to 24 inches apart.

Care & Problems—Moisture and fertilization are the keys to growing healthy astilbes. Fertilize astilbe with a low-nitrogen slow-release fertilizer in the spring before growth begins or in the fall as plants are going dormant. Astilbe can take a year or two to get growing. Regular dividing every three years seems to help revitalize them.

Hardiness—Throughout the Midwest

Seasonal Color—White, pink, red, salmon, and lavender

Peak Season—Summer blooms

Mature Size (H x W)—1 to 4 ft. x 2 to 3 ft.

Water Needs—Evenly moist soil is best.

BAPTISIA
Baptisia australis

Why It's Special—Attractive blue-green foliage, topped with blue flowers and subsequent decorative black seedpods, helped this large North American native win a Perennial Plant of the Year title.

How to Plant & Grow—Start plants from scarified seeds (whose seedcoats have been "nicked") to enhance germination. Purchase small plants as they recover more quickly from transplanting. Plant dormant plants after severe weather has passed and the soil is workable. Plant hardened-off transplants in the garden after the danger of frost has passed. Space 3 feet apart.

Care & Problems—This is a low-maintenance plant when properly sited. Avoid high-nitrogen fertilizers, excess fertilization, and heavy shade that can lead to floppy open growth. Be patient as these plants take several years to get established. By the third year they quickly fill in and flourish. Pinch off faded flowers to encourage more blooms or skip the extra bloom and enjoy the seedpods earlier.

Hardiness—Throughout the Midwest

Seasonal Color—Blue flowers; black seedpods

Peak Season—May and June blooms, fall & winter seedpods

Mature Size (H x W)—3 to 4 ft. x 3 to 4 ft.

Water Needs—Drought tolerant once established.

BEEBALM
Monarda didyma

Why It's Special—This lovely flower fits in formal, informal, or naturalized settings. The unique, almost Dr. Seuss-like in character, flowers sit atop fragrant foliage. The tubular flowers attract hummingbirds, butterflies, and, as the common name suggests, bees.

How to Plant & Grow—Plant from seeds indoors or directly in the garden. Place dormant plants in the garden as soon as the soil is workable. Plant hardened-off transplants throughout the season. Space plants at least 2 feet apart.

Care & Problems—Drought-stressed plants are less attractive and more susceptible to powdery mildew. Those grown in shade are also more susceptible to powdery mildew and tend to spread faster. Avoid high-nitrogen and excess fertilizer, and select mildew-resistant plants when possible. Remove one-fourth of the plant's stems in early spring to increase stem sturdiness and reduce disease. Deadhead for added bloom and to limit unwanted seedlings. Divide plants every three years or as needed to control its spread.

Hardiness—Zones 4 to 9

Seasonal Color—Red or violet

Peak Season—Summer bloom

Mature Size (H x W)—Up to 4 ft. x 3 ft.

Water Needs—Evenly moist soil is best.

BELLFLOWER
Campanula species

Why It's Special—Bellflowers' beautiful blue-and-white, bell-shaped flowers are unmistakable. They grow equally well in formal or more naturalized settings.

How to Plant & Grow—Plant dormant bellflowers in the spring after the danger of severe weather has passed. Plant hardened-off transplants anytime during the growing season. Divide overgrown and poorly flowering bellflowers in early spring for best results. Do not plant European or creeping bellflower, *Campanula rapunculoides*; these quickly spread and engulf any plant in its path. Space 12 to 24 inches apart.

Care & Problems—Bellflowers have a difficult time surviving cold winters in poorly drained soils. Avoid excess nitrogen fertilizer that leads to floppy growth and poor flowering. Cut back floppy plants after blooming to encourage fresh compact growth. Stake clustered bellflower and other cultivars subject to flopping. Remove faded flowers to encourage repeat blooming and reduce problems with reseeding. Be careful not to remove the developing buds.

Hardiness—Throughout the Midwest

Seasonal Color—Blue, purple, and white

Peak Season—Late spring to summer

Mature Size (H x W)—6 to 36 in. x 6 to 36 in.

Water Needs—Evenly moist soil is ideal.

BERGENIA
Bergenia species

Why It's Special—The large, cabbagelike leaves are green through the growing season, turning a purplish red in fall through winter. Include the long-lasting flowers in spring bouquets and the bold leaves in flower arrangements.

How to Plant and Grow—Start seeds indoors or directly in the garden in spring. Plant dormant plants in spring as soon as the soil is workable and severe weather has passed. Plant hardened-off transplants in the garden throughout the growing season. Space plants 12 inches apart.

Care and Problems—Divide bergenia growing in moist soils every four years. Those on drier sites will seldom need dividing. Leaves may be tattered and brown after a harsh or open winter. Remove damaged leaves in spring before or as new growth emerges. And don't be discouraged when flower buds are damaged in cold winters; the foliage is still an asset.

Hardiness—Throughout the Midwest

Seasonal Color—Pink, salmon, red, white, violet flowers; red fall color

Peak Season—Early to late spring bloom; fall through winter foliage

Mature Size (H x W)—12 to 18 in. x 12 in.

Water Needs— Drought tolerant once established.

BLACK COHOSH
Actaea racemosa

Why It's Special—The long wand-like white flowers are held on dark stems high above the foliage. The stems disappear in the shade, making the flowers appear to be floating in the air. This perennial beauty goes by many names including black snakeroot, black cohosh, bugbane, and its previous Latin name of *Cimicifuga*.

How to Plant & Grow—Plant dormant plants in spring as soon as possible and plant hardened-off transplants after the danger of frost has passed. Grow in cooler areas of the garden in moist organic soils for best results. Space 2 to 3 feet apart.

Care & Problems—These plants rarely need dividing. If more plants are desired, divide the summer-blooming black cohosh in spring or fall and the fall bloomers in spring for best results. Leaves will scorch in hot dry conditions. Leave the seedpods on the plants to feed the birds and add winter interest to the landscape.

Hardiness—Throughout the Midwest

Seasonal Color—White flowers

Peak Season—Late June to July

Mature Size (H x W)—4 to 6 ft. (in bloom) x 2 to 4 ft.

Water Needs—Evenly moist soil is best.

BLACK-EYED SUSAN
Rudbeckia species

Why It's Special—Black-eyed Susans are sure to attract the attention of your neighbors as well as passing butterflies and birds. Their yellow flowers brighten formal, informal, and naturalized plantings. They bloom continuously throughout summer and fall without deadheading. As the flowers fade, attractive seedheads form for you and the finches to enjoy.

How to Plant & Grow—Sow seeds in early spring or fall. See the chapter introduction for planting tips. Space plants at least 2 to 3 feet apart.

Care & Problems—Black-eyed Susans will quickly grow and crowd out weeds. Powdery mildew can be a cosmetic problem on some species. Select mildew-resistant plants and grow them in areas with full sun and good air circulation. Several fungal and a bacterial leaf spot diseases have recently attacked rudbeckias. Remove infested leaves and do a thorough fall cleanup. Some gardeners report fewer problems on *R. fulgida* and *R. fulgida* 'Viette's Little Suzy'.

Hardiness—Throughout the Midwest

Seasonal Color—Yellow blooms with black centers

Peak Season—Summer and fall blooms; winter seedheads

Mature Size (H x W)—24 to 36 in. x 18 to 48 in.

Water Needs—Drought tolerant once established.

BLEEDING HEART
Dicentra spectabilis

Why It's Special—Bleeding heart is an old-fashioned favorite grown as much for sentimental as ornamental reasons. The beautiful, heart-shaped flowers add interest and color to shade gardens and cut flower arrangements.

How to Plant & Grow—Plant bleeding hearts in the spring. See the chapter introduction for details. Divide plants in early spring to start new plants or to reduce the size of those that have outgrown their location. It will turn yellow and go dormant earlier than normal when they are grown in full sun and dry soils. Space plants 24 to 30 inches apart.

Care & Problems—Remove faded flowers to encourage a longer bloom period and discourage reseeding. The leaves normally turn yellow and brown and the plants go dormant in July. Prune bleeding heart plants back halfway after flowering to avoid the summer dormancy and encourage new growth. Or try the lower growing fringed bleeding heart (*Dicentra exima*). It blooms a bit later and longer and the foliage lasts all season.

Hardiness—Throughout the Midwest

Seasonal Color—Rose-red and white

Peak Season—Spring to early summer

Mature Size (H x W)—2 to 3 ft. x 3 ft.

Water Needs—Evenly moist soil is best.

BLUE FESCUE
Festuca glauca

Why It's Special—This small grass is a good fit in large and even small city lots. The blue-green leaves that contrast nicely with bold textured perennials and shrubs and makes a nice groundcover in well-drained soils. Plus it's fully or semi-evergreen and tolerant of deicing salt.

How to Plant & Grow—Plant spring and early summer to establish before winter. Divide and transplant blue fescue in the spring. Grow in well-drained soil spaced 1 foot apart.

Care & Problems—Blue fescue is a relatively low-maintenance plant. Avoid poorly drained soils, overwatering, and overfertilizing, which can lead to poor growth, root rot, and dead plants. Try dividing blue fescue every three or four years to increase its vigor in heavy soils. You can trim back the older leaves in late winter before growth begins, or just let the new growth mask the old leaves as they fade away. A light combing with your fingers through the foliage will help dislodge the brown leaves. In colder areas, it partially browns out in winter.

Hardiness—Throughout the Midwest

Seasonal Color—Blue-green foliage and flowers; beige seedheads

Peak Season—Foliage all season; flowers midsummer

Mature Size (H x W)—6 to 10 in. x 10 in.

Water Needs—Drought tolerant once established.

BLUE OAT GRASS
Helictotrichon sempervirens

Why It's Special—Slightly larger and coarser textured than blue fescue, blue oat grass seems to perform better in the heavier soils. Its larger size makes it easier to see through the snow, and the leaves tend to hold their blue color better than blue fescue.

How to Plant & Grow—Plant container-grown blue oat grass during the growing season, though spring and early summer planting gives the grass time to establish before winter. Divide and transplant blue oat grass in the spring. Plant blue oat grass in areas with full sun and well-drained soil. Space the plants 24 to 30 inches apart.

Care & Problems—Avoid overwatering and overfertilizing that can lead to root rot and plant decline. Rust, a fungal disease, can occasionally be a problem during wet, humid weather. Adjust watering if necessary and remove infected leaves as soon as they appear.

Hardiness—Throughout the Midwest

Seasonal Color—Blue-green foliage; pale blue flowers; beige seedheads

Peak Season—Evergreen foliage & flowers in early summer; seedheads in fall

Mature Size (H x W)—2 to 3 ft. x 2 to 3 ft.

Water Needs—Drought tolerant once established.

BUTTERFLY WEED
Asclepias tuberosa

Why It's Special—This is no "weed" that needs to be removed from the garden. The deep orange flowers and the monarch butterflies they attract brighten the landscape from midsummer into fall.

How to Plant & Grow—Sow purchased seeds in early spring. Butterfly weed is difficult to transplant, so plant seeds in their permanent location. Move, propagate, transplant, and divide butterfly weed in early spring. Space plants 12 inches apart.

Care & Problems—Butterfly weed is slow to establish and the seedlings that plant themselves often do the best. Mark their location, as butterfly weeds are late to emerge in the spring. Deadhead the first set of flowers to encourage a second flush of blooms. Allow the seedpods to form for added interest and additional plants. Aphids are a problem. Let the ladybugs take care of them. If further intervention is needed dislodge aphids with a strong blast of water or insecticidal soap that won't harm the monarch caterpillars.

Hardiness—Zones 4 to 9

Seasonal Color—Orange, red, and yellow blooms

Peak Season—Summer into fall blooms

Mature Size (H x W)—18 to 30 in. x 12 in.

Water Needs—Drought tolerant once established.

CATMINT
Nepeta x faassenii

Why It's Special—Catmint is out of the doghouse and into the garden thanks to the non-aggressive cultivars now available. Catmint's fragrant gray-green foliage is covered with lavender to blue flowers from June through August attracting bees and butterflies to the garden.

How to Plant and Grow—Plant dormant plants as soon as the soil is workable and hardened-off transplants anytime throughout the growing season. Space plants 18 to 24 inches apart.

Care & Problems—Overwatering and rainy seasons can lead to yellow foliage and floppy growth. Avoid high-nitrogen fertilizers that can also result in floppy growth. Select sterile and less aggressive cultivars like 'Walker's Low', 'Walker's Low Junior', and 'Six Hills Giant'. They offer all the beauty without fighting to keep the plant inbounds. Deadheading is not needed for repeat bloom. Remove spent flowers for a tidier appearance or to prevent reseeding. Cut back floppy plants by two thirds after the first flush of blooms. This encourages more compact growth and prevents open centers.

Hardiness—Throughout the Midwest

Seasonal Color—Lavender to blue

Peak Season—Late spring through fall

Mature Size (H x W)—18 to 30 in. x 10 to 30 in.

Water Needs—Drought tolerant once established.

COLUMBINE
Aquilegia hybrids

Why It's Special—This delicate beauty has blue-green leaves and uniquely shaped flowers that attract hummingbirds and butterflies. Be sure to situate them in the garden where you can sit and watch the hummingbirds feed. And plant extras to enjoy indoors as well.

How to Plant & Grow—See the chapter introduction for planting tips. Columbine seldom needs dividing. You can divide plants in late summer. Space plants 12 inches apart.

Care & Problems—Plants will deteriorate in dry soil and rot in overly wet conditions. Remove faded flowers to encourage rebloom and prevent reseeding. Deadheading also channels energy back into the roots, increasing hybrid's longevity. Leafminers create white, snake-like patterns in the leaves. It doesn't hurt the plant; it just looks bad. Cut severely damaged plants back to ground level after flowering to encourage fresh new foliage. Columbine sawfly eats the leaves but is not harmful to the plants.

Hardiness—Throughout the Midwest

Seasonal Color—Yellow, red, pink, blue, purple, and white blooms

Peak Season—Late spring to early summer

Mature Size (H x W)—1 to 3 ft. x 1 to 2 ft.

Water Needs—Evenly moist soil is best.

CORALBELLS
Heuchera sanguinea

Why It's Special—Use coralbells as groundcovers, edging plants, or specimens in sun or shade locations. The foliage looks good throughout the growing season and in mild winters. The small bell-shaped flowers are held high above the leaves attracting hummingbirds and butterflies.

How to Plant & Grow—Plant in spring and early summer for best results. See the chapter introduction for planting details. Coralbells perform best in partial shade with moist, well-drained soil but will tolerate dry shade. Heavy shade allows nice foliage but fewer flowers. Some cultivars will scorch in the hot afternoon sun. Space plants 12 inches apart.

Care & Problems—Shallow-rooted coralbells are subject to frost heaving. Dig and divide these plants about every three years to prevent woody stems or when they outgrow their location. Try cultivars of the *Heuchera villosa* if your coralbells tend to melt out in the heat and humidity of summer.

Hardiness—Throughout the Midwest

Seasonal Color—Red, pink, and white blooms

Peak Season—Late spring to early summer

Mature Size (H x W)—12 to 20 in. x 12 to 20 in.

Water Needs—Moist well-drained soil is best but it tolerates dry shade.

COREOPSIS
Coreopsis species

Why It's Special—Coreopsis is a good choice for sunny, dry gardens. The small daisy-like flowers are great for cutting and for attracting butterflies. Use them in formal and informal perennial gardens or in wildflower and naturalized plantings. Threadleaf coreopsis (*Coreopsis verticillata*) is a good choice for beginning gardeners and low-maintenance gardens.

How to Plant & Grow—Plant seeds in early spring and hardened-off transplants anytime throughout the growing season. Dig and divide threadleaf coreopsis about every four years to increase its vigor and eliminate the need for deadheading. Space plants 12 to 24 inches apart.

Care & Problems—Proper soil preparation, plant selection, and planting will help reduce future maintenance. Avoid high-nitrogen fertilizer and excess fertilization that can decrease flowering and increase floppiness. Some coreopsis species need deadheading. This encourages a second flush of flowers and reduces problems with self-seeding. A little deadheading and spring weeding will help keep self-seeders under control.

Hardiness—Throughout the Midwest

Seasonal Color—Yellow

Peak Season—Late spring to late summer

Mature Size (H x W)—18 to 36 in. x 18 to 36 in.

Water Needs—Most are drought tolerant once established.

CRANESBILL GERANIUM
Geranium sanguineum

Why It's Special—Use this long-blooming plant to provide several seasons of interest in your landscape. The fragrant, lobed leaves form an attractive mound. The white, pink, or lavender blooms appear in late spring through early summer. Watch for hummingbirds and butterflies looking for a meal from this garden beauty. In the fall, the leaves turn red and will often persist through a mild winter.

How to Plant & Grow—Transplants can be planted throughout the growing season. See the chapter introduction for planting details. Dig and divide geraniums when they outgrow their location. Space plants 18 to 24 inches apart.

Care & Problems—Deadheading will not increase the sporadic bloom. Trim plants back after the main flower display when the leaves are spotted, discolored, or unkempt. The new leaves will grow quickly, giving the plant a fresh new look. Geraniums occasionally suffer from leaf spot and rust. Clean-up will usually control these.

Hardiness—Throughout the Midwest

Seasonal Color—Pink, lavender, and white flowers

Peak Season—Late spring through summer

Mature Size (H x W)—8 to 15 in. x 24 in.

Water Needs—Established plants will tolerate drought.

DAYLILY
Hemerocallis species and hybrids

Why It's Special—Use these versatile plants as groundcovers, cut flowers, edibles, or in perennial gardens and mixed borders. The individual flowers last a day, but the flower display can last up to one month on an individual plant. The newer, repeat-blooming hybrids provide a summer-long floral display.

How to Plant & Grow—Pastel-colored daylilies tend to fade in full sun, and poor flowering and floppy growth may occur on any daylily growing in heavy shade. Divide plants every three years to make digging through the tangle of fleshy roots easier. Space plants 1½ to 3 feet apart.

Care & Problems—Avoid excess nitrogen that can cause unattractive growth and poor flowering. Repeat bloomers benefit from regular division and light fertilization in spring. Meticulous gardeners may find these a bit high maintenance. Daily deadheading and regular deleafing will keep plants looking neat and tidy. Animals also love the blossoms.

Hardiness—Throughout the Midwest

Seasonal Color—blooms in most colors

Peak Season—Summer through fall

Mature Size (H x W)—11 to 4 ft. x 2 to 3 ft.

Water Needs—Drought tolerant once established.

DELPHINIUM
Delphinium elatum

Why It's Special—Stately spikes of blue-and-white delphinium flowers stir up visions of an English cottage garden. These visions may have enticed you, like many gardeners, to add these high-maintenance plants to your garden.

How to Plant & Grow—Plant and divide early in the season for best results. Grow in a cool sunny locations or an area with light afternoon shade. Space plants 24 inches apart.

Care & Problems—Summer heat and poor drainage, especially in winter, shorten their lives and increase the risk of pest problems. Fertilize delphiniums lightly in the spring as growth begins and again in the summer, after you clip back the faded foliage. Deadhead flowers to encourage a second flush of blossoms. Prune back plants once all the flowers have faded to encourage new growth and blossoms. Consider skipping the fall bloom the first year to increase the chance of winter survival. Stake tall cultivars and check plants frequently for insects and disease problems.

Hardiness—Throughout the Midwest

Seasonal Color—Blue, purple, white, red, pink, and yellow blooms

Peak Season—Early to midsummer

Mature Size (H x W)—4 to 6 ft. x 2 ft.

Water Needs—Evenly moist, well-drained soil is ideal.

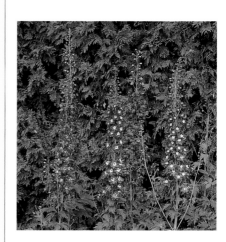

FEATHER REED GRASS
Calamagrostis x *acutiflora* 'Stricta'

Why It's Special—Feather reed grass has demonstrated its hardiness, durability, and beauty for many years in our landscapes. The wheat-like seedheads and stiff, upright leaves provide year-round interest. Feather reed grass is tall enough to demand attention in a large yard yet small enough to fit into more limited spaces.

How to Plant & Grow—Plant during the growing season, though planting in spring and early summer gives the grass time to get established before winter. Divide and transplant feather reed grass in the spring. It prefers moist, well-drained soil but will tolerate clay and wet soil with good drainage. Space plants at least 2 feet apart.

Care & Problems—Feather reed grass is a low-maintenance and salt-tolerant plant. Cut it back to just above ground level in late winter before growth begins.

Hardiness—Throughout the Midwest

Seasonal Color—Pink blooms; beige seedheads

Peak Season—Year-round

Mature Size (H x W)—4 to 5 ft. x 2 ft.

Water Needs—Moist soil is best but it tolerates wet soil that drains well.

FERNS
Athyrium, Matteuccia, Osmunda et al.

Why It's Special—Ferns' wonderful textures, shades of green, and interesting forms can add interest to shady gardens. Ferns also come in a variety of sizes and leaf shapes. Some are even suited for the sun, making them a plant for any garden.

How to Plant & Grow—Plant dormant ferns in the spring after the danger of severe weather has passed. Hardened-off transplants can be planted anytime during the season. Plant tender ferns early in the season to give them time to establish before winter. Space 12 to 36 inches, depending on the variety.

Care & Problems—Fast-growing ferns benefit from division while slow-growing ones seldom need attention. Divide overgrown ferns in the spring as growth begins. Let fronds stand for winter adding beauty to the winter garden and increasing winter hardiness. Prune out old fronds in late winter or allow the new growth to mask the old leaves.

Hardiness—Throughout the Midwest

Seasonal Color—Green foliage, some with silver and red stems or variegation

Peak Season—All season; some are evergreen

Mature Size (H x W)—1 to 5 ft. x 1 to 3 ft.

Water Needs—Evenly moist soil is best.

FOUNTAIN GRASS
Pennisetum setaceum

Why It's Special—Its light airy texture makes fountain grass a great filler in annual, perennial, and container gardens. Use it as a vertical accent in your planters. Fountain grass has feathery foxtail flowers that extend beyond the leaves and attract birds to the garden. In late fall, the seedheads will shatter and the leaves will brown, but the plant form will remain intact to provide winter interest.

How to Plant & Grow—Sow seeds in late winter according to seed packet directions. Move hardened-off transplant into the garden after the danger of frost. Space plants 1 or 2 feet apart.

Care & Problems—It prefers moist, well-drained soil but will tolerate a wide range of conditions including clay soil. Excessive shade can result in poor flowering and floppy plants. No deadheading is needed to keep this plant covered with flowers throughout the growing season. Perennial fountain grass (*Pennisetum alopecuroides*) is marginally hardy in Zone 4a.

Hardiness—Annual

Seasonal Color—Pink to purplish pink blooms

Peak Season—Season-long; midsummer through fall blooms

Mature Size (H x W)—3 ft. x 18 to 24 in.

Water Needs— Evenly moist soil is best.

FOXGLOVE
Digitalis purpurea

Why It's Special—Its large stature and shade tolerance has helped maintain this biennial's popularity. Foxgloves work well in a cottage-style or woodland gardens and make a nice backdrop for any style shade garden. Use them as a transition plant between trees and shrubs and perennial borders.

How to Plant & Grow—Plant hardened-off transplants early in the season. Sow seeds directly in the garden in late spring or early summer up to two months prior to the first fall frost. These plants will bloom the following year. Or start seeds indoors in spring. Most foxgloves will self-seed in the garden. Plant this biennial two years in a row for yearly blooms. Space plants 15 to 18 inches apart.

Care & Problems—Poorly drained soils, heavy mulch, pre-emergent weedkillers, and overzealous weeders are the biggest threat to these self-seeding plants. Powdery mildew, leaf spot, stem rot, Japanese beetles, and aphids may cause damage.

Hardiness—Throughout the Midwest

Seasonal Color—White, pink, mauve, rust, and yellow

Peak Season—Late spring to early summer

Mature Size (H x W)—2 to 5 ft. x 1 to 2 ft.

Water Needs—Moist, well-drained soil is ideal.

GAYFEATHER
Liatris spicata

Why It's Special—This late-season bloomer adds color and attracts birds and butterflies to the late summer and fall garden. Cut a few flowers to enjoy in a garden bouquet and leave plants standing for winter. Then watch for birds feeding on the seeds hidden in the fluffy seedheads.

How to Plant & Grow—Plant gayfeather rhizomes in the spring or fall. Place the woody corm or rhizome 1 to 2 inches below the soil surface. Plant transplants anytime during the growing season. Divide overgrown plants in the spring as growth begins. Space plants 15 to 20 inches apart.

Care & Problems—Avoid high-nitrogen fertilizer and excess fertilization, which can lead to floppy growth and poor flowering. Deadhead plants when most of the flower spike has bloomed to encourage a second flush of flowers. The plants will self-seed if the seedheads are left on the plant. Gayfeather plants seldom need staking.

Hardiness—Throughout the Midwest

Seasonal Color—Lavender, rose, and white blooms; fluffy seedpods in winter

Peak Season—Midsummer to fall

Mature Size (H x W)—12 to 36 in. x 18 in.

Water Needs—Drought tolerant once established.

GOLDENROD
Solidago species

Why It's Special—A hillside filled with New England aster and goldenrod mimics a Monet painting. Most goldenrod prefer full sun and well-drained soils though some do like a bit moister soils. All make great cutflowers and none of the species is the cause of hay fever.

How to Plant & Grow—Start seed indoors in spring. Plant transplants in the garden throughout the growing season. Divide overgrown plants in spring for best results and minimal impact on flowering. Space plants 1 to 2 feet apart, giving self-seeding varieties plenty of room to naturalize with other equally assertive plants.

Care & Problems—Avoid excess fertilization and high-nitrogen fertilizers that can promote rampant growth. Deadhead plants for increased bloom and to reduce reseeding. Mildew, rust, and leaf spot are usually only a problem when goldenrod is improperly sited, overplanted, or during cool, wet weather. Remove diseased plants in fall. Otherwise let the plants stand for winter.

Hardiness—Throughout the Midwest

Seasonal Color—Yellow flowers

Peak Season—Midsummer to fall bloom; winter interest

Mature Size (H x W)—2 to 6 ft. x 1 to 3 ft.

Water Needs—Most are drought tolerant once established.

HAKONECHLOA
Hakonechloa macra 'Aureola'

Why It's Special—Consider this award-winning plant if you're looking for something different for your shade or container garden. Its unique features along with its shade and moisture tolerance won it a Perennial Plant of the Year title.

How to Plant & Grow—Plant and transplant hakonechloa early in the season to give this slow-to-establish plant time to root. Keep the soil moist, but not wet, throughout the season. Mulching will help conserve water and minimize weeds. This is key to establishing these plants. Space plants 18 to 24 inches apart.

Care & Problems—Leaf scorch or brown-leaf edges can occur on plants grown in full sun or in dry soil. Loss of variegation is common in heavily shaded areas. Extremely cold and fluctuating winter temperatures as well as poor drainage can kill this plant. Use a winter mulch to help it survive the cold.

Hardiness—Zones 4 to 9

Seasonal Color—Colorful foliage; blooms tinged with pink

Peak Season—Foliage all season; late summer blooms

Mature Size (H x W)—20 to 24 in. x 20 to 24 in.

Water Needs—Keep soil evenly moist.

HELLEBORE
Helleborus orientalis

Why It's Special—The evergreen foliage, long bloom, and low maintenance make this a good choice for most gardeners. And the deer usually leave it be. If you have planted hellebores in the past and failed, don't worry. It often takes a couple tries.

How to Plant & Grow—You can start plants from seed though you will have better results transplanting the seedlings your plants produce. See the chapter introduction for planting guidelines. Divide plants as needed or to propagate new plants in spring. Make sure each division has several leaf buds and roots. Space 12 to 15 inches apart

Care & Problems—Plants may not bloom the first year after planting. Hellebores' evergreen foliage may be tattered or scorched after an extremely harsh or open winter. Blackspot and crown rot are usually only a problem in wet weather and poorly drained soils.

Hardiness—Varies with the species

Seasonal Color—Purple, pink, white, black, red, yellow, and green flowers; evergreen foliage

Peak Season—Early spring blooms

Mature Size (H x W)—15 to 18 in. x 15 in.

Water Needs—Keep soil moist but they will tolerate drought once established.

HOLLYHOCK
Alcea rosea

Why It's Special—Many gardeners like this old-fashioned favorite as much for the childhood memories as for its beauty. Hollyhock is classified as a biennial or short-lived perennial. Don't worry; they reseed readily, and you will have plenty for your landscape *and* twenty of your closest friends.

How to Plant & Grow—Start hollyhock seeds indoors in late February or March for flowers the first summer. Or start them outdoors in spring or early summer at least two months prior to the first fall frost. These plants will bloom the following summer. Or start from transplants. Space plants 18 to 36 inches apart.

Care & Problems—Avoid excess nitrogen fertilization that can increase risk of disease. Lacy leaves are the result of a caterpillar, hollyhock weevil, or Japanese beetle feeding on the plant. Orange-and-brown spotted leaves are caused by the fungal disease called rust. None of these is life threatening. Mask damage with nearby plantings.

Hardiness—Throughout the Midwest

Seasonal Color—White, yellow, pink, red, lavender, and nearly black flowers

Peak Season—Midsummer to early fall

Mature Size (H x W)—Up to 8 ft. x 2 ft.

Water Needs—Moist, well-drained soil is needed.

HOSTA
Hosta species and cultivars

Why It's Special—Hostas are low-maintenance, quick-growing, shade-tolerant perennials. The variety of leaf sizes, shapes, colors, and textures and its yellow fall color adds to its landscape value. The white or lavender, sometimes fragrant, flowers attract hummingbirds in summer and juncos feeding on the seeds in winter.

How to Plant & Grow—See the chapter introduction for planting details. You can divide hostas almost any time during the growing season. Grow hosta in partial shade for the best foliage color. Spacing depends on size of the variety grown.

Care & Problems—Hostas will scorch in hot afternoon sun and dry soil. Early-sprouting plants may suffer frost damage. New growth will help mask some of the browned leaves. Slugs and earwigs are the major pests. See pest management strategies on page 16. Deer and rabbits *love* hosta. Repellents, scare tactics, and fences around small perennial plantings may help, or you can replace hosta with the more deer-resistant *Pulmonaria*.

Hardiness— Throughout the Midwest

Seasonal Color—Colorful foliage, white and lavender bloom

Peak Season—Summer and fall foliage; yellow fall color

Mature Size (H x W)—6 to 36 in. x 36 in.

Water Needs—Keep hostas moist.

JOE-PYE WEED
Eupatorium species

Why It's Special—Bold and beautiful, these large plants provide fresh color to the late summer and fall landscape. Their towering size and dramatic flower heads provide an architectural accent in the landscape.

How to Plant & Grow—Plants can be started indoors from seeds. Plant transplants in the garden any time during the growing season. Dig and divide overgrown plants in early spring. Space plants 3 feet apart.

Care & Problems—Keep soil moist for best results. Plants growing in shade tend to grow tall and leggy, and those growing in droughty soils are not as robust and attractive. Cut plants back to 6 inches in early June to reduce their height by several feet. Or select a shorter cultivar if desired. Regular division keeps the plants vigorous and needing less deadheading. Leave the seedheads on and plants standing for winter interest. Leaf spot disease and powdery mildew are occasional problems. Good cleanup is usually sufficient to control these diseases.

Hardiness—Zones 4 to 8

Seasonal Color—Purple flowers

Peak Season—Mid- to late summer through fall

Mature Size (H x W)—Up to 8 ft. x 3 ft.

Water Needs—Moist soil is a must.

LAVENDER
Lavandula angustifolia

Why It's Special—The wonderful fragrance, silvery gray foliage and beautiful purple summer blooms make lavender worthy of a spot in the garden. Enjoy it in the garden, flower arrangement, at the dinner table, or in a sachet.

How to Plant and Grow—Start seeds indoors six to eight weeks prior to last spring frost. A five-week cold treatment (stratification) may increase germination success. Or purchase transplants from garden catalogs or garden centers; they may be in the perennials or herb section. 'Hidcote' and 'Munstead' are the most winter hardy. See the chapter introduction for planting instructions. Plant lavender early in the season so plants have time to establish before winter. Space 12 inches apart.

Care & Problems—Overwatering and poor drainage, especially in winter, can kill lavender. Skip the mulch if your soils tend to be damp or wet. Avoid high-nitrogen fertilizers and excess fertilization. Wait for new growth to begin before pruning.

Hardiness—Zones 4 to 9

Seasonal Color—Lavender and purple blooms

Peak Season—Summer

Mature Size (H x W)—12 to 24 x 12 – 24 inches

Water Needs—Drought tolerant once established.

LITTLE BLUESTEM
Schizachyrium scoparium

Why It's Special—Its year-round beauty and bird appeal have helped this native grass find its way into the home landscape. The fine-textured green to blue-green foliage fits well in naturalized or perennial gardens. The late-summer flowers quickly give way to showy silvery white seedheads and striking orange-red fall color.

How to Plant & Grow—Seed large plantings of little bluestem in the spring or fall. The seed must be stratified (cold treated) to germinate. Plant container-grown little bluestem during the growing season. Divide and transplant in the spring. Space plants at least 2 feet apart.

Care & Problems—When placed in an appropriate spot, little bluestem requires very little maintenance. Avoid overfertilizing and rich soils where plants are more likely to flop. Dig up struggling plants in the early spring and move them to a location with better drainage, or replace with varieties like 'Blue Heaven' and 'The Blues' that are more upright.

Hardiness—Throughout the Midwest

Seasonal Color—Orange-red fall foliage; pinkish white blooms

Peak Season—Year-round interest

Mature Size (H x W)—1½ to 3 ft. x 2 ft.

Water Needs—Drought tolerant once established.

MISCANTHUS
Miscanthus sinensis

Why It's Special—This is one of the most dramatic ornamental grasses for the landscape with its fluffy white seedheads providing fall and winter interest. Some gardeners call this hardy pampas grass, a common name shared by several grasses. Miscanthus provides the height of a shrub without the width, making it great for locations needing narrow screens and vertical accents.

How to Plant & Grow—Plant anytime during the growing season. Divide and transplant miscanthus in the spring. It will tolerate clay soil. Space plants at least 3 feet apart.

Care & Problems—Do *not* plant the aggressive Chinese silver banner grass (*Miscanthus sacchariflorus*) or unnamed *Miscanthus* cultivars as these plants have become invasive. Visit miscanthus.cfans.umn.edu for more details. Plants are slow to emerge in spring, so be patient. Root prune in place to invigorate sparsely leaved plants struggling after a hard winter. Cut the plants back in late winter before new growth begins.

Hardiness—Throughout the Midwest

Seasonal Color—Pale pink to red bloom; beige seedheads

Peak Season—Year-round

Mature Size (H x W)—3 to 7 ft. x 4 ft

Water Needs—Keep soil evenly moist to slightly dry.

MOOR GRASS
Molinia caerulea

Why It's Special—The fine, airy blooms held above the tuft of low-growing foliage makes this an easy addition to most landscapes. Plus it is more tolerant of wet soils than most grasses.

How to Plant & Grow—Plant any time during the growing season, though early plantings allow this slow-to-establish grass time to root in before winter. Divide and transplant moor grass in the spring. Grow in moist, well-drained soil, 18 to 24 inches apart.

Care & Problems—Mulch the soil surrounding the grass to help keep roots moist. Water thoroughly as needed during dry spells. Some gardeners have reported problems with voles feeding on the roots and crowns of this grass. Watch for damage and dig, divide, and replant healthy sections in the spring. Moor grass is self-cleaning; the leaves and flower stems drop from the plants in the winter. A little spring cleanup may be all that is needed.

Hardiness—Throughout the Midwest

Seasonal Color—Purple blooms; beige seedheads; yellow fall foliage

Peak Season—Midsummer blooms; fall into winter seedheads

Mature Size (H x W)—1 to 2 ft. x 1 to 2 ft.

Water Needs—Evenly moist soil is best.

MUM
Chrysanthemum x morifolium

Why It's Special—Mums provide a last bit of color in the garden and just one plant can provide over a hundred blossoms for cutting and garden use. Consider adding a few mums to your perennial gardens, annual flower display or fall container gardens. Thanks to the University of Minnesota's breeding programs, there are new hardy mums being introduced into the market.

How to Plant & Grow—Plant in the spring or late summer. Spring planting increases plant hardiness and overwintering success. Or, treat them like annuals. Space plants 2 to 3 feet apart.

Care & Problems—Pinch back taller cultivars for compact growth and increased flower production. Start pinching mums back to 6 inches in late May or early June. Stop pinching by late June in the north or the first week of July in southern parts of the Midwest so blooming will occur prior to snowfall. Leave the plants intact for the winter for increased hardiness.

Hardiness—Throughout the Midwest (though hardiness varies with variety)

Seasonal Color—Yellow, orange, rust, red, bronze, white, and lavender

Peak Season—Late summer through frost

Mature Size (H x W)—1 to 2 ft. x 1 to 2 ft.

Water Needs—Moist, well-drained soil is best.

ORIENTAL POPPY

Papaver orientale

Why It's Special—The colorful bold flowers make this a standout in the garden. Once you help them settle into the garden they will provide years of beauty. Poppies make great cut flowers and the dried seedpods add interest to wreaths and dried arrangements.

How to Plant & Grow—Plant hardened-off transplants in spring about 2 feet apart. Divide poppies, only if needed, in August and September. Good soil drainage is critical for their growing success.

Care & Problems—Established poppies are low-maintenance plants. Winter-mulch new late season plantings with evergreen branches after the ground lightly freezes. This will help them through their first winter and increase establishment success. There's no need to deadhead. Consider leaving the large, attractive seedheads for added interest. Remove the faded leaves in midsummer. A small rosette of leaves may develop in the fall; leave these in place over the winter.

Hardiness—Throughout the Midwest

Seasonal Color—Orange-red, red, pink, and white

Peak Season—Late spring to early summer blooms

Mature Size (H x W)—1 to 4 ft. x 2 ft.

Water Needs—They are moderately drought tolerant but need well-drained soil.

PEONY

Paeonia hybrids

Why It's Special—Peonies provide a long season of interest in the landscape. The new growth emerges red and soon turns green. The large flowers can be single, semi-double, or double. Many are fragrant, and all of them work well as cut flowers. The leaves remain attractive throughout the season, turning a nice purple in the fall.

How to Plant & Grow—Plant rhizomes with the buds (eyes) 2 inches below the soil surface in the fall before the ground freezes or in the spring after the danger of severe weather has passed. Plant transplants anytime during the growing season. Divide in late summer or early fall. Space peonies 3 feet apart.

Care & Problems—Disbud to achieved desired flower display. Stake peonies subject to flopping. Plants can fail to bloom the spring after transplanting and when grown in too much shade, planted too deep, or overfertilized. Peonies are subject to several fungal diseases. Control these with fall cleanup.

Hardiness—Throughout the Midwest

Seasonal Color—White, pink, red, and salmon

Peak Season—Late spring to early summer

Mature Size (H x W)—3 ft. x 3 ft.

Water Needs—Moist, well-drained soil is needed.

PHLOX
Phlox species

Why It's Special—Fragrance, versatility, and butterfly and hummingbird appeal make phlox a traditional favorite. Use a few creeping phlox for added pizzazz in your spring landscape. Include tall garden phlox as a vertical accent, added color in the back of the perennial garden and for cutting.

How to Plant & Grow—Plant phlox anytime during the growing season. See the chapter introductions for planting directions. Creeping phlox prefer well-drained soils and are drought tolerant; garden phlox prefer moist, well-drained soil. Space creeping phlox 12 inches apart and garden phlox 18 to 24 inches apart.

Care & Problems—Cut back creeping phlox halfway after flowering. Deadhead garden phlox to extend its bloom time. Powdery mildew is the biggest problem of garden phlox. Select mildew-resistant cultivars whenever possible. Remove one-third of the stems in the spring to improve air circulation and reduce mildew problems. Deer *love* phlox. Repellents, netting, and fencing can help reduce the damage. Vary controls and *be persistent.*

Hardiness—Throughout the Midwest

Seasonal Color—Blue, purple, pink, rose, red, and white

Peak Season—Spring or summer to fall

Mature Size (H x W)—3 to 48 in. x 24 in.

Water Needs—Water requirements vary with the species.

PRAIRIE DROPSEED
Sporobolus heterolepis

Why It's Special—The airy foliage of this native combines nicely with ornamental shrubs, dwarf conifers, and perennials to provide year-round interest. In late summer, the grassy leaves are topped with fragrant delicate flowers. The leaves turn a yellow-orange in fall and eventually fade to beige. The seedheads persist through winter, capturing dew and ice crystals to add a little sheen to the garden.

How to Plant & Grow—Sow seeds in spring or fall. Plant bare-root plants as soon as they arrive and container plants throughout the season. Grow prairie dropseed in full sun and well-drained soils. Space 2 feet apart.

Care & Problems—This native grass is low maintenance and basically pest free. It takes several years to dig its roots in and start blooming. So be patient. Allow the plants to stand for winter interest. Cut them back in late winter and compost the leaf debris.

Hardiness—Throughout the Midwest

Seasonal Color—Pale pink blooms; fall foliage; beige seedheads

Peak Season—Summer bloom, fall and winter seedheads

Mature Size (H x W)—3 to 3½ ft. x 24 in.

Water Needs—Drought tolerant once established.

PURPLE CONEFLOWER
Echinacea purpurea

Why It's Special—Purple coneflower is at home in its native environment or in the home landscape. A few coneflowers can create a mass of color in the fall garden or cutflower arrangements and will help attract butterflies. Start small since one plant goes a long way.

How to Plant & Grow—Sow seeds outdoors in the fall or early spring. These plants will bloom in several years. Plant transplants anytime during the growing season. Excess shade and overfertilization will cause poor growth and flowering. Space plants 24 inches apart.

Care & Problems—Encourage more compact growth by cutting the plants back by half in mid-June. Deadheading is not necessary but will give the plants and garden a neater appearance. Stop deadheading by early September to allow seedheads to form. Coneflowers suffer from leaf spot diseases, stem wilt, and aster yellows (green and distorted flowers). Remove spotted leaves, prune out wilted stems, and remove aster yellows-infested plants.

Hardiness—Throughout the Midwest

Seasonal Color—Purple, white, yellow, and pink

Peak Season—Summer through fall

Mature Size (H x W)—2 to 4 ft. x 2 ft.

Water Needs—Drought tolerant once established.

RUSSIAN SAGE
Perovskia atriplicifolia

Why It's Special—Russian sage provides year-round interest in the landscape. Its fine leaves and flowers give it an airy texture, making it a good filler plant. Try using young plants and small cultivars as a vertical accent in container plantings.

How to Plant & Grow—Plant hardened-off transplants anytime during the growing season. Good drainage is essential for vigorous growth and winter survival. Space plants 30 to 36 inches apart.

Care & Problems—Plants will flop in wet soil and shade. Prune back to 4 to 6 inches above the ground in spring to remove the dead stems and encourage sturdy new growth. Mature plants, even when pruned in spring, may topple. Cut these plants back by half when they reach 12 inches tall. Or try one of the more compact cultivars that are less likely to flop. Leave plants standing for winter interest and increased hardiness. The silvery stems and some of the foliage will last throughout the winter.

Hardiness—Zones 4 to 9

Seasonal Color—Blue

Peak Season—Midsummer through fall

Mature Size (H x W)—3 to 5 ft. x 3 to 4 ft.

Water Needs—Drought tolerant once established.

SALVIA
Salvia species

Why It's Special—The spikes of blue and pink flowers add charm to the garden and color to flower arrangements. Plant a few of these long-blooming perennials near a window or patio so you can enjoy the butterflies and hummingbirds that come to visit.

How to Plant & Grow—Plant dormant salvias in the spring after the danger of severe weather has passed. Plant hardened-off transplants anytime during the growing season. Divide overgrown salvia in spring. Plants tend to flop in excess shade and rich soils. Space plants 18 inches apart.

Care & Problems—They grow better and flower longer in cool temperatures and moist soil. Deadhead salvia to extend its bloom time. Prune back by half after the second flush of flowers. Some salvia become floppy and open in the center during flowering. In that case, skip the deadheading and prune plants back after the first flush of flowers. Leave plants standing for winter to increase hardiness.

Hardiness—Throughout the Midwest

Seasonal Color—Blue, violet, and rose-pink

Peak Season—Summer

Mature Size (H x W)—2 to 3 ft. x 3 to 4 ft.

Water Needs—Moist well-drained soil is best but it's drought tolerant once established.

SEDGE
Carex species

Why It's Special—Sedges are good alternatives for grass in moist shady areas. Use it as a groundcover in shady locations. Though it's not a true grass, it has the same texture and growth habit. Their long narrow leaves make nice fillers and provide contrast to the bold textures of hosta, ginger, and ligularia, which are often found in shade gardens.

How to Plant and Grow—Plant bare-root sedges as soon as they arrive. Container-grown sedges can be planted throughout the season. Most sedges prefer full to part shade and moist to wet soils. Space 12 to 18 inches apart.

Care and Problems—Hardiness can be a problem in northern areas and when grown in clay soils that stay excessively wet in winter. Let plants stand for winter. They provide interest and increases hardiness. Cut back the dead foliage in spring or allow the new leaves to grow through the old.

Hardiness—Throughout the Midwest

Seasonal Color—Late spring colorful foliage

Peak Season—Foliage all season

Mature Size (H x W)—6 to 24 in. x 6 to 24 in.

Water Needs—Keep plants evenly moist.

SEDUM
Sedum species

Why It's Special—Sedums have long been known and used for their ability to grow in difficult locations. Low maintenance, heat and drought tolerant, and flowers with butterfly appeal make sedums a great choice for beginning, busy, or just about any gardener.

How to Plant & Grow—Plant dormant sedums in the spring after the danger of severe weather has passed. Place hardened-off transplants in the garden anytime during the growing season. Divide overgrown sedums anytime during the season. Spacing varies with the species.

Care & Problems—There are no serious pest problems on healthy palnts. Avoid overwatering and overfertilization, which can lead to floppy growth and root rot. Some taller sedums like 'Autumn Joy' can become floppy. Grow in full sun with well-drained soil to avoid this problem. Control floppiness on problem plants with proper pruning. Pinch back 8-inch-tall stems to 4 inches in June. Let the plants stand for winter interest.

Hardiness—Throughout the Midwest

Seasonal Color—Yellow, pink, red, and white

Peak Season—Summer and fall blooms

Mature Size (H x W)—2 to 24 in. x 2 to 24 in.

Water Needs—Drought tolerant once established.

SHASTA DAISY
Chrysanthemum x superbum

Why It's Special—Shasta daisies provide a profusion of white flowers from summer until frost. The large daisy-like flowers are good for cutting, attracting butterflies, or providing a long season of bloom in the garden. You will also find it listed as *Leucanthemum x superbum*.

How to Plant & Grow—Plant seeds outdoors in spring. Plant hardened-off transplants in the spring or early summer. Good drainage is important for winter survival. Space plants 18 to 24 inches apart.

Care & Problems—Shasta daisies tend to be short lived. They do great for several years, and then one spring, they fail to return. Regular dividing, every two to three years, seems to keep the plants vigorous and prolongs their life. Divide Shasta daisies in early spring every two to three years. Staking is often needed for the species and taller cultivars. Spring pruning will help encourage more compact growth. Pinch back tall cultivars to 6 inches in late May or early June. Deadheading will prolong bloom.

Hardiness—Zones 4 to 9

Seasonal Color—White flowers with yellow center

Peak Season—Summer until frost

Mature Size (H x W)—1 to 3 ft. x 1 ft.

Water Needs—Moist, well-drained soil is needed.

SIBERIAN BUGLOSS
Brunnera macrophylla

Why It's Special—Brighten up the shade with this Perennial Plant of the Year, *Brunnera* 'Jack Frost'. The heart-shaped leaves have silvery variegation that looks good all season long. The blue flowers resemble forget-me-nots and cover the plant in spring.

How to Plant & Grow—Seeds may be hard to find and most will need a chill before planting. Follow planting directions on the package. Plant dormant container and bare-root plants in spring after severe weather has passed. Plant hardened-off plants anytime during the growing season after the danger of frost has passed. Divide in spring when the center of the plant dies out, or when you want to start new plants. Space 12 inches apart.

Care & Problems—Hot afternoon sun, extreme heat, and dry soil can cause leaf browning (scorch). Plant may die out in extremely cold winter. They reseed though they may not retain their variegation. Seedlings can be invasive. Slugs can be a problem in cool wet weather.

Hardiness—Throughout the Midwest

Seasonal Color—Forget-me-not–blue flowers

Peak Season—Early to late spring

Mature Size (H x W)—12 to 18 in. x 18 in.

Water Needs—Keep plants moist.

SWITCHGRASS
Panicum virgatum

Why It's Special—Bring a little of our native prairie into your backyard. The colorful flowers look like fireworks exploding 1 to 2 feet above the leaves that turn a beautiful golden yellow in fall. And watch for the finches feeding on the seeds and the larvae of several types of caterpillars munching on the leaves.

How to Plant & Grow—Seed large areas of switchgrass in the spring or fall using a local seed source. Plant switchgrass plants during the growing season. Divide and transplant in spring. Switchgrass prefers moist soil but will tolerate wet to dry soil and exposure to deicing salt. Space plants 30 to 36 inches.

Care & Problems—The straight species should only be used in large natural areas where it has room to spread. Grow cultivated varieties, which are much less aggressive, for home gardens and landscapes. Shade-grown plants tend to be more open and fall over.

Hardiness—Throughout the Midwest

Seasonal Color—Pink to red to silver blooms

Peak Season—Midsummer through winter

Mature Size (H x W)—3 to 8 ft. x 3 ft.

Water Needs—Prefers moist soil but is drought tolerant once established.

TURTLEHEAD

Chelone species

Why It's Special—Turtlehead is a blooming perennial that tolerates wet or damp soil in shady locations and rain gardens. It will go unnoticed for most of the season until the pink and purple flowers appear adding a fresh splash of color to the garden.

How to Plant & Grow—Start plants from seeds following the directions on the seed packet. See the chapter introduction for planting directions. Divide overgrown plants in spring or fall. Space 18 to 24 inches apart.

Care & Problems—Turtlehead usually does not need staking but plants growing in heavy shade may need support from a stake or sturdy neighbor. Don't deadhead. Instead, leave the seedheads intact and plants standing for winter interest. Turtleheads are late to emerge so mark their location or leave a few stems intact until growth begins. Pinch plants in spring when they are about 6 inches tall to encourage fuller growth. Powdery mildew may be a problem in heavy shade or droughty conditions.

Hardiness—Throughout the Midwest

Seasonal Color—Pink and purple flowers

Peak Season—Late summer to early fall

Mature Size (H x W)—3 ft. x 2 ft.

Water Needs—Moist soil is best.

VARIEGATED SOLOMON'S SEAL

Polygonatum odoratum 'Variegatum'

Why It's Special—The 2- to 4-foot-tall upright arching branches provide vertical interest in the shade garden. Fragrant, white, bell-shaped flowers hang below the branches in spring. The white variegation on leaf edges brightens the shade all summer long then turns golden in the fall. It can also be used in flower arrangements. Its durability and beauty helped it become a Perennial Plant of the Year.

How to Plant & Grow—Sow seed in the fall in cold frames following planting directions on the seed packet. Or plant rhizomes just below the soil surface. Wait for the severe weather to pass before planting dormant plants. Place hardened off transplants in the garden anytime during the growing season. See the chapter introduction for planting details. Space plants 18 to 24 inches apart.

Care & Problems—Solomon's seals are low maintenance with no real pest problems. Some gardeners have reported problems with slugs. Dig, divide, and share as needed.

Hardiness—Throughout the Midwest

Seasonal Color—White flowers, variegated foliage

Peak Season—Early spring

Mature Size (H x W)—18 to 36 in x 18 to 36 in.

Water Needs—Tolerates dry shade once established.

VERONICA

Veronica species

Why It's Special—Veronicas are versatile plants that fit into many garden situations. Spike speedwell blends nicely with other perennials in both formal and informal settings. Many of the low-growing veronicas are fast growing, mat forming, and great as groundcovers.

How to Plant and Grow—Plant dormant veronicas in the spring after the danger of severe weather has passed. Plant hardened-off potted and container-grown perennials anytime during the growing season. Space plants 18 to 24 inches apart.

Care & Problems—The upright types of veronica and those grown in heavy shade, poorly drained soils, or when overfertilized tend to open in the center and flop. Stake taller plants or select cultivars with sturdier stems that resist flopping. Deadhead to extend the flower display; prune back halfway after the second flush of flowers to encourage compact growth. Divide floppy and overgrown veronicas in the spring. Most cultivars benefit from being divided every two or three years.

Hardiness—Throughout the Midwest

Seasonal Color—Blue, red, and white

Peak Season—Late spring to summer

Mature Size (H x W)—4 to 36 in. x 6 to 24 in.

Water Needs—Drought tolerant once established.

VIRGINIA BLUEBELL
Mertensia pulmonarioides

Why It's Special—Virginia bluebell is one of the early spring bloomers that let us know winter is on its way out. Plus the bell-shaped flowers are a beautiful blue, a sought-after garden flower color.

How to Plant & Grow—Virginia bluebells are available as plants or tuberous roots. Plant tuberous roots in spring or fall with the growing point 1 to 2 inches below the soil surface. Plant hardened-off, container-grown, and field-potted perennials anytime during the growing season, though transplants will be leafless summer through fall. Space plants 12 inches apart.

Care & Problems—Divide bluebells in early spring as new growth emerges. Regular dividing can help prevent the bluebells from taking over the garden. Mask the large declining leaves with hosta or other shade tolerant planting companions. Leaf spot is an occasional problem in extremely wet seasons. Clean up and a bit drier weather will usually control this seldom seen problem.

Hardiness—Throughout the Midwest

Seasonal Color—Blue

Peak Season—Early spring

Mature Size (H x W)—12 to 24 in. x 18 in.

Water Needs—Water thoroughly and often enough to keep soil slightly moist when plants are actively growing.

YARROW
Achillea filipendulina

Why It's Special—Yarrow is a good low-maintenance perennial that is heat and drought tolerant, attracts butterflies, and can be used fresh or dried in flower arrangements. Select your plant carefully as some are well mannered and others can become weeds. The common yarrow, *Achillea millefolium*, is an aggressive plant you will see listed in weed books, wildflower books, *and* garden catalogs.

How to Plant & Grow—Plant dormant yarrow plants in the spring after the danger of severe weather has passed. Plant hardened-off transplants anytime during the growing season. Space plants 2 to 3 feet apart.

Care & Problems—Yarrow tends to flop when grown in shade, fertile soil, or overfertilized gardens. Deadhead yarrow to remove unattractive seedheads and to encourage longer blooming. This also reduces reseeding of the more weedy species. Prune plants back to fresh new growth after the final bloom. The foliage will continue to look attractive into the winter. Divide overgrown, leggy, or poorly flowering plants in the spring.

Hardiness—Throughout the Midwest

Seasonal Color—Yellow

Peak Season—Summer

Mature Size (H x W)—1 to 4 ft. x 3 ft.

Water Needs—Drought tolerant once established.

YUCCA
Yucca filamentosa

Why It's Special—Yucca grows in hot, dry areas where other plants fail to thrive. Use yucca as a vertical accent in the garden or shrub bed. The tall flower stalk is quite impressive and attracts hummingbirds to your garden.

How to Plant & Grow—Start new plants from offsets in spring. Treat them like cuttings, rooting them before planting. See the chapter introduction for planting tips. Space plants 24 inches apart.

Care & Problems—Avoid high-nitrogen fertilizers and excess fertilization, which can prevent flowering. Clip off faded flowers for a neater appearance or allow the seedheads to develop. These as well as the evergreen leaves add winter interest. The new growth in the spring will mask the fading leaves. Or for a tidier look, remove older leaves as new leaves appear. Yucca may suffer leaf spot disease in cool wet seasons.

Hardiness—Throughout the Midwest

Seasonal Color—White blooms

Peak Season—July blooms; evergreen foliage

Mature Size (H x W)—2 to 3 ft. (foliage) x 3 ft. to 12 ft. (in bloom)

Water Needs—Drought tolerant once established.

BUY THE RIGHT NUMBER OF PLANTS

Avoid overbuying and the temptation to overplant by buying the right number of plants for the available space. Consider planting groups of odd-numbered plants (one, three, five) for a more informal appearance. Use larger groupings for a bolder display of color. To calculate the number of plants you will need:

1. Measure the length and width of the garden. Multiply these numbers for the total square footage of the perennial garden. This will give you an idea of the total space available for planting.

2. Now review your garden design. Calculate (length times width) the planting area of each drift, mass, or cluster of plants. Then evaluate the area you have for each plant.

3. Check the space requirements of the individual plants. Use the spacing chart below to calculate the number of plants you will need.

4. Multiply the square footage of the planting area times the number of plants needed per square foot to get the number of plants needed for your garden. For example, if your garden is 100 square feet, and you decide to cover 9 square feet with spike speedwell at 18 inches apart, then your calculation would be:

9 square feet x 0.45 = 4 plants of Spike Speedwell

PLANT SPACING	# OF PLANTS PER SQ. FT.
12 inches	1.0
15 inches	0.64
18 inches	0.45
24 inches	0.25
36 inches	0.11

DIVIDING PERENNIALS

Divide perennials that have poor flowering, open centers, or floppy growth. Some plants, such as Shasta daisy and 'Moonshine' yarrow, benefit from transplanting every few years. Others, such as purple coneflower and perennial geraniums, can go many years without division. Let the plant, not the calendar, be your guide.

- Begin digging and dividing existing plants as new growth appears. Try to move them when they are less than 3 to 4 inches tall. Cut back taller plants to reduce the stress of transplanting.

- Early spring is a good time to transplant summer- and fall-blooming perennials. Transplanting spring-blooming perennials in spring may delay or eliminate this year's flowers.

- Dig and divide spring-flowering plants in late August or early September. You can dig and divide most perennials anytime as long as you can give them proper post-planting care.

- Use a shovel or garden fork to dig the clump to be divided. Lift the clump and set it on the soil surface. Use a sharp knife or two shovels or garden forks to divide the clumps. Cut into smaller pieces. Plant one division in the original hole after amending the soil. Use the others in new and existing gardens.

- Amend the soil when dividing and transplanting perennials. Add several inches of compost, peat moss, or other organic matter into the soil. Plant the division at the same depth as it was growing originally. Gently tamp the soil, and water to remove any air pockets.

INVASIVE WEED REMOVAL

Ground ivy, quackgrass, and bindweed are perennial weeds that can quickly take over your garden. Handpulling does not usually work on these deeply rooted plants. Cultivation just breaks the plants into smaller pieces that can start lots of new plants. Use a total vegetation killer to control these pesky weeds. These products kill the tops and roots of the weeds and any growing plant they touch. Several applications may be needed.

Paint, sponge, or wipe the total vegetation killer on the weed leaves. The chemical moves through the leaves, down the stems, and into the roots. Here is a quick tip for making the job easier:

1. Remove the top and bottom of a plastic milk jug.

2. Cover the weed with the plastic milk jug.

3. Spray the total vegetation killer on the weed inside the milk jug. The jug will protect the surrounding plants from the harmful weed-killer. Remove the jug after the herbicide on the weed dries.

A sharp shovel makes digging and dividing perennials an easier task

JANUARY

- Pack away the holiday decorations and break out the photos, video, and journal of last year's gardens and landscape. Review these materials before you start planning this year's additions. Look for areas to convert to perennial gardens as well as locations for adding a few new plants.

- Perennials can be started indoors much like annuals. Some seeds need to be stratified (a cold treatment) for weeks, soaked in tepid water overnight, or scarified (the seed coat scratched) prior to planting. Check the label directions for seed treatment, timing, and planting directions. See page 40 for details on starting plants from seed.

- Recycle your holiday trees and trimmings by converting them into windbreaks and mulch. Cut branches off the trees and lay them over your perennial gardens.

- Place a few holiday trees in a snow bank for storage. They provide shelter for the birds and easy storage, just in case you need to convert them into mulch.

- Check for tracks, chewed bark, and other signs of vole (meadow mouse) damage. High vole populations may start nibbling on the roots of Siberian iris and hostas. Chipmunks and squirrels can also damage perennials by digging up the plants and leaving the roots exposed to cold winter temperatures. There is not much you can do when the plants are buried in the snow. Next year, plan ahead and try to prevent the damage.

FEBRUARY

- Check out catalogs (hard copies and online) for newer and harder to find perennials. They can also be a source of information.

- Monitor plantings for frost heaving caused by the freezing and thawing of unmulched gardens. The fluctuating temperatures cause the soil to shift and often push shallow-rooted perennials right out of the soil. Gently tamp these back into the soil as soon as they are discovered. Make a note to mulch these areas next fall after the ground freezes.

- Avoid damping off (a fungal disease) of seedlings by using sterile containers and seed-starter mix. Infected plants suddenly collapse and rot at the soil line. Remove any diseased seedlings as soon as they appear. Apply a fungicide as a soil drench to infected plantings. Make sure the product is labeled to control damping off disease on perennial seedlings.

- Wait for the worst of winter to pass before cleaning out the garden. Many borderline hardy perennials survive better when the stems are left standing for winter.

MARCH

- Wait until the soil thaws and dries before getting out the shovel. Working wet soil causes damage that takes years to repair.

- Most catalogs send bare-root plants just prior to the planting time for our area. Dormant plants can be planted directly outdoors if the soil is workable. Store dormant bare-root plants in a cool, dark location. Plant and grow indoors, those that started growing.

- Wait until temperatures consistently hover near freezing before removing the mulch. Remove the mulch if plants are starting to grow. Keep some handy to protect the tender tips of early sprouting hostas, primroses, and other early sprouters that may be damaged by a sudden drop in temperature.

- It is time to get busy cleaning up the garden once the snow disappears and before perennials start to grow. Remove any dead leaves, stems, and seedpods left for winter interest. Remove only the dead leaves on evergreen perennials, such as lungwort (*Pulmonaria*), barrenwort (*Epimedium*), and coralbells (*Heuchera*). This makes a more attractive display as the new foliage fills in. Remove dead foliage on lamb's ear. The old leaves tend to mat down over winter and will lead to rot if not removed.

- Cut back ornamental grasses before the new growth begins. Use a weedwhip, hedge shears, or hand pruners to clip the plants back to several inches above the soil. Smaller grasses, such as blue fescue and blue oat grass, can be clipped back or left intact.

- Prune back Russian sage and butterfly bush to 4 to 6 inches above the soil. Both plants (often classed as sub-shrubs) usually die back in winter. Use a lopper or hand pruners to cut stems above an outward facing bud.

- Cut back only the dead tips of candytuft, lavender, and thyme. Cut them back even further in late spring if the plants become leggy.

APRIL

- Start a bloom chart in your garden journal. Record the name and bloom time of various plants in the landscape. This will help you fill any flowering voids when planning next year's additions.

- Begin planting once the soil is prepared and the plants are available. Plant dormant bare-root plants as soon as they arrive and the weather permits. Soak the roots several hours prior to planting. Trim off any broken roots. Dig a hole large enough to accommodate the roots. Place the plant in the hole and spread out the roots. Fill the hole with soil, keeping the crown of the plant (where stem joins the roots) just below the soil surface. Gently tamp and water.

- Watch for late-emerging perennials, such as butterfly weed and hardy hibiscus. Use a plant label or consider adding spring-flowering bulbs next fall to mark their location. This will help you avoid damaging them in the spring.

- Perennials grown in properly amended soil need very little fertilizer. Always follow soil test recommendations. Spread several inches of compost or aged manure over the surface of existing gardens. Apply organic matter every two to four years to keep perennials healthy and well fed.

- Use netting and repellents to protect emerging plants from animal damage. Start early to encourage animals to go elsewhere to feed. Reapply repellents after severe weather or as recommended on label directions.

MAY

- Harden off plants that were started indoors or in the greenhouse before planting outdoors. Use a cold frame or protected location for this process. See page 22 in the book's introduction for details on hardening off. Label plants and record the planting information on your landscape plan and in your journal. Make a note of the cultivar (variety), planting date, and plant source.

- Dig and divide overgrown perennials or those you want to propagate. Spring is the best time to divide summer- and fall-blooming perennials. Wait until after flowering or late August to divide spring-flowering perennials.

- Dig and divide your woodland wildflowers after blooming. Do this only if you must move existing plants or to start new plantings; otherwise, leave your wildflowers alone.

- Move or remove unwanted perennial seedlings. Coneflowers, black-eyed Susans, and other prolific seeders may provide more offspring than needed. Dig and share with friends or donate surplus plants to nearby schools, community beautification groups, and master gardeners.

- Put stakes, peony cages, and trellises in place. It is always easier to train young plants through the cages or onto the stakes than manipulate mature plants into submission.

- Check columbine plants for leafminer, sawfly, and stalk borer. Healthy plants can tolerate the leafminer and sawfly. Remove wilted stems and destroy the borer.

- As the garden comes to life, so does the opportunity to spend time in the garden. Deadhead (remove faded flowers) early blooming perennials. Shear phlox, pinks, and candytuft to encourage a new flush of foliage. Use hand pruners or pruning shears.

- Pinch back mums and asters. Keep them 4 to 6 inches tall throughout the months of May and June.

- Pinch back Shasta daisy, beebalm, garden phlox, and obedient plants to control height and stagger bloom times. Disbud (remove side flower buds) peonies if you want fewer but larger flowers.

- Thin garden phlox, beebalm, and other powdery mildew-susceptible plants when the stems are 8 inches tall. Remove one-fourth to one-third (leaving at least four to five) of the stems. Thinning increases light and air to the plant, decreasing the risk of powdery mildew.

JUNE

- Keep planting. The soil is warm, and there are still lots of perennials available at local garden centers and perennial nurseries. See the label and the plant profiles for any specific planting and care information.

- This is a good time to transplant bleeding heart and dig and divide overgrown perennials.

- Cool, wet springs mean lots of diseases. Remove spotted, blotchy, or discolored leaves as soon as they are found. Sanitation is the best control for disease problems.

- Watch for leafhoppers, aphids, mites, and spittlebugs. These insects all suck out plant juices, causing leaves to yellow, brown, and die. Control high populations with insecticidal soap. Repeat weekly as needed.

- Get out the flashlight, and check your garden for nighttime feeders. Slugs and earwigs eat holes in leaves and flowers at night. Fill a shallow dish sunk in the ground with beer. The slugs are attracted to the beer, crawl inside, and die.

- Check the garden for signs of wildlife. Deer and rabbits love hostas, phlox, and other perennials. Apply repellents or use scare tactics such as noisemakers and whirligigs, and fence gardens to discourage feeding.

- Deadhead valerian, columbine, and other heavy seeders to prevent unwanted seedlings. Do not deadhead Siberian iris. Leave some seedpods to provide added interest in the summer, fall, and winter garden.

- Consider removing the flowers of lamb's ear as soon as they form. This encourages better foliage.

- Keep mums and asters 6 inches tall throughout the month. Cut back amsonia and wild blue indigo (Baptisia) by one-third to prevent sprawling, open centers. Prune back by one-half Russian sage that flopped in the past.

- You can pinch or cut back an outer ring of stems or scattered plants of purple coneflower, heliopsis, garden phlox, balloon flower, and veronica. The pinched-back plants will be shorter and bloom later. They act as a living support for the rest of the plant and extend the bloom period.

- Pinch out the growing tips or cut back 8-inch stems to 4 inches on 'Autumn Joy' sedum that may have tended to flop in your garden. Or try moving it to a sunnier location with less fertile but well-drained soil.

- Cut back bleeding heart as the flowers fade. This reduces reseeding and encourages new growth that may last all season. Mulch the soil and water to help preserve the leaves.

JULY

- Dig and divide or take root cuttings of spring-blooming poppies, bleeding heart, and bearded iris (six to eight weeks after bloom).

- Consider fertilizing heavy feeders and those cut back for rebloom. Use a low-nitrogen, slow-release fertilizer to avoid burn.

- Check the leaf surfaces and stems for aphids and mites. Spray plants with a strong blast of water to dislodge these insects. Use insecticidal soap to treat damaging populations. This is a soap formulated to kill soft-bodied insects, but it is not harmful to the plant or the environment.

- Check for plantbugs whenever you see speckled and spotted leaves and stems. Insecticidal soap or other environmentally friendly insecticides labeled for controlling plantbugs on flowers can be used.

- Watch for lacy leaves caused by Japanese beetles. Healthy plants can tolerate the damage. Control them by knocking them into a can of soapy water. Be careful when using insecticides that can harm beneficial insects like honeybees as well as kill the beetles.

- Continue deadheading and pinching back straggly plants, such as lavender. Prune back silvermound artemisia before flowering. Prune back to fresh new growth to avoid open centers. Cut back old stems of delphiniums to the fresh growth at the base of the plant. This encourages new growth and a second flush of flowers. Prune back yellow foliage of bleeding heart to ground level.

AUGUST

- Dig and divide overgrown irises, poppies, and other spring-blooming perennials.

- Do not fertilize. Late-season fertilization encourages problems with winter survival. Use this time to evaluate the health and vigor of your plantings. Make note of those areas that need topdressing or fertilization next spring.

- Check beebalm, garden phlox, and other perennials for signs of white, powdery mildew. This fungal disease causes leaves to eventually yellow and brown. Consider moving infected

plants into an area with full sun and good air circulation. Or substitute mildew-resistant cultivars of mildew-susceptible plants in next year's garden.

- Try cutting back short-lived perennials, such as blanket flowers (Gaillardia) and 'Butterfly Blue' pincushion flower (Scabiosa). Late-season pruning will stimulate new green growth and may help extend the plant's life.

- Pick flowers at midday to harvest flowers used for drying. Remove leaves and combine in small bundles. Use rubber bands to hold the stems together. As the stems shrink, the rubber bands will contract, holding the stems tight. Use a spring-type clothespin to attach drying flowers to a line, nail, or other support.

SEPTEMBER

- Move self-sown biennials to their desired location. Transplant early in the month so the seedlings will have time to get re-established before winter.

- Add mums to the fall garden. Fall-planted garden mums are not always hardy in our area. Leave them stand for winter and add winter mulch after the ground freezes. Many botanical gardens and estates use them as an annual for fall interest.

- Finish digging and dividing perennials, including iris. Wait until spring to divide Siberian iris, astilbe, delphinium, or other slow-to-establish perennials.

- Stop deadheading plants you want to develop seedpods for winter interest, such as fall-blooming rudbeckias, coneflowers, astilbes, and sedums. Continue deadheading to prevent seed set on perennials that are overtaking your garden.

- Dig and divide peonies, only if needed, now through right after the tops have been killed by frost. Use a spading fork to dig the rhizomes. Dig a hole wider than the plant to avoid damaging the root system. Cut the clump into smaller pieces, leaving at least three to five eyes per division. Prepare the planting site by adding several inches of compost into the top 12 inches of soil. Replant the divisions, keeping the eyes no more than 1 to 2 inches below the soil surface.

OCTOBER

- Finish planting early in the month. The later you plant, the less time your perennials will have to get established and the greater the risk of winterkill. Try to limit planting to hardier perennials that are suited to our cold winters.

- Locate a place to overwinter less hardy transplants and those scheduled for spring planting. Sink the pots into the ground. Once the soil freezes, mulch with evergreen branches or straw for extra protection.

- Collect and sow seeds of coneflowers, rudbeckias, and other late summer- and fall-blooming perennials. Spread the seeds outdoors on well-prepared soil.

- Leave stems, flower heads, and seedpods standing for winter interest. Remove only those infected by pests or those that tend to reseed more than you desire.

- Carefully blow or rake tree and shrub leaves off your perennial gardens. Large leaves get wet, mat down, and provide poor insulation for your plants. Shred fallen leaves and use them as a soil mulch or amendment for new plantings. Or rake and bag them for use in next year's garden.

- Check last winter's notes on wildlife damage. Consider control options if voles have been a problem in the past. Some gardeners choose to cut down their gardens in fall to eliminate the vole's habitat. Others depend on nature, hawks, owls, temperature extremes, and the neighbors' cats to control these rodents.

NOVEMBER

- Collect and save seeds of coneflowers, black-eyed Susans, and other perennials you want to plant next spring. Remove seeds from the seedpod and allow them to dry, then place the seeds in an envelope. Label the envelope, and place in an airtight container in the refrigerator for the needed cold treatment (stratification). The seeds will be ready to plant next spring.

- Give your perennials growing aboveground extra care for the winter. Place planters in an unheated garage, porch, or other protected area where temperatures hover near freezing. Insulate the roots with packing peanuts or other material. Water whenever the soil is thawed and dry. Or sink perennials growing in weatherproof containers into a vacant garden area for the winter. Or add potted perennials to the garden.

- Leave the stems or place markers by butterfly weed, balloon flower, and other late-emerging perennials. Plant bulbs next to these perennials to mark their locations and to prevent accidental damage in early spring.

DECEMBER

- Finish garden clean-up. Do not worry if you have waited too long and the snow has buried all your good intentions. Wait until the first thaw or spring to finish garden cleanup. Use evergreen branches, straw, or marsh hay for winter mulch. These will protect tender perennials and prevent frost heaving.

- Make sure the garden hose is safely stored for winter. Turn off the water or insulate outside faucets to prevent freezing.

- Don't throw away that holiday tree. Use it in your winter landscape. Collect the discarded trees in your neighborhood to use as mulch in your garden. Prune off the branches and cover perennial and bulb gardens. The soil is usually frozen by the holidays and we have not yet had the damaging winter thaw.

- Or leave the tree intact and use it as a windbreak for other plants in the landscape. In snowy winters, I prop trees in a snowdrift for winter interest. The trees provide shelter for the birds that like to feed on the seeds of coneflower, rudbeckia, and liatris in the perennial garden.

MIX OF CONEFLOWERS AND DAYLILIES

ROSES
for the Midwest

Roses are not just for the experienced gardener or those willing to invest lots of time managing high-maintenance plants. Now everyone can enjoy roses in their landscape. The wide selection of hardy beautiful repeat blooming varieties requiring varying levels of care make it possible for all to enjoy. Go eco-friendly with Earth-Kind award-winning roses. They were selected for their superior pest tolerance, low water usage, and outstanding landscape performance. And for those looking for a challenge, you still have lots of choices.

Use roses to add color, fragrance, and year-round beauty to your landscape. They can be grown *en masse*, as specimen plants, planted in a mixed border, shrub bed, or in a container.

With proper selection, siting and care, you can keep pest problems to a minimum and increase winter survival. There are many roses from hardy to finicky for you to choose from and more are being introduced every year. So keep checking catalogs and garden centers for showier, hardier, and more pest-resistant plants that best suit your gardening style.

Once selected plant roses in moist, well-drained soil where they receive good air circulation and at least six hours of sun per day. Select a site with morning sun, such as an east-facing location, that will dry morning dew off the leaves, thus helping reduce disease problems.

BUYING ROSES

Roses are available from catalogs, garden centers, and nurseries. Roses are available bare root, potted, and in containers. Bare-root roses are often sold according to grades 1, 1½, and 2. Grade 1 plants are the most expensive with three or four heavy canes that are about 18 inches long. Grade 1½ and 2 plants have a smaller root system and fewer canes that are shorter and thinner. Store bare-root plants in a cool, shaded, frost-free location until they can be planted outdoors. Heel them in outdoors in a protected location, or pack the roots in peat moss or sawdust and place in the refrigerator to keep them from drying out.

Bare-root plants that have begun to grow in transit or storage need special care. Plant them and move these and any greenhouse-grown or early-sprouting container plants to a sunny location free from frost. Provide water as needed. Gradually introduce the plants (harden off) to the outdoor conditions. Plant outdoors once danger of frost has passed.

PLANTING ROSES

Soil preparation is critical to successful rose growing. Spread 2 to 4 inches of organic matter over the soil surface and work it into the top 12 inches of soil. Plant bare-root roses in the spring while they are still dormant. Soak the roots for twenty-four hours before planting. Container plants can be planted throughout the season and dormant plants as soon as the ground is workable. Plant less hardy varieties early in the season to allow the plants time to get well established before winter.

Some roses are grafted. A bud from the desired plant is attached to a hardy root system. The bud graft is the swollen knob where all the branches are formed. This portion of the plant is very susceptible to winter damage. Plant the graft 2 inches below the soil surface for added winter protection. Roses grown on their own roots can be planted at the same level they were growing in the container. Dig the planting hole at least two times wider than the root system. For bare-root roses, create a cone of soil in the middle of the planting hole. Set the roots on top of the cone so the graft is 2 inches below the surface and the roots are positioned over the cone and throughout the hole.

Container grown roses have a more established root system. They can be planted like other shrubs or like potted roses to insure transplant success. Potted roses are bare-root plants that were potted just a few months prior to sale and should be handled with care. Cut off the bottom of the container. Set the plant (pot and all) in the planting hole, making sure the graft will be 2 inches below the soil surface. Now slice the side of the pot and peel it away, leaving the rootball intact. Fill the hole with soil and water. Mulch and keep the soil moist, but not wet, throughout the growing season.

MAINTENANCE

Roses do best when they receive 1 inch of water per week from rainfall or irrigation. Once established, shrub roses are fairly drought tolerant. Mulch roses with an organic material to conserve moisture, reduce weed problems, and improve the soil.

Test the soil to determine its nutrient content and then fertilize roses according to the test recommendations. In lieu of a test, apply a low-nitrogen fertilizer in spring once new growth is well established. Most of our soils are high to excessive in phosphorous and potassium so only use complete fertilizers such as 10-10-10 and 12-12-12 if your soil is lacking in phosphorus and potassium. Additional fertilizing can be done as needed, but do not fertilize in late summer as this can stimulate late-season growth more subject to winter injury.

PRUNING

Pruning requirements vary for each type of rose. For all roses, remove the suckers that form from the rootstock of grafted roses. Cut suckers below the soil to discourage resprouting. Wait until spring to do the majority of pruning.

Climbers: Only prune dead and damaged wood during the first few years. All climbers should be pruned after flowering, and plants should not be cut back for winter protection. Each spring, cut only the dead stems back to ground level. After blooming you can remove one-third of the older canes. Single bloomers can be pruned back by two-thirds of their size. Trim side branches by two-thirds also. Prune after flowering throughout the season. This improves air circulation and reduces problems with powdery mildew.

Floribunda, Grandiflora, and Hybrid teas: Prune these roses in the spring as buds swell, before growth begins—about the same time the forsythias bloom. Start by removing dead and diseased wood. Prune back to healthy live portions of the canes where the stem is green and center is white. This may be to ground level some years. If needed, prune floribundas back to 10 inches, hybrid teas back to 16-18 inches and grandifloras to the desired height. Next, thin out the center of the plant. Remove old and crossed canes first. Cut back stems ¼ inch above an outward-facing bud. You may want to seal pruning cuts to keep borers out.

Miniature: Start pruning miniature roses after winter protection is removed and the buds swell but before growth begins. Prune to open the center by removing twiggy growth. Cut the plants back to the desired height. Make cuts ¼ inch above an outward-facing bud. You can seal pruning cuts to keep borers out.

Shrub: Remove dead and crowded stems in the spring before growth begins and cut back older stems to keep growth in bounds.

Deadheading and cutting roses for arrangements are also forms of pruning. When properly done, this will encourage strong, new growth and repeat blooms. Deadhead by removing only individual flowers in clusters as they fade. Once all the flowers in the cluster have bloomed, prune back the flower stem to the first five-leaflet leaf. Deadhead single-flowered roses back to the first five-leaflet leaf. This encourages stouter and stronger branch development. You can prune back farther on established plants as long as you leave at least two five-leaflet leaves behind. Stop harvesting large bouquets and deadheading in late summer to allow plants to prepare for winter and form hips (fruit) for you and the birds to enjoy.

PESTS

Roses are subject to many insect and disease problems. Select the most pest-resistant cultivars available. Blackspot, powdery mildew, and rust are the most common disease problems. Remove infected leaves as soon as they appear. Fall cleanup will also help reduce the source of disease for the

Prune the flowering stem back to the first set of 5 leaflet leaves once all the flowers in the cluster fade.

next growing season. Many gardeners spray disease-susceptible plants with a fungicide on a regular basis. New plant-derived, more environmentally friendly products are available. Check with your local garden center for availability in your area.

Insect pests, including Japanese beetles, aphids, mites, leafhoppers, beetles, sawflies, and caterpillars, feed on the leaves of rose bushes. Healthy plants can usually tolerate the damage. Aphids, mites, and leafhoppers suck plant juices, causing leaf discoloration and curling. Strong blasts of water or several applications of insecticidal soap will control these pests. Handpicking or applying insecticides appropriate for roses will take care of the others that chew holes in leaves or flowers. Be sure to read and follow label directions to minimize impact on our bees and butterflies.

Deer and rabbits are also fond of roses. Using scare tactics, repellents, and fencing may provide relief from these bigger pests. Apply repellents before animals start feeding and repeat as recommended for increased success. Make sure fencing is tight to the ground and high enough to keep animals out. Continue to monitor for damage, change tactics as needed and try a multifaceted approach for increased success.

WINTER PROTECTION

Provide winter protection when growing grafted and borderline hardy plants. There are as many ways to protect roses from winter weather as there are rose gardeners; but proper timing is the key to the success of each method. We often protect the roses when we get cold, *not* when the roses need it. Wait to cover rose bushes after we have had a week of consistently freezing temperatures. Start removing winter protection in the spring when the mercury again starts hovering near freezing. Limit fall pruning; remove only just what is needed to apply winter protection and do not prune climbers.

Hybrid tea and all grafted roses need extra care to survive cold Midwest winters. You can do nothing and hope for the best. Some winters this actually works. The soil mound method works well. Start after that week of cold to start mulching plants. Loosely tie the canes. Many gardeners surround the plants with chicken wire sunk into the ground (prior to the ground freezing) to hold the soil and mulch in place and keep rodents out. Cover the bottom 8 to 10 inches of the rose plant with soil. You may need to raid the compost pile, or bring in soil. Let the soil mound freeze and then mulch with evergreen branches, marsh hay, or straw.

Or try the leaf method for rose beds. Surround planting beds with a 4-foot-high fence of hardware cloth before the ground freezes. Sink the fencing several inches into the soil to keep out the rodents. Prune roses back to 18 inches once the ground freezes, then fill the rose bed with 3 feet of tightly packed dry leaves or bark mulch. Remove the leaves in spring and recycle them in your compost pile or use as mulch in the garden.

Rose cones are a favorite but often misused technique. The same timing applies to this method. Prune back roses to fit under the cone. Mulch roses and cover with cone. Anchor to hold the cone in place. Be sure to ventilate cones on sunny winter days.

The Minnesota Tip method is much more labor intensive but has the greatest survival rate in the upper Midwest. In fall use a spade to cut through the roots about a foot from the stems on one side of the plant. Tip the plant over so it is lying flat on the ground. Cover with soil. Once the soil covering freezes, mulch with straw or evergreen boughs for added insulation. This method works well for climbers and tree roses.

Nonhardy climbers growing in protected areas may survive if left in place. Mound the base of grafted climbers with soil. Then wrap the plant with burlap and fill with evergreen boughs or straw for extra insulation.

Roses growing in pots may need extra care starting in fall. Non-grafted or those roses two zones hardier than your zone and growing in a weatherproof pot can survive outdoors. For less hardy plants, sink the pot in a vacant part of the garden. Once cold weather arrives use one of the above winter protection methods. Or move the rose, pot and all, into an unheated garage. Pack insulating materials around the pot for added insulation. Water the soil anytime the soil is thawed and dry. Or move miniatures and other smaller roses indoors. Though challenging you can grow it like a houseplant in a cool sunny location watering as needed.

Tree roses are usually grafted in two places and need special winter care. Grow them in a pot and winter as above or follow the recommendations for winter care of climbing roses. It's a little extra work but worth it if you want your tree rose to survive the winter.

Winter-damaged roses may die back to ground level. Those growing on their own roots will recover and eventually regain the mature size. Grafted roses suffer a different fate. If the graft union survives the plant will send out new growth with the desirable flowers. If the tender bud graft dies and the roots survives you end up with thick, thorny stems and no or different flowers. You can either enjoy the surprise or replace it with the desired rose.

There are many wonderful roses, too many to mention here. Look for hardy, pest-resistant introductions that fit your landscape and garden design. Contact your nearby botanical garden for their list of favorite roses, check out the All-America Rose Selections (www.rose.org) and American Rose Society (www.ars.org) websites and then start creating your own list of favorites.

FLORIBUNDA ROSE 'PLEASURE' WITH JOHNNY JUMP-UPS

CLIMBING
Rosa x hybrida

Why It's Special—The climbing rose is a versatile beauty. Use climbers as vertical accents, flowering specimens, or screens. Ramblers are large, fast-growing, hardy climbing roses that require little care and no winter protection. The large-flowered climbing roses come from a variety of sources including mutations of hybrid tea, grandiflora, and multiflora roses.

How to Plant & Grow—Plant climbers near a fence, trellis, or arbor that is large and sturdy enough to handle the size and weight of the mature plant. Train and attach climbers to their support as they grow. See the chapter introduction for planting tips.

Care & Problems—Water thoroughly whenever the top few inches of soil starts to dry. Proper watering, fertilization, pest management, and pruning are critical for growing beautiful climbers. Follow pruning guidelines in the chapter introduction. Provide winter protection if the variety is not hardy in your area. See the tips on overwintering roses in cold climates.

Hardiness—Varies with species

Bloom Color—Various, including red, pink, salmon, yellow, and white

Bloom Period—Once, or repeat blooming summer through fall

Mature Size (H x W)—6 to 20 ft. x 3 to 6 ft.

Water Needs—Established roses are fairly drought tolerant.

FLORIBUNDA
Rosa x hybrida

Why It's Special—These long-blooming, often fragrant roses make nice additions to the landscape and flower arrangements. They are the result of crossing polyantha and hybrid tea roses. The polyanthas imparted increased hardiness, while the hybrid teas passed on larger attractive flowers and pest susceptibility. Select one of the hardier, more pest-resistant cultivars available in a variety of colors.

How to Plant & Grow—Plant your floribundas early in the season in a sunny, well-drained location. Use floribunda roses in mass plantings, hedges, or mixed borders. Follow planting guidelines in the introductions to roses.

Care & Problems—Provide adequate water and fertilization and monitor plants for insects and diseases throughout the season. Deadhead throughout the season to encourage new blooms and thick sturdy growth. Stop deadheading toward the end of the season to slow growth and increase winter hardiness. Many floribundas benefit from winter protection in the upper Midwest. (See the chapter introduction also.)

Hardiness—Varies with variety

Bloom Color—Variety of colors

Bloom Period—Summer

Mature Size (H x W)—3 ft. x 3 ft.

Water Needs—Evenly moist to slightly dry soil is best.

GRANDIFLORA
Rosa x hybrida

Why It's Special— The long-lasting flowers, extended bloom time, and increased hardiness make these a nice addition to the landscape. Though the flowers often lack fragrance, their large size, long stems, and variety of colors make them suited to cutting.

How to Plant & Grow—Plant grandifloras early in the season to give them time to get established before winter. They prefer full sun and moist, well-drained soil. These large plants can be used as background plants in a flower garden or mixed with other roses and shrubs. See the planting tips in the chapter introduction.

Care & Problems—Water, fertilize, prune properly for best growth and bloom. Deadhead to encourage more bloom. Monitor for insect and disease problems though susceptibility varies with cultivars. Winter protection is usually needed in the upper Midwest. (See the chapter introduction for details.)

Hardiness—Varies with variety

Bloom Color—A variety of solids, blends, and bicolors

Bloom Period—Summer

Mature Size (H x W)—4 to 5 ft. x 3 to 4 ft.

Water Needs—Soil should be evenly moist to slightly dry.

HYBRID TEA
Rosa x hybrida

Why It's Special—Their beautiful, large flowers put on quite a show in the garden or in a vase. But there is a price for their beauty. Hybrid tea roses require some time and effort on your part. Consider incorporating some All America Rose Selections (AARS) winners selected for their flower form, pest resistance, fragrance, growth habit, and other features.

How to Plant & Grow—Like all roses, hybrid teas benefit from early season planting in sunny, well-drained locations. Grow hybrid teas in rose gardens, in containers, as specimen plants, or incorporate them into planting beds. See the chapter introduction for general rose planting guidelines.

Care & Problems—Water and fertilize as needed. Prune hybrid tea roses in the spring as buds swell but before growth begins. Hybrid teas benefit from winter protection throughout central and the upper Midwest, though some gardeners choose to do nothing.

Hardiness—Winter protection is needed in central and upper Midwest.

Bloom Color—Variety of colors

Bloom Period—Summer

Mature Size (H x W)—3 ft. x 3 ft.

Water Needs—Keep soil evenly moist.

MINIATURE
Rosa x hybrida

Why It's Special—Miniatures are just that—miniature versions of hybrid teas or floribunda roses. These free-flowering small roses will fit in any landscape. Look for the American Rose Society Award of Excellence the next time you shop for miniature roses. Winners are selected for their outstanding performance in such areas as novelty, bud and flower form, plant habit, quantity of blooms, vigor, foliage, and disease/insect resistance.

How to Plant & Grow—Plant in full sun and moist, well-drained soil. Use minis as an edging plant in the garden, a specimen in a rock garden, or in containers. Move container plantings indoors or to a protected location for the winter. Or you may want to try growing miniatures as a flowering houseplant in a south-facing window or under artificial lights.

Care & Problems—Just like all roses, miniatures benefit from adequate water and fertilization. Miniatures are subject to insect and disease problems. Susceptibility varies with the cultivar, so reduce problems by selecting the most pest-resistant cultivars available. Even though miniatures are hardier than the hybrid teas, many benefit from some winter protection. This is especially true in upper Midwest. (See the chapter introduction for details.)

Hardiness—Minis benefits from winter protection in the upper Midwest.

Bloom Color—Variety of colors

Bloom Period—Summer

Mature Size (H x W)—6 to 24 in. x 8 to 24 in.

Water Needs—Keep soil evenly moist to slightly dry.

SHRUB
Rosa species and hybrids

Why It's Special—Hardy, vigorous, and low maintenance make these roses a good choice for any gardener. Many shrub roses have showy flowers, long and repeat bloom, and good fall color. They also provide winter interest with their abundant attractive fruit.

How to Plant & Grow—These hardier roses are much more tolerant of late-season planting than other roses. Grow shrub roses in full sun and moist, well-drained soil. Their size and growth habit will help determine their suitability for use as climbers, hedges, specimens, borders, and for winter interest. See the chapter introduction for planting tips.

Care & Problems—Shrub roses require much less care and pruning. Fertilize as needed in the spring after new growth has developed. Shrub roses are generally resistant to insects and disease and do not need winter protection. Select a rose that's hardy for your part of the Midwest.

Hardiness—Varies with species

Bloom Color—Variety of colors

Bloom Period— Early summer and many repeat throughout summer

Mature Size (H x W)—2 to 8 ft. x 2 to 8 ft.

Water Needs—Drought tolerant once established.

COMMON DISEASES

Select the most pest-resistant roses whenever possible. Your best defense against pest problems is a healthy plant, but even healthy plants can be infested by disease. Sanitation is sometimes enough to keep diseases under control. If you choose to use a fungicide, be sure to read and follow all label directions carefully. Select a fungicide labeled to control several diseases. This will give you a great range of control with one product. Here are some of the more common rose diseases and the recommended controls:

- Blackspot is one of the most common and most serious fungal diseases on roses. It causes black spots and yellowing of the leaves. Once a planting is infected, it is likely to develop the disease in the future. Remove infected and fallen leaves throughout the season. Fall cleanup helps reduce the source of infection for the next season. Apply fungicides labeled to control blackspot on roses in mid-June or at the first sign of this disease. Repeat every seven days throughout the growing season. You can lengthen the time between applications during dry weather.

- Powdery mildew is a fungal disease that appears as a white powder on the leaf surface. It is a common problem during periods of fluctuating humidity. Properly spaced plants growing in full sun are less likely to develop this disease. Apply fungicides as soon as the disease appears and repeat every seven to fourteen days. Use a product labeled for controlling powdery mildew on roses. Several universities and botanical gardens have successfully used weekly applications of a mixture of 1 tablespoon baking soda, ½ tablespoon lightweight horticultural oil or insecticidal soap, and 1 gallon of water to control powdery mildew.

- Botrytis blight is a fungal disease that causes flower buds to turn black and fail to open. It is most common on pink and white roses and occurs during wet weather. Prune off and destroy infected blossoms. Sanitation and drier weather are usually enough to keep this disease under control.

- Cankers are sunken and discolored areas that develop due to weather, mechanical injury, or disease. Prune out infected canes beneath the canker. Disinfect tools between cuts. Provide plants with proper care and winter protection to minimize this problem.

COMMON INSECT PROBLEMS

A variety of insects attack roses. Small populations can usually be removed by hand. You may choose to use an insecticide to control larger populations that are damaging the plant. Many rose fertilizers contain insecticides. Check your fertilizer and pesticide labels before applying these materials.

- Aphids and mites suck out the plant juices causing the leaves to appear speckled, yellow, and distorted. Many rose fertilizers contain insecticides labeled for controlling these pests. Lightweight horticulture (summer) oils and insecticidal soap are more environmentally friendly products that will control these pests.

Blackspot is one of the most common and serious fungal diseases on roses.

- Leafhoppers often go undetected but can cause plants to be weak and stunted. These greenish yellow insects feed on the underside of the leaves. They hop sideways when disturbed. Insecticidal soap and many other insecticides will control these insects.

- Budworms and other caterpillars feed on flower buds and leaves. Remove and destroy the caterpillars as they are found. *Bacillius thuringiensis*, sold as Bt, Dipel, or Thuricide, will control these insects without harming other beneficial insects.

- Rose slugs are really sawflies that feed on the leaves. Healthy plants tolerate the damage but these insects annoy gardeners. Live with the damage or use an environmentally friendly insecticide labeled for their control.

- Rose chafers are most common in areas with sandy soil. These beetles eat the leaf tissue, leaving the veins intact. They feed on roses from late June through July. Small populations can be removed and destroyed by hand. Insecticides labeled to control chafers on roses may be used to control larger populations or insects on large plantings. Make sure the insects are still present prior to spraying. The damage is often noticed after the insects have left.

- Japanese beetles have been found throughout the Midwest. Watch for this pest in June through August. Knock adults into a can of soapy water or use an insecticide labeled for controlling this pest on roses.

- Earwigs are reddish brown beetles with pinchers on their back end. They eat holes in leaves and flower petals. To trap and kill damaging earwigs, set a crumpled paper under a flowerpot. The earwigs will hide in the folds of the paper during the day. Move fast to capture and crush the hiding earwigs. Environmentally friendly insecticides can also be used to control these pests.

HOW TO KNOW IF THE GRAFT UNION HAS DIED

Extremely harsh weather, improper winter protection, or shallow planting can cause the death of the bud graft (the swollen portion of the stem). This delicate union joins the hardy root system with the desired rose. Since the graft is planted belowground, the damage is not always discovered immediately. After the graft dies, the rootstock takes over. If the graft has died, replace the rose and plant the new rose with the graft 2 inches below the soil surface.

The following changes in growth may mean the graft has died:

- Canes are thicker, with more thorns and fewer leaves.

- The plant fails to bloom or produces flowers that are different than those produced in the past.

CUTTING ROSES FOR VASES

- Cut rose flowers early in the morning just as the top of the bud is starting to open. Make the cut on a slight angle above an outward facing, five-leaflet leaf. Cut flowers back to a three-leaflet leaf on young plants that may not tolerate this amount of pruning.

- Remove the lower leaves on the stem.

- Recut the bottom of the stem on an angle just before placing in a vase.

GROWING ROSES IN CONTAINERS

If your planting space is limited, or if you need a little color on your patio, consider growing container roses. Tree roses, miniature roses, and hybrid teas can all be grown in containers.

1. Leave the rose in the nursery pot for easier winter care.

2. Select a decorative container with drainage holes that is one to two sizes larger than the original pot.

3. Place pebbles in the bottom of the decorative pot if it lacks drainage holes and set the rose on the pebbles inside the decorative pot.

4. Water when the soil dries.

5. Fertilize with any flowering houseplant fertilizer. The higher phosphorus will help promote flowering. Follow label for rate and frequency. Stop fertilizing in early August.

6. Next season move the rose into a larger pot filled with a well-drained potting mix. Incorporate a low-nitrogen, slow-release fertilizer into the soil at planting. This will eliminate the need to fertilize through most or all of the growing season.

OVERWINTERING ROSES INDOORS

1. Locate a cool sunny area to grow the plants over winter.

2. Over the next few weeks, gradually reduce the amount of light the plants receive.

3. Quarantine (isolate) the roses for several weeks. Watch and control insects prior to introducing them into your indoor plant collection.

4. Move plants to their permanent indoor location. Keep soil slightly moist and continue to watch for insects and disease.

HARVEST ROSES FOR WINTER ENJOYMENT

1. Line a solid cardboard box with a plastic bag. Use a 10 x 14-inch or other box of a convenient size.

2. Move the box to the basement, crawl space, or other location where it will stay cool, but above 40 degrees Fahrenheit.

3. Fill the box with wet sand once it is in its permanent location. It may be too heavy to move once filled.

4. Pick roses that are in full bud and show a little color.

5. Remove the leaves and submerge the stems (with the flowers above the water) in warm water for forty-five to sixty minutes.

6. Make a hole in the sand for the rose stem. Stand roses in the sand so that the stems are covered and the buds are just above the sand.

7. Remove flowers to enjoy throughout winter. Recut the stem and place in hot water.

ROSE TYPES

Modern roses are those roses introduced after 1867. These include hybrid teas, polyanthas, floribundas, and grandifloras.

Hybrid tea roses are grafted onto a hardy rootstock. They grow 3 to 5 feet tall and produce single or double flowers on long stems.

Polyanthas are hybrids that grow up to 2 feet tall and produce a proliferation of small flowers in clusters. They are hardier than hybrid teas but less popular than floribundas.

Floribundas are the result of crossing hybrid teas with polyanthas. These 3-foot-tall plants are usually grafted and produce many small flowers in clusters.

Grandifloras are grafted and grow up to 6 feet tall. They produce flowers similar to the hybrid teas, though the blooms are smaller and are clustered in groups of five to seven.

Tree roses can be any type of rose, though hybrid teas and floribundas are the most popular choices. A straight trunk is grafted onto a hardy rootstock. The desired rose is then grafted to the top of the trunk. During cold weather, both grafts need to be covered or the plants should be moved indoors for winter.

Climbing roses can grow to over 6 feet tall and can be trained over fences, on trellises, or up walls. These plants produce long canes that can be tied to the support structure.

Large-flowered climbers have thick stiff canes, bloom twice a season, and are climbing versions (mutations) of other roses. Some are grafted, and most benefit from winter protection. Some large hardy shrub roses like 'William Baffin' 'Ramblin' Red' and 'John Cabot' can be grown as climbers and need no winter protection.

Ramblers are much hardier climbers. They flower once a year on long, thin, flexible canes.

Miniature roses are small versions of floribundas and hybrid teas that produce smaller leaves and flowers on 6- to 18-inch-tall plants.

Always select the hardiest and most pest-resistant rose available. Visit local botanical gardens to find out which roses perform the best for them. You may find that many of these are labeled AARS. This means they are one of the All America Rose Selections. These award-winning roses have been tested at over twenty-five locations in the United States. They were selected as winners based upon their flower form, pest resistance, fragrance, growth habit, or other feature. See www.rose.org for more information.

FIGHTING OFF DEER AND RABBITS

Deer and rabbits will feed on roses anytime they can reach the plants. A variety of techniques may be needed to control these pests.

- Fence in small areas. Use a black or green fine mesh material to fence in the garden. This material allows you to see the garden while providing a barrier to the animals. The fence should be 5 feet tall with the bottom few inches sunk into the ground. The deer will stay out of these small areas and the rabbits can't get in.

- Homemade or commercial repellents may provide some relief. Hot pepper sprinkled on the plants has provided some relief. One landscape professional swears by this method, while another says the deer prefer the "seasoned" plants. Or try bloodmeal, Messina Animal Stopper, TreeGuard, Ropel, and other commercial repellents. Apply them early and repeat after heavy rains. Try a variety of products.

- Scare tactics such as clanging pans, blasting radios, white balloons on a stick, and other devices may help keep animals away. Vary these tactics for continued success. Urban animals are not scared by people, noises, and smells. They are too used to dining undisturbed in our landscape.

- Trapping is not always a humane method for controlling rabbits. This practice can separate a mother from her young babies. Releasing animals in a strange environment can be stressful and even deadly. Besides, who needs more rabbits? Parks, farmers, and other gardeners probably have enough rabbits of their own.

TRANSPLANTING ROSES

1. Make sure the soil around the rose is moist, not wet. Water dry soils the night before transplanting roses. The moist soil will hold together during transplanting.

2. Dig out as much of the root system (2 feet or more in diameter) as possible. Make the rootball only as large as you are able to handle. Digging up and dropping a large rootball is worse than starting with a smaller one.

3. Use your shovel or spading fork to lift the rose out of the planting hole. You may need to cut attached roots with your pruning shears.

4. Slide a plastic or burlap tarp under the rootball. This makes transporting the plant easier and reduces the risk of damaging the rootball.

5. Slide the plant off the tarp and into the planting hole. Plant it at the same depth as it was growing before. The graft on grafted roses should be 2 inches below the soil surface.

6. Fill with soil and water.

JANUARY

- The catalogs are pouring in and, like all gardeners, you are planning all the new additions to your landscape, including roses. Select the most pest-resistant varieties available.

- Monitor the health of any roses overwintering indoors. Keep plants in a cool room in front of a southern or other sunny window and water thoroughly and often enough to keep the soil slightly moist. Watch for mites and aphids that cause speckled and yellow leaves and stunted growth. Apply a strong blast of water to dislodge these pests. Then spray the upper and lower leaf surfaces with insecticidal soap if needed.

- Check outdoor roses to make sure winter and animal protection is secure. Try scare tactics and repellents on uncovered roses that are suffering damage.

FEBRUARY

- Attend a meeting of your local rose society. These local experts can give you great insight into growing roses in your part of the Midwest.

- Place your rose order if you have not already. Select a place to store roses that arrive prior to planting. Select Grade I roses for the best quality. The bare-root roses should be dormant, have firm canes, and be free of pests. Bare-root roses should be kept in a cool, dark place until planting.

- Water roses overwintering in the garage whenever the soil is thawed and dry.

MARCH

- Store dormant bare-root roses in a cool, dark location and monitor until planting. Dormant roses can be stored in a spare refrigerator, root cellar, or other location where temperatures remain above freezing. Keep the roots moist and covered with peat moss or sawdust.

- Or heel in bare-root roses outdoors if they cannot be planted within several days. Dig a trench with one sloping side. Place the roots and the graft (if present) in the trench with the plant leaning on the side. Cover with soil.

- Roses that started to grow in transit or storage will need different care. Plant in pots and grow indoors. Keep them near a sunny window. Water thoroughly, and allow the top few inches of soil to dry before watering again. These roses can be moved outdoors after the danger of frost has passed.

- Uncover roses when the weather begins to consistently hover near freezing. Gradually remove the protective covering, but keep some handy in case of an extreme drop in temperature. Many gardeners let the spring rains wash away the soil mounded over the crown.

APRIL

- Tip climbers and tree roses back into an upright position. Firm the soil around the roots and water. Attach climbing roses to trellises and tree roses to stakes as needed.

- Move container roses out of the garage or in-ground storage after severe weather has passed. Water thoroughly as needed. This is also a good time to transplant, if needed, into a slightly larger pot.

- Fertilize old garden, shrub, species, and climbing roses as their buds begin to swell. Apply the amount and type of fertilizer recommended by your soil test. If this information is not available, apply 2 pounds per 100 square feet, or 2 heaping tablespoons per plant of a low-nitrogen slow-release fertilizer. Wait to fertilize hybrid teas.

- Assess animal and winter damage. Remove only dead and damaged canes on old roses, including climbers. These roses bloom on the previous season's growth. Major pruning is done after flowering.

- Prune hybrid tea and other modern roses just before growth begins. Remove old and winter damaged canes and tips on repeat-blooming shrub roses. See the chapter introduction for pruning tips.

- Seal fresh pruning cuts to prevent cane borer. This is particularly important for roses with a history of this pest. Dab cut ends with pruning paint, yellow shellac, or white glue to prevent the borer from entering through this opening.

MAY

- Evaluate the health and survival rate of existing plants. The aboveground growth may be dead, but the graft and roots may still be alive. Watch for signs of new growth emerging above the graft union.

- Wait for the danger of frost to pass to move roses overwintered indoors to the outside. Gradually introduce them to the outdoors. This is also a good time to repot roses that have outgrown their pots and will remain in containers throughout the season. Move them to slightly larger (about I to 2 inches bigger in diameter) containers and fill with a well-drained potting mix. Water, but do not fertilize for several weeks.

- Fertilize hybrid teas and other modern roses at the same rate as old roses (see April), once their new spring growth is full size.

- Wait three to four weeks after planting to fertilize new roses.

- Fertilize roses growing in planters once in spring with a slow-release fertilizer or more often (per label directions) for fast-release flowering plant fertilizer.

JUNE

- Remove dead and struggling plants. Select an appropriate replacement that may, or may not, be another rose. If roses keep dying in a location, it's time to find another place for your roses.

- Leave the fading flowers on spring-blooming old roses. The faded flowers on these one-time bloomers will soon be replaced by colorful fruit known as rose hips. The hips turn orange or red and often persist through fall and winter. They are decorative in the landscape or floral arrangements, high in vitamin C, and help attract birds to the winter landscape.

- Deadhead repeat bloomers and hybrid tea roses. This improves the appearance and increases bloom time. See the chapter introduction.

- Hybrid tea roses are often disbudded to increase flower size. Remove side buds that form along the stem. This allows the plant to focus all its energy into forming one large on a long stem. Harvest or deadhead them back to the first 5-leaflet leaf.

- Now is the time to shape old garden, species, shrub, and climbing roses. Shrub and species roses are hardy and need very little pruning. Allow them to grow to their normal size and shape. See the chapter introduction for details.

- Sanitation and proper care are critical in pest management. Check for pests at least once a week. Small populations detected early are much easier to control.

JULY

- It is not too late to mulch roses. A 2- to 3-inch layer of organic matter over the soil surface can help conserve moisture and suppress weeds. Weed the garden prior to mulching. Avoid piling the mulch around the crown of the plant.

- Repellents, fences, and scare tactics may provide some relief from deer and rabbits.

- Continue monitoring plants for problems like blackspot, powdery mildew, and canker diseases. Aphids, mites, leafhoppers, caterpillars, and beetle populations are starting to reach damaging levels. Early detection and sanitation can reduce pest populations with fewer pesticides. Always read and follow all label directions whenever using any chemical.

AUGUST

- Finish planting containerized hybrid teas early in the month. The later you plant, the greater the risk of winterkill.

- Stop fertilizing. Late applications of fertilizer will encourage late season growth that is more susceptible to winter injury.

- Remove suckers that appear at the base of roses. Cut them off belowground to reduce the chance of re-sprouting. These canes are growing from the hardy rootstock and can diminish the vigor and beauty of the desired, grafted rose.

- Prune off any cankered, dead, or damaged canes. Between cuts, disinfect tools with a solution of one part bleach to nine parts water. This will help reduce the spread of diseases.

- If the weather is hot and dry, the insect populations will be thriving. Watch for aphids, mites, and leafhoppers.

SEPTEMBER

- You can still plant hardy shrub and landscape roses. Make sure they get proper post-planting care to reduce transplant shock and speed up establishment.

- Some gardeners overwinter miniatures, tree, and other roses indoors. Start preparing these roses for their new indoor location.

- Continue to monitor and control insects and diseases. Maintaining a healthy, relatively pest-free plant throughout the season is the best start to winter protection. Prune off canes with sunken or discolored areas. Remove and rake away any diseased foliage. Continue fungicide treatments as needed.

OCTOBER

- Hybrid teas, grafted, and marginally hardy roses benefit from winter protection. Hardy shrub and species roses will survive with little or no winter protection in much of the Midwest.

- Wait for a week of freezing temperatures before applying winter protection. Mulching and covering plants too early can lead to heat buildup, disease problems, and death of plants. Remove diseased leaves and insects prior to applying winter protection. See the chapter introduction for options.

- Wait until spring to prune your roses. Cut back roses only enough to apply winter protection. Do not prune ramblers, climbers, or once-blooming shrub roses since they bloom on old wood.

- Continue watering as needed until the ground freezes.

- Watch for signs of animal damage. If deer have been nibbling on the garden all summer, they will continue dining throughout the winter. Repellents and winter protection will help minimize the damage.

NOVEMBER

- Protect any roses you purchased that did not get planted. Find an unused garden area in a sheltered location. Sink the pot in the soil. Once the ground freezes, protect this rose just like all the others. Move it to its permanent location once the ground is workable next spring.

- Care for roses overwintering indoors as you would your other houseplants. Grow them in a cool, sunny location. They will continue to drop leaves as they adjust to their new location. Keep the soil slightly moist and continue to watch for pests. Mites are a common problem on indoor roses.

- Fall cleanup will help to minimize future problems. Rake and destroy fallen and disease-infested leaves.

DECEMBER

- Record any unusually warm weather that can delay dormancy or stimulate unwanted growth. These weather changes are hard on the plants, and the damage often doesn't show up until next spring. We can't change the weather but we can enjoy the surprises it brings, like rose blossoms in December.

- Complete winter protection after a week of freezing temperatures. Check on winter protection already in place. Make sure rose cones and mulches are secure.

- Check roses growing in containers in winter storage and water anytime the soil is dry and not frozen.

Brighten your winter by forcing a few stems of flowering trees and shrubs into bloom. Prune a few for this purpose or save branches when pruning crabapples, magnolias, forsythia, and pussy willows.

- Recut the stems and place in a bucket of water in a cool (60°F), brightly lit location.

- Mist the branches several times a day if possible until the stems start to bloom.

- Flowering stems can be used in arrangements with other flowers or by themselves.

- Prolong the blossoms by storing the blooming stems in a cooler spot (40°F) at night.

SHRUBS
for the Midwest

Shrubs have long been shoved up against home foundations or strung out along the lot line. Consider expanding the use of shrubs in your landscape. Look for opportunities and spaces that could use the facelift shrubs can provide.

Use shrubs to create a focal point, provide winter interest, screen a bad view, serve as a barrier, or provide food and shelter for birds and butterflies.

PLANNING

Now that you see the possibilities, break out the landscape plan. Select the shrubs that are best suited to the growing conditions and your design goals. Proper planning will give you an attractive landscape with a lot less work.

Evaluate the light, soil, wind, and other environmental factors that affect plant growth. Plant shrubs suited to the growing conditions.

Consider the ornamental value of the shrubs selected. Include evergreens for year-round foliage, lilacs and other flowering shrubs for an added splash of color, or plants such as red twig dogwoods with decorative bark.

Match your gardening style with the plant's maintenance requirements. Minimize your workload by planting drought-tolerant and pest-resistant shrubs. Avoid fast-growing shrubs that will grow too large for the location and will require frequent pruning.

Make sure the plants will still fit in the space once they reach full size. Check the heights of windows, distance to structures, and mature size of nearby plants. Provide the space needed to minimize future pruning and frustration caused by trying to keep a 6-foot shrub contained in 3 feet of space.

PURCHASING

Once the plan is complete, you are ready for the trip to the nursery or garden center.

Hook up the trailer or clear out the trunk to make room for your purchases. Throw a couple of tarps in the car. Use them to protect the seats and carpet in your vehicle or to cover leafed-out shrubs transported in the open air of a pickup truck or trailer.

Purchase healthy plants free of damaged stems, discolored or brown leaves, or other signs of pests and stress. Avoid unhealthy bargain plants that can end up costing you more money and time when they need replacing.

PLANTING

The planting process starts with a call to 811, a free utility-locating service. Call 811 at least three working days before planting. This service marks the location of all underground utilities. Working with utility-locating services can prevent costly damage to underground utilities and may save your life.

Most shrubs are sold in containers. The majority of these are grown in the container, but others are dug out of the field and placed in the container or recently potted bare-root plants. We will call these potted plants. The remainder, mostly evergreens and a few select flowering shrubs, are sold as balled-and-burlapped plants.

All types of shrubs benefit from proper planting. Start by reviewing your plan and adjust planting locations to avoid conflicts with both underground and overhead utilities.

Then locate the crown (the place where roots and stem meet) and pull away any excess soil covering it. Dig a hole that is the same as or slightly shallower than the depth of the crown to the bottom of the rootball. Make it at least two times as wide as the roots.

Roughen the sides of the planting hole to avoid glazing. Smooth-sided holes prevent roots from growing out of the planting hole and into the surrounding soil. Use your shovel or garden fork to nick or scratch the sides of the planting hole.

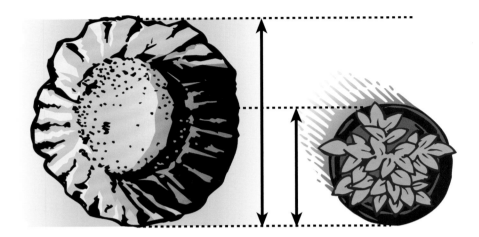

Dig a hole the same depth, but at least twice as wide as, the rootball.

Carefully remove the plant from container. Potted plants need special care since their root systems may not be well established in the container. Minimize root disturbance by using this technique: Cut off the bottom of the pot and place it in the planting hole. Slice the pot lengthwise and peel it away.

Loosen the roots of potbound container-grown shrubs. Use a sharp knife to slice through the rootball. Make several shallow slices (running top to bottom of the rootball) through the surface of the roots. This will encourage roots to grow out into the surrounding soil.

Use a similar technique with balled-and-burlapped plants. Place the shrub in the hole. Remove the twine and peel back the burlap. Cut away the fabric and wire basket.

Once the plant is in the hole, make sure it is setting straight and its best side is facing the way you prefer. Now fill the hole with the existing soil. Use water, not your foot or a heavy tool, to settle the soil.

Water the planting hole and surrounding soil. Cover the soil surface with shredded bark or woodchips to conserve moisture, insulate roots, and reduce weeds.

POST-PLANTING CARE

New plantings need help to become established. Be sure they receive about an inch of water each week. You may have to water if nature doesn't take care of the job. Check shrubs growing in clay soil every seven to ten days. Those growing in sandy soils should be checked twice a week. Water when the top 3 to 4 inches are crumbly and moist. Water thoroughly enough to moisten the top 12 inches of soil.

Some container-grown shrubs are planted in soilless mixes. The rootball of these shrubs will dry out faster than the surrounding soil. You will need to water the root system more frequently than the surrounding soil to keep both moist, but not wet.

Established shrubs will need to be watered during drought conditions. Thoroughly water the soil when the top few inches begin to dry. This is about once a week in clay soils and twice a week in sandy soil.

Mulch the soil to conserve moisture and reduce weed problems. Use a 2- to 3-inch layer of woodchips, shredded bark, or other organic materials. These help improve the soil as they decompose. Don't bury the base of the shrub and do not use weed barrier fabrics under these organic mulches. Weeds end up growing into the fabric, creating a real mess in several years.

Wait a year to fertilize new plantings. Fertilizer can damage the young tender roots and interfere with establishment. And only remove branches that were damaged in the transport and planting process. The more branches left on the plant, the more leaves that will be formed and the more energy will be produced for the plant.

PRUNING

No other gardening chore evokes such a wide range of emotions as pruning. Feelings range from pruning paranoia (fear of killing or maiming the plant) to visions of a chainsaw massacre.

Before breaking out the tools, make sure there is a reason to prune. Prune to maintain size; improve flowering, fruiting, and bark color; or remove damaged or diseased branches. When and how you prune are equally important.

Prune spring-flowering shrubs, such as lilac, bridal wreath spirea, and forsythia, in spring right after flowering. Spring bloomers flower on the previous season's growth. Pruning in late summer or winter removes the flower buds and eliminates the spring display.

Trim summer-blooming plants, like hills-of-snow hydrangeas, potentilla, and summer-blooming spireas, during the dormant season. These shrubs flower on the current season's growth.

You can remove dead, damaged, or disease-infected branches whenever they are found.

Disinfect tools between cuts to prevent the spread of disease. Use rubbing alcohol or a solution of one part bleach to nine parts water as a disinfectant.

The "how" of pruning is a little trickier. Match the type of pruning to the plant and your landscape goals. Some plants, such as cotoneasters and barberries, need very little pruning, while forsythia and common lilacs need regular attention. Use thinning cuts and renewal pruning to contain plant size while maintaining the plant's natural appearance. Shearing transforms shrubs into rectangular hedges or spheres of green.

Where you make the pruning cut is equally important. Prune on a slight angle above a healthy bud, where a branch joins another branch, or where a branch joins the trunk. These cuts close quickly and reduce the risk of insects and disease entering the plant. The location of the pruning cut also influences the plant's appearance and future growth.

Use thinning cuts to open up the plant and reduce the size while maintaining its natural appearance. Prune off branches where they join the main stem, another branch or back to ground level. Thinning cuts allow air and light to penetrate the plant, improving flowering, fruiting, and bark color. It also helps reduce some disease problems.

Use heading cuts to reduce the height and spread of shrubs. Limit the number and vary the location of heading cuts to maintain the plant's natural appearance. Prune branches back to a shorter side shoot or above a healthy bud. Excessive heading can lead to a tuft of growth at the end of a long, bare stem.

Reserve shearing for only the most formal settings. This technique is easy on the gardener but hard on the plant. Shearing makes indiscriminant cuts, leaving stubs that make perfect entryways for insects and disease. Prune so that the bottom of the plant is wider than the top. This allows light to reach all parts, top to the bottom, of the plant.

Use renewal pruning to manage overgrown shrubs, contain growth, and stimulate new, healthy, and more attractive stems. Start by removing one-third of the older (larger) canes to ground level. Reduce the height of the remaining stems by one-third if needed. Repeat the process the next two years for overgrown shrubs. By the end of the third year, the shrub will be smaller, more attractive, and healthier. Continue to remove older canes as needed throughout the life of the shrubs.

Employ rejuvenation pruning to manage the size of some fast-growing and overgrown shrubs. Make sure the plant will tolerate this severe pruning. Cut all stems back to 4 inches above the soil line during the dormant season. Late winter through early spring before growth begins is the best time. The plant will soon begin to grow and recover.

FERTILIZING

Shrubs receive most of their nutrients from fertilizers applied to nearby plantings and lawn areas. Organic mulches also add small amounts of nutrients as they decompose.

Start with a soil test to determine if fertilizer is needed. The soil test report will indicate what type and how much fertilizer you will need.

Wait a year to fertilize new shrub plantings. Follow your soil test recommendations for the type and amount of fertilizer to use. If this information is not available, you can use a nitrogen fertilizer such as 16-8-8 or 21-0-0 at a rate of 2 pounds per 100 square feet of shrub beds. Or better yet, use a low-nitrogen slow-release fertilizer. It releases small amounts of fertilizer to the plants throughout the growing season. The formulation is also goof proof, eliminating damage caused by overfertilization.

Spread the fertilizer on the soil surface. Keep the fertilizer off the shrubs. Rake the fertilizer into the soil surface and water well. Fertilizer can be applied over organic mulch and raked into the soil below.

Young shrubs can be fertilized in late fall after the plants are dormant or in early spring before growth begins. Fertilizing every few years encourages rapid growth on young shrubs. Established shrubs need little if any fertilizer.

PESTS

Pest control starts by selecting the right plant for the growing conditions and providing proper care. Healthy plants are more resistant to insects and disease and better able to tolerate damage when it occurs.

Use the following plant profiles to help you select the best shrubs for your Midwest garden.

RHODODENDRON

ABELIA
Abelia x grandiflora

Why It's Special—This fast-growing multi-stem shrub puts on a magnificent floral display in spring. The sepals persist, providing added color into fall. Use it in natural or informal settings where its relaxed form can be appreciated. The green leaves turn a red to purple bronze color in fall and may persist into winter, adding to its appeal.

How to Plant & Grow—Abelia transplants easily and prefers slightly acidic, moist but well-drained soil. Plants may suffer chlorosis in alkaline (high pH soils). Once established, they are fairly drought tolerant. Space plants 3 to 4 feet apart.

Care & Problems—Abelia has no serious pest problems. It will die back to the ground in the northern portion of its hardiness zone or when temperatures drop below -5 degrees. Prune dead wood back to the ground in early spring. Regular removal of older stems will encourage more dense and controlled growth.

Hardiness—Zone 5 (dieback); Zones 6 to 9

Seasonal Color—White flushed pink blooms

Peak Season—Spring; sepals last into fall

Mature Size (H x W)—3 to 6 ft. x 3 to 6 ft.

Water Needs—Moist, well-drained soil is best.

ARBORVITAE
Thuja occidentalis

Why It's Special—Arborvitaes are a favorite evergreen of deer and gardeners alike. Though not a true cedar, *Cedrus*, it is often called white cedar by Midwest gardeners. Use it as a screen, foundation plant, or tall evergreen hedge.

How to Plant & Grow—Cultivated arborvitaes prefer moist, well-drained soil, even though native plants will tolerate wetter locations. Plants grown in heavy shade tend to become loose and open. Avoid exposed areas and those open to drying northwest winter winds and winter sun from the south. Space 3 to 4 feet apart.

Care & Problems—Arborvitaes need minimal pruning if the right size cultivar is selected. Overgrown specimens can be topped but will be more subject to damage from heavy snow loads. Multi-stemmed arborvitae tend to split apart under the weight of heavy snow. Prevent the problem by loosely tying the upright stems together in the fall. Manage deer damage with fencing, repellents, and scare tactics.

Hardiness—Throughout the Midwest

Seasonal Color—Evergreen, some golden cultivars

Peak Season—Year-round evergreen foliage

Mature Size (H x W)—3 to 40 ft. x 4 to 15 ft.

Water Needs—Moist, well-drained soil is best.

BLUE MIST SPIREA

Caryopteris x clandonensis

Why It's Special—The blue-gray foliage is a nice addition to the perennial border. The true blue flowers can't be beat for a late summer through fall display and bee appeal. Don't worry; the bees won't bother you or others who pass by the plants.

How to Plant & Grow—Often listed as only hardy to Zone 5 or 6, it has successfully been grown in Zone 4. See the chapter introduction for planting details. Blue mist spirea will tolerate most soils, but good drainage, especially in winter, is important for survival. Space 2½ to 3 feet apart.

Care & Problems—Winter kill is the only real problem. Let the plants stand for winter for added winter beauty and increased hardiness. Avoid excess fertilization that stimulates growth (which is more likely to be winter killed). Prune to 6 inches height in late winter or early spring. The plant will quickly reach its full size and still flower in late summer. Plants may reseed.

Hardiness—Zones 5 through 9

Seasonal Color—Blue flowers

Peak Season—Late summer through frost

Mature Size (H x W)—3 ft. x 3 ft.

Water Needs—Drought tolerant once established.

BOXWOOD

Buxus microphylla

Why It's Special—These shade-tolerant broadleaf evergreens have long been used as hedges and edging plants in formal gardens. They are naturally compact, dense growers with a round growth habit. Use them as the framework in informal mixed borders or shady gardens.

How to Plant & Grow—Plant in spring and early summer so plants can establish before our harsh winter. Follow planting directions in the chapter introduction. Grow boxwood in protected locations sheltered from winter wind and winter sun for best results. Space plants 2½ to 3 feet apart.

Care & Problems—Proper cultivar selection, placement, and watering throughout the season will help decrease winter browning. A burlap wrap, decorative windbreak, or cylinder of hardware cloth filled with evergreen boughs or straw can reduce winter damage on more tender cultivars or plants exposed to winter wind and sun. Non-sheared boxwoods require very little pruning. Cut long branches back to a side branch in midsummer.

Hardiness—Zones 4 to 9, depending on cultivar

Seasonal Color—White blooms; evergreen foliage

Peak Season—Year-round foliage

Mature Size (H x W)—3 to 4 ft. x 3 to 4 ft.

Water Needs—Moist, well-drained soil is best.

BUSH HONEYSUCKLE
Diervilla species

Why It's Special—This native beauty is not related to the invasive honeysuckle shrub that shares part of its common name. Use bush honeysuckle to attract bees, bumblebees, butterflies, and hummingbirds as well as providing four seasons of interest in the garden. The variegated cultivar 'Cool Splash' brightens up a shady spot.

How to Plant & Grow—Plant container-grown bush honeysuckle spring through fall. The suckering nature of this shrub makes it a good choice for bank stabilization and erosion control on a hillside. They are shade tolerant but grow and flower best in part to full sun. These adaptable plants plant tolerate a wide range of soils including poor rocky soils to clay. Space 4 feet apart.

Care & Problems—Prune, if needed, in late winter or early spring before growth begins. Renewal pruning will encourage full growth and maintain desired plant size. See "Pruning" on page 161.

Hardiness—Varies with species

Seasonal Color—Yellow flowers

Peak Season—June to July

Mature Size (H x W)—2 to 3 ft. x 3 or more ft. (suckering)

Water Needs—Drought tolerant once established.

BUTTERFLY BUSH
Buddleja davidii

Why It's Special—The fragrant long-lasting blooms and the large number of butterflies and hummingbirds drawn to this plant makes this shrub worth a first, second, or even third try. The flowers resemble lilac blooms, inspiring its other common name of summer lilac.

How to Plant & Grow—Plant container-grown butterfly bushes in the spring and early summer to give plants maximum time to establish before winter. Space plants 4 to 5 feet apart.

Care & Problems—Leave the plants stand for winter. The seedheads and plant form add to your landscape's winter interest and increase hardiness. Prune the plants back to 4 to 6 inches above ground level in late winter or early spring. Be patient; the plants are slow to emerge in cool spring. Even with a late start butterfly bush plants will quickly reach mature full size and bloom in midsummer and continue through frost. Butterfly bush benefits from regular fertilizing.

Hardiness—Zones 4 to 9

Seasonal Color—Purple, white, pink, and yellow

Peak Season—July through frost

Mature Size (H x W)—5 to 8 ft. x 5 to 8 ft.

Water Needs—Drought tolerant once established.

CHOKEBERRY
Aronia melanocarpa

Why It's Special—Chokeberry is a great four-season plant suited to the Midwest. Use this as an accent plant with evergreens. The flowers, fruit, and birds it attracts, and fall color add life to evergreen screens, mixed borders, and hedges.

How to Plant & Grow—Plant container-grown plants anytime during the growing season. They tolerate a wide range of soil, including wet and dry, but prefer moist, well-drained soils. Space plants 2½ to 3 feet apart.

Care & Problems—Chokeberries may be slow to start but eventually sucker and can form a colony. Give them plenty of space to take advantage of this growth habit. Avoid excess nitrogen, which can limit flowering and fall color. Regular renewal pruning controls the overall size. You may see problems with leaf spot or powdery mildew in wet seasons when diseases are prevalent. Rake and destroy infested leaves as they drop.

Hardiness—Throughout the Midwest

Seasonal Color—White flowers; red or black fruit; red fall color

Peak Season—Spring flowers

Mature Size (H x W)—3 to 5 ft. x 5 ft. or more

Water Needs—Tolerates wet and dry soils once established.

COTONEASTER
Cotoneaster species

Why It's Special—Low growing, spreading, weeping, or tall and upright: these terms all describe the popular cotoneaster. With the many sizes and forms available, it can be used in a variety of ways throughout the landscape.

How to Plant & Grow—Plant throughout the growing season. Cotoneasters tolerate a wide range of soil conditions, as long as the soil is well drained. These tough plants tolerate dry soil and roadside salt. Spacing varies with each variety.

Care & Problems—Established shrubs can be pruned in late winter or early spring before growth begins. Remove old, diseased, and damaged stems at ground level. You can prune back overgrown shrubs by one-third. Rabbits live under and will feed on cotoneaster. Fencing is the best control option but is often not practical. A variety of repellents and scare tactics may discourage the rabbits.

Hardiness—Throughout, varies with species

Seasonal Color—White and pink blooms; red fruit

Peak Season—Spring to summer blooms; fall and winter fruit

Mature Size (H x W)—1 ½ to 25 ft. x 6 to 15 ft.

Water Needs—Drought tolerant once established.

DOGWOOD
Cornus species

Why It's Special—Our native dogwoods are prominent members of our landscapes. They can be used in natural settings, informal landscapes, or formal gardens. The flower show varies with species, but they all provide food and shelter for the birds and year-round interest in the landscape.

How to Plant and Grow—Most prefer moist soil; many tolerate wet sites. Plant bare-root dogwoods in the spring before growth begins and container-grown plants throughout the season. Spacing varies with variety.

Care and Problems—Wait a year to fertilize new plantings. Regular fertilization will encourage rapid growth on young shrubs. Established shrubs need minimal fertilization. Prune established shrubs in late winter or early spring if needed. Remove old, diseased, or damaged canes on redtwig, gray, and variegated dogwoods at ground level. Stressed plants can suffer from scale insects and drought-induced cankers. Proper watering and regular pruning will reduce these problems.

Hardiness—Throughout the Midwest but varies with species

Seasonal Color—White, yellow, pink flowers; colorful fruit; fall color; interesting bark

Peak Season—Spring to summer blooms; fall foliage

Mature Size (H x W)—5 to 15 ft. x 5 to 15 ft.

Water Needs—Moist soil is best.

ELDERBERRY
Sambucus species

Why It's Special—The purplish black berries of the native American elderberry have long been used for jelly, pies, and, of course, wine. Many cultivars have attractive foliage. Use these adaptable plants in rain gardens, moist areas, natural plantings, and in large containers. The flowers of elderberry attract butterflies and bees, adding color to the landscape. Be sure to leave some fruit on the plants to encourage birds to visit your landscape.

How to Plant & Grow—These adaptable plants prefer moist soil but will tolerate drier conditions once established. This makes them well suited to rain gardens. Plant container-grown plants throughout the growing season. Spacing varies with species.

Care & Problems—They will tolerate shaded locations but flowering, fruiting, and foliage color may suffer. Elderberries are basically pest-free. Allow plants to sucker and form dense thickets if you are naturalizing them. Prune established plants to maintain a more refined growth habit.

Hardiness—Throughout the Midwest

Seasonal Color—White flowers; purplish black fruit

Peak Season—June to July bloom

Mature Size (H x W)—5 to 20 ft. x 5 to 20 ft. (varies by species)

Water Needs—Prefers moist soil, but soil can be drier once established.

FIRETHORN

Pyracantha coccinea

Why It's Special—This medium- to fast-growing shrub provides year-round interest in the landscape. The foliage is fully evergreen in milder parts of the Midwest and turns a brownish color in colder or unprotected areas. The green leaves provide a nice backdrop to the white flowers and orange-red fruit. Use it as a hedge, thorny barrier planting, or espaliered against a wall.

How to Plant & Grow—Plant container-grown pyracanthas in spring. Wear long sleeves and gloves to protect yourself from the thorns. Space plants at least 6 feet apart.

Care & Problems—Excess shade reduces flowering and fruiting. Overfertilization also reduces flowering and increases the risk of disease. Thorns make maintenance difficult but the abundant fruit make it worth the scratches and scrapes. Fireblight and scale can be problems. Plant fireblight-resistant cultivars to avoid this problem. Proper pruning and care will reduce the risk of scale.

Hardiness—Zones 6 to 9

Seasonal Color—White flowers; orange-red fruit; evergreen

Peak Season—Spring bloom; fall to winter fruit

Mature Size (H x W)—6 to 18 ft. x 6 to 18 ft.

Water Needs—Tolerates dry soil.

FORSYTHIA

Forsythia hybrids

Why It's Special—The bright yellow flowers of forsythia signal the start of spring. Though the plant may be hardy and thriving in your garden, the flower buds are frequently killed in cold winters of the northern Midwest. Fortunately, there are varieties with hardy flower buds that will reliably flower in spring. Enjoy the bright yellow flowers in the garden or spring arrangements.

How to Plant & Grow—Plant bare-root forsythia in the spring before growth begins and container-grown plants throughout the season. They will tolerate any soil pH, as well as urban conditions. Follow planting directions in the chapter introduction. Space depends on the size and spread of the cultivar grown.

Care & Problems—Lack of flowers is the major problem of forsythia; this is caused by cold temperatures, poorly timed pruning, excess nitrogen, and too much shade. Prune established shrubs in the spring after flowering to preserve next year's blooms and control size. Bring a bit of spring indoors by forcing a few forsythia branches.

Hardiness—Throughout the Midwest; varies with the species

Seasonal Color—Yellow flowers

Peak Season—Early spring

Mature Size (H x W)—1 to 10 ft. x 4 to 10 ft.

Water Needs—Forsythia needs lots of water when newly planted but lives on average rainfall once established.

FOTHERGILLA
Fothergilla gardenii

Why It's Special—The fragrant white flowers, attractive dark green to blue-green leaves that look good all season, and the yellow to orange to scarlet foliage in fall gives this shrub multi-season appeal. Use this big-impact low-maintenance plant in partially shaded areas, moist spaces, cottage gardens, mixed borders, or shrub beds.

How to Plant & Grow—Plant balled-and-burlapped plants soon after they are purchased. Plant container-grown fothergilla throughout the growing season. This plant prefers moist but well-drained acidic soil. Place a few fothergillas in front of evergreens; the green provides a year-round backdrop that maximizes the impact of its spring flowers and fall color. Space 1½ to 3 feet apart.

Care & Problems—Fothergilla is basically pest-free and needs minimal pruning. Wait until the flowers fade but before growth begins to do any pruning. Watch for and protect this plant from hungry rabbits over the winter.

Hardiness—Zones 4 to 8

Seasonal Color—White flowers; blue-green leaves

Peak Season—Spring blooms; colorful fall foliage

Mature Size (H x W)—2 to 3 ft. x 2 to 3 ft.

Water Needs—Moist, well-drained soil is best.

HYDRANGEA
Hydrangea species

Why It's Special—Hydrangeas can put on a dramatic floral display even in the shade. Cultivars of smooth hydrangeas, *Hydrangea arborescens*, often called snowball bush, are the most shade tolerant. *Hydrangea paniculata* specimens are larger, hardier, and bloom later. The big leaf hydrangeas, *Hydrangea macrophylla*, have blue flowers in acidic soil and pink in alkaline soil.

How to Plant & Grow—Plant throughout the season, keeping soil moist until established.

Care & Problems—Prune snowball-type hydrangeas to 12 inches above the ground every spring. Panicle hydrangeas require very little pruning. Lack of flowers is the biggest problem on the blue- and pink-flowering hydrangeas in colder parts of the Midwest. These plants typically bloom on old wood so when they die back over winter the plants fail to bloom. Keep the soil moist and fertilize with an organic nitrogen fertilizer like Milorganite® in spring to promote flowering on newer repeat bloomers. Use aluminum sulfate on big leaf types to encourage blue flowers in alkaline soil.

Hardiness—Throughout the Midwest; varies with species

Seasonal Color—White, pink, or blue blooms

Peak Season—Summer

Mature Size (H x W)—3 to 15 ft. x 10 to 15 ft.

Water Needs—Moist well-drained soil is best.

JUNIPER
Juniperus species

Why It's Special—Its wide variety of sizes, shapes, and foliage colors make juniper a valuable landscape plant. These tough evergreens can be used as windbreaks, groundcovers, screens, hedges, or rock garden plants. Select the hardiest, most disease-resistant cultivars best suited to your landscape design. And don't forget to enjoy the fruit display and the birds that feed upon them.

How to Plant & Grow—See the chapter introduction for planting tips. Grow junipers in well-drained soil. Spacing varies with cultivar selected.

Care & Problems—Established junipers need little, if any, fertilizer. Reduce snow and ice damage on upright junipers by loosely tying the stems in fall. Prune junipers in the spring before growth begins or in midsummer during their semi-dormant period. Wear long sleeves and gloves. When properly sited and spaced, junipers need little pruning. Prune spreading and creeping junipers by selectively removing the longest branches back to a shorter side branch or main stem. Winter damage, phomopsis blight, and cedar rust are the most common problems.

Hardiness—Throughout the Midwest

Seasonal Color—Evergreen foliage

Peak Season—Year-round

Mature Size (H x W)—Up to 20 ft. x 10 ft.

Water Needs—Drought tolerant once established.

LILAC
Syringa species and cultivars

Why It's Special—Add a lilac or two to your landscape and enjoy beautiful spring flowers, fragrance, and the butterflies and hummingbirds they attract. The new repeat-blooming 'Bloomerang®' is perfect for those who can't get enough lilac flowers and fragrance.

How to Plant and Grow—See the chapter introduction for planting directions. Spacing varies with species grown.

Care & Problems—Lack of bloom seems to be the biggest concern. Overfertilization, shade, or poorly timed pruning can prevent flowering. Lilacs set their flower buds in the summer prior to spring bloom. Prune established lilacs right after flowering, if needed, so you won't eliminate the following spring's bloom. Remove old flower heads to encourage flowering. Powdery mildew is the most common disease. Grow less susceptible varieties in full sun with good air circulation to reduce this problem. Bacterial blight and scale insects are usually controlled with proper pruning. Regular pruning helps reduce the risk of these problems.

Hardiness—Throughout the Midwest; varies with cultivar

Seasonal Color—White, blue, purple, pink, and magenta flowers

Peak Season—Spring blooms

Mature Size (H x W)—4 to 15 ft. x 4 to 15 ft.

Water Needs—Lilac prefers moist, well-drained soil.

MOCKORANGE
Philadelphus coronarius

Why It's Special—Mockorange is an old-time favorite. The sweet, citrus fragrance and bright white flowers won this plant a place in the landscape. Select cultivars carefully. Many are subject to winter injury in northern areas of the Midwest, eliminating the spring flower display. Other cultivars lack fragrance, which is the main reason gardeners grow this plant.

How to Plant & Grow—Plant container-grown plants throughout the season. Place plants where their fragrant flowers can be enjoyed but not steal space from plants with more year round appeal. Space plants 3 to 6 feet apart depending on the mature size of the variety grown.

Care & Problems—Lack of bloom is the biggest problem. Established shrubs need little, if any, fertilizer. Avoid high-nitrogen fertilizers that can prevent flowering. Mockorange blooms on the previous season's growth. Prune established mockorange shrubs, if needed, in the spring after flowering. Regular renewal pruning will control size and improve this plant's overall appearance.

Hardiness—Zones 4 to 8

Seasonal Color—White flowers

Peak Season—Spring

Mature Size (H x W)—Up to 10 ft. x 10 ft.

Water Needs—Moist, well-drained soil is best.

NINEBARK
Physocarpus opulifolius

Why It's Special—Ninebark is a big bold plant that offers a dramatic silhouette against the winter sky. Often overlooked for more ornamental shrubs, ninebark's drought tolerance, adaptability, and many of the new colorful cultivars, like 'Diablo', 'Center Glow', and 'Amber Jubilee', make it a good choice for Midwest gardeners.

How to Plant & Grow—Ninebark can be planted throughout the growing season. It tolerates acidic to alkaline soils as well as drought. Space plants 5 to 6 feet apart.

Care & Problems—Minimal care is needed for these tough plants. Regular pruning will improve their appearance including the winter show the stout peeling stems provide. Powdery mildew is a problem on 'Diablo' and a few other cultivars. Grow in full sun, avoid overhead irrigation, and properly prune to reduce this problem. Borers may also attack. Remove infested stems as they're discovered and regularly prune to manage this pest.

Hardiness—Throughout the Midwest

Seasonal Color—White or pinkish flowers in spring; red fall color; interesting bark

Peak Season—Year-round

Mature Size (H x W)—5 to 10 ft. x 5 to 10 ft.

Water Needs—Drought tolerant once established.

PIERIS
Pieris japonica

Why It's Special—The lightly fragrant, white urn-shaped blooms and colorful emerging foliage make this a standout in the spring landscape. Use it as a specimen plant backed by evergreens or in the mixed border.

How to Plant & Grow—Plant container-grown plants anytime during the growing season. See the chapter introduction for planting details. Pieris prefers slightly acidic soil and good drainage is a must. Provide a bit of afternoon shade where summers are hot. Space plants 4 to 6 feet apart.

Care & Problems—This is a slow grower, so be patient. Lace bugs can be a problem, and wet heavy soils can weaken and eventually kill these plants. Pieris can struggle a bit in the northern and southern limits of the hardiness zone. Prune right after flowering, if needed. These plants, like lilac and forsythia, form their flower buds the summer prior to spring bloom.

Hardiness—Zones 4 to 7

Seasonal Color—White flowers; red tinged spring foliage

Peak Season—Spring

Mature Size (H x W)—Up to 12 ft. x 8 ft.

Water Needs—Moist, well-drained soil is best.

POTENTILLA
Potentilla fruticosa

Why It's Special—Potentilla's bright yellow blossoms add color to the summer landscape. Its color, dense habit, drought tolerance, and pest-free nature made it popular. But just like with any tough plant, gardeners can push it beyond its limits. Proper cultivar and site selection and correct pruning will keep potentillas looking good in the landscape.

How to Plant & Grow—Plant them anytime during the growing season. Grow potentillas in full sun and well-drained soil for best results. Space plants 2½ to 3 feet apart.

Care & Problems—Potentilla needs regular pruning to remain attractive. Prune overgrown and floppy potentillas in late winter or early spring before growth begins. Cut the plants back halfway to the ground. Remove about one-third to one-half of the larger stems to ground level. Or prune all the stems back to just above ground level. This rejuvenation pruning can be done every second or third year as needed. Potentillas pruned this way are often more floppy.

Hardiness—Throughout the Midwest

Seasonal Color—Pink, lavender, and white flowers

Peak Season—Late spring through summer

Mature Size (H x W)—8 to 15 in. x 24 in.

Water Needs—Established plants will tolerate drought.

RHODODENDRON
Rhododendron species

Why It's Special—Rhododendrons' large, beautiful, and often fragrant flowers cannot be duplicated by another spring-flowering plant. Their unique beauty has driven gardeners to expend time and money amending the soil and providing winter protection.

How to Plant & Grow—Azaleas are a type of rhododendron; they look similar and require the same care. Both prefer moist, well-drained acidic soil. Plant early in the season to establish them before winter. Avoid growing where the leaves will be subject to drying by winter wind and sun. An east-facing location works well. Space them about 3 to 6 feet apart.

Care & Problems—Rhododendrons require little pruning. Remove any winter damage and thin out overcrowded branches in the spring after flowering, or when they should have flowered. Proper siting, soil preparation, and care along with winter protection will help rhododendrons through cold Midwest winters. Young plants and those growing in exposed sites benefit from additional winter protection.

Hardiness—Zones 3b to 8; varies with cultivar

Seasonal Color—Variety of flower colors, some evergreen

Peak Season—Spring blooms

Mature Size (H x W)—Up to 6 ft. x 6 ft.

Water Needs—Moist, well-drained soil is best.

ROSE-OF-SHARON
Hibiscus syriacus

Why It's Special—Add some late season color and bring in the hummingbirds and butterflies with this traditional garden favorite. Many of the newer cultivars have larger and longer-lasting flowers.

How to Plant & Grow—Those in northern areas should plant early in the season so rose-of-Sharon can establish itself before winter. Space plants 4 to 6 feet apart.

Care & Problems—Established and slower growing rose-of-Sharon plants tend to have a greater rate of winter survival. Wait a year or two to fertilize new plantings and avoid excess fertilization and high-nitrogen fertilizers. Prune established plants yearly to remove dead wood and increase flower size. Prune the main branches and shorten side shoots to two or three buds for an impressive flower display. Rose-of-Sharon can be severely damaged or killed in extremely cold winters. They are often slow to leaf out in the spring. Give them plenty of time to leaf out before declaring them dead and replacing them.

Hardiness—Zones 5 to 8

Seasonal Color—Blue, lavender, and white flowers

Peak Season—Summer to fall blooms

Mature Size (H x W)—8 ft. x 5 ft.

Water Needs—Moist, well-drained soil is needed.

SMOKEBUSH
Cotinus coggygria

Why It's Special—Outstanding foliage, unique ornamental seedheads, and adaptability to a wide range of soil types and pH allow many gardeners to include this plant in the landscape. Purple, maroon, and golden leaf cultivars add to its multi-season appeal. Use it in small groups, mixed borders, and shrub beds. Space at least 6 to 8 feet apart.

How to Plant & Grow—Plant anytime during the growing season. Smokebush is adaptable to a wide range of conditions, but it prefers moist well-drained soils and a full sun location.

Care & Problems—Smokebush is late to leaf out, so be patient. These plants may experience top dieback in Zones 4 and 5. Prune winter-killed stems back to the ground and wait for new growth to appear. Consider pruning colorful cultivars back to the ground in early spring to force vigorous new growth with better foliage color. Seedheads can last all summer in cooler parts of the Midwest.

Hardiness—Zones 4 to 8

Seasonal Color—Smoky pink seedheads; fall foliage

Peak Season—Summer through fall

Mature Size (H x W)—Up to 10 to 15 ft. x 10 to 15 ft.

Water Needs—Drought tolerant once established.

SPIREA
Spirea species

Why It's Special—Spireas are adaptable, colorful plants that have been used extensively in the landscape. These shrubs require little maintenance and tolerate the stresses of urban landscapes. Let the plants stand for winter. The chestnut brown stems, growth habit, and dried seedheads can add to your winter landscape.

How to Plant & Grow—Spireas tolerate a wide range of soils, except for wet sites. Follow the planting directions in the chapter introduction. Spacing varies with species grown.

Care & Problems—Spireas are fast growers and need minimal fertilizer especially once they are established. Spring-blooming spireas flower on the previous season's growth. Renewal prune, if needed, right after flowering. Pruning at any other time will eliminate the flowers. Summer-blooming spireas flower on new growth. Prune in late winter before growth begins. Prune like *Potentilla*; see page 174. Lightly shear summer-blooming spireas as the flowers fade to encourage a second and even third flush of flowers.

Hardiness—Throughout the Midwest

Seasonal Color—White, pink, and rose

Peak Season—Spring or summer blooms

Mature Size (H x W)—2 to 8 ft. x 2 to 8 ft.

Water Needs—Most are drought tolerant once established.

SUMMERSWEET
Clethra alnifolia

Why It's Special—Summersweet adds color, fragrance, and attracts hummingbirds and butterflies to the summer landscape. It finishes off the season with a yellow to golden fall color. This tough shrub tolerates shade, moist soils, and salt making it a beautiful solution to difficult growing conditions. The dwarf variety 'Hummingbird' has all the outstanding characteristics on a smaller plant.

How to Plant & Grow—Plant anytime during the growing season. It can sucker to form a large colony so give the plant room to grow. See the planting details in the chapter introduction. Space plants 3 to 6 feet apart.

Care & Problems—Prune in early spring as needed. It is late to leaf out in spring, so be patient. Poor flowering can result from droughty conditions. Water thoroughly whenever the top few inches of soil are crumbly and moist. It is relatively pest free, though mites can be a problem in hot dry summers.

Hardiness—Zones 4 to 9

Seasonal Color—White flowers

Peak Season—Summer

Mature Size (H x W)—4 to 8 ft. x 4 to 8 ft.

Water Needs— Keep soil moist.

VIBURNUM
Viburnum species

Why It's Special—Viburnums' flowers, some fragrant, fall foliage, and the red, blue, or black berries add color and attract birds to your landscape. These ornamental features combined with the diversity of sizes and shapes make viburnums worth adding to your landscape.

How to Plant & Grow—Plant hardy species throughout the season and, tender species early in the season so they can establish before winter. Most viburnums tolerate full sun to partial shade and prefer moist soil. Some species are drought tolerant. Spacing varies with the species.

Care & Problems—Slow-growing viburnums need little pruning. Remove dead, damaged, and unwanted branches back to an adjoining branch or main stem. Use renewal pruning described on page 161 for fast-growing suckering types. Viburnum borers feed at the base of the plants, killing individual stems. Regular pruning and proper care will reduce the risk.

Hardiness—Throughout the Midwest

Seasonal Color—White flowers; fall color; red, black, or blue fruit

Peak Season—Spring blooms; fall color; winter fruit

Mature Size (H x W)—2 to 15 ft. x 2 to 10 ft.

Water Needs—Most viburnum species prefer moist, well-drained soil.

WEIGELA
Weigela florida

Why It's Special—You'll bring in the birds, butterflies, and hummingbirds with this traditional garden favorite. The large, arching growth habit makes it a perfect fit in heirloom landscapes, natural plantings, and wildlife gardens. The many new cultivars have colorful foliage, intense flowers, and more compact growth habit expanding their use in both small and large landscapes.

How to Plant & Grow—Plant throughout the season. Follow planting instructions in the chapter introduction. Space plants 3 to 4 feet apart.

Care & Problems—Young weigelas need very little pruning. Remove any dead wood as it is discovered. Prune established shrubs in early summer after the first flush of flowers. Reduce the overall shrub size by cutting back long flowering stems to older upright growth. Remove several older stems to ground level each season. You can prune overgrown weigela back to ground level. Weigelas frequently suffer winter injury, especially those in poorly drained soils.

Hardiness—Zones 4 to 8

Seasonal Color—Pink, red, white, and purplish red flowers

Peak Season—Spring through summer

Mature Size (H x W)—Up to 6 ft. x 9 to 12 ft.

Water Needs—Drought tolerant once established.

WINTERBERRY
Ilex verticillata

Why It's Special—Add bright red berries to the winter landscape and bring in the birds with this deciduous holly. This native holly also provides nectar for bees as well as food and habitat for birds. You'll need one male for every five female plants for pollination and fruit set. Use the berries in winter arrangements with greenery.

How to Plant & Grow—Grow winterberry in full sun to light shade for the best fruit display. Plants will tolerate partial shade and damp soils. These, like most hollies, prefer moist organic soils. Follow the planting directions in the chapter introduction. Space plants 3 to 4 feet apart.

Care & Problems—Winterberry need minimal pruning. Remove any damaged, dead, or rubbing branches. This plant is low maintenance when grown in the right conditions. Fruit may drop during drought. Leaves may yellow in high pH soils. Use an acidifying fertilizer, move into a container, or transplant to a more suitable location.

Hardiness—Throughout the Midwest

Seasonal Color—Red berry-like fruits

Peak Season—Fall to winter berries

Mature Size (H x W)—6 to 10 ft. x 6 to 10 ft.

Water Needs—Moist soil is a must.

WITCHHAZEL
Hamamelis virginiana

Why It's Special—Witchhazel's fragrant, yellow flowers are the last of the season. They open in mid-October or November as the leaves turn yellow and drop from the plant. Its close relative vernal witchhazel (*Hamamelis vernalis*) has yellow, orange, or red flowers in late February or March; it is hardy to Zone 4.

How to Plant & Grow—Plant throughout the season. Witchhazel grows well in sun or shade and performs best in moist soil though it will tolerate some extremes. Space at least 5 to 6 feet apart.

Care & Problems—Avoid high-nitrogen fertilizers that may inhibit flowering. Witchhazel leaves may yellow in alkaline soil. Use acidifying fertilizers, such as ammonium sulfate, to minimize this problem. Keep pruning to a minimum with witchhazels. They are slow growing and respond slowly to pruning. Remove dead, damaged, or wayward branches in the spring. Prune them back to young healthy growth. Protect plants from rabbit damage.

Hardiness—Throughout the Midwest

Seasonal Color—Yellow flowers; fall color

Peak Season—Fall blooms

Mature Size (H x W)—10 to 15 ft. x 10 to 15 ft.

Water Needs—Tolerates dry shade once established.

YEW
Taxus species

Why It's Special—The variety of shapes and sizes available, along with the yew's ability to grow in sun or shade, make the cultivated yew adaptable to many landscape situations.

How to Plant & Grow—Plant evergreens by October 1 to give them time to establish before winter. Avoid areas with drying winter winds to minimize the risk of winter burn. Good drainage is essential. Spacing varies with type.

Care & Problems—Yews are traditionally sheared but are quite attractive and healthier when grown in their natural form. Prune yews, if needed in the spring before growth begins, or lightly in midsummer when they are semi-dormant. Maintain the yew's natural form by pruning branches back to a healthy bud, where the branch joins another branch, or back to the main trunk. Yews will also tolerate severe pruning, but be patient—it takes time for the plants to recover. Prune out any browning caused by winter damage or disease.

Hardiness—Zones 4 to 7

Seasonal Color—Evergreen foliage

Peak Season—Year-round

Mature Size (H x W)—20 ft. x 10 ft.

Water Needs—Moist, well-drained soil is best.

TRANSPLANTING SHRUBS

Start transplanting when the ground thaws and soil is moist. Complete this garden task before growth begins.

1. Loosely tie the branches to prevent damage and keep them out of your way.

2. Dig a trench around the shrub slightly larger and deeper than the desired rootball.

3. Undercut the rootball with your shovel. A sharp spade will make the job easier. Use hand pruners and loppers for larger or tougher roots.

4. Slide a piece of burlap or canvas under the rootball. Have several friends lend a hand. Extra hands and strong backs will make the job easier and reduce the risk of dropping the shrub and damaging the rootball.

5. Set the shrub in the prepared site. Carefully cut away or slide the tarp away from the shrub.

6. Backfill the hole with existing soil, water, and mulch.

Use a garden hose to mark the outline for a hole that is at least two or three times the diameter of the root ball of the shrub you wish to plant.

JANUARY

- Shake off the post-holiday blues and a few pounds with a walk around the block. Find out how friends and neighbors are using shrubs to add year-round interest to their landscape. Expand your search to include nearby botanical gardens and arboretums.

- Monitor the landscape for snow, deicing salt, and animal damage. Do not shake or brush frozen snow off the plants. This can cause more damage than if the snow was left in place. Make a note on your calendar to prevent plant damage next season.

- This is a quiet time in the landscape, but a good time to spring a surprise attack on many garden pests. A little preventative pest management can help reduce plant damage, pesticide use, and your summer workload.

- Check the base of viburnum, euonymus, and spirea stems for round, swollen growths called galls. These galls eventually girdle and kill the stem. Prune out infected stems below the gall, and discard. Disinfect your tools between cuts with rubbing alcohol or a solution of one part bleach to nine parts water.

FEBRUARY

- Late winter pruning is a good time to look for and control certain pests. Look for and remove black knot cankers on plums and cherries. These appear as swollen areas on the twigs. Remove and destroy eastern tent caterpillar egg masses. The eggs look like a shiny glob of mud on the stem.

- Check dogwood for signs of golden canker. This fungal disease is common on dogwoods that have suffered heat and drought stress in summer. The twigs turn gold and die. Prune out infected stems. Disinfect tools between cuts.

- Try bringing a little spring indoors. Prune a few branches from spring flowering shrubs to force for indoor bloom. Forsythia, quince, and pussy willows make nice additions to arrangements or in a vase on their own.

MARCH

- Late winter through early spring is the best time to transplant shrubs. Moving large, established shrubs can be tricky and heavy work. Replacing overgrown or misplaced shrubs may be easier, cheaper, and more successful.

- Wait until after flowering to prune lilacs, forsythia, bridal wreath spirea, and other spring-blooming shrubs. These shrubs have already set flower buds for this spring. Pruning at other times will not harm the plants but eliminates the bloom—the reason they are planted.

- Prune summer- and fall-blooming shrubs now. Late winter pruning will not interfere with summer flowering and allows the plants to recover quickly. See the "Pruning" section in the chapter introduction for specific information on pruning.

APRIL

- A few catalogs and garden centers sell bare-root shrubs. These plants are cheaper, often have a lower survival rate, and require your immediate attention for good results. Store bare-root plants in a cool, shaded location. Pack roots in peat moss and keep them moist. Soak roots overnight before planting. Place the shrubs in the planting hole at the same depth they were growing in the nursery.

- Move aboveground planters out of winter storage. Wait until temperatures hover around freezing if the leaves have begun to grow.

- Continue to locate and destroy egg masses of eastern tent caterpillars. The eggs hatch and the caterpillars start building their webbed tents when the saucer magnolias (*Magnolia soulangeana*) are in the pink bud stage. Prune out and destroy tents as they are found.

- Watch for European pine sawflies on mugo pine when the saucer magnolias begin dropping their petals. These wormlike insects feed in large groups, devouring pine needles a branch at a time. Smash them with a leather glove-clad hand or prune out and destroy the infested branch.

MAY

- Gradually move shrubs outdoors that were wintered indoors. Those stored in heated garages, the basement, or other warm locations need to gradually adapt to the cooler, harsher outdoor conditions.

- Water aboveground planters whenever the top few inches of soil begin to dry. Water thoroughly so that the excess drains out the bottom. Check planters every few days, daily during hot weather.

- Treat mugo and other pines infested with pine needle scale that appear as white flecks on the needles. Apply insecticidal soap when the Vanhoutte (bridal wreath) spirea is in bloom and again seven to ten days later.

- Check and treat lilacs, dogwoods, and other deciduous shrubs infested with oyster shell scale. These hard-shelled insects look like miniature oyster shells. Spray the stems and leaves with an ultrafine oil or insecticide labeled for use on shrubs with scale. Spray when the Vanhoutte (bridal wreath) spirea are in bloom and again when the hills-of-snow hydrangea blossoms change from white to green.

- Watch for phomopsis blight on junipers. Infected plants have cankered branches (sunken discolored areas) with brown and dead needles. Prune out infected branches 9 inches below the canker. Disinfect your tools between cuts.

JUNE

- Finish pruning spring-flowering shrubs early this month. This gives the plants plenty of time to develop flower buds for next spring's display.

- Shear and shape hedges after new growth has emerged. Prune so that the top of the hedge is narrower than the bottom. This allows light to reach all parts of the shrub. Better light penetration means leaves from top to bottom.

- Consider removing grass and creating planting beds around shrubs. Grass is a big competitor with shrubs for water and nutrients. The weed whips and mowers used to cut the grass often damage the shrubs. Reduce maintenance and improve the health of your shrubs by mulching around shrubs. Kill or remove grass and cover with woodchips or shredded bark.

- Treat borer-infested viburnum in early June when mockorange shrubs bloom and ten to fourteen days later. Spray the bottom 2 feet of stems with an insecticide labeled for this use.

- Check burning bush and other euonymus for signs of the euonymus caterpillar. These worm-like insects build webbed nests and feed on the leaves. Use a stick to knock out the nests and remove the insects as soon as they are found. Large populations can be treated with *Bacillus thuringiensis* var. *kurstacki*. This bacterial insecticide kills only true caterpillars and will not harm beneficial insects, wildlife, or people.

- Look for white, hard flecks on the leaves and stems of euonymus. Treat these scale insects with insecticidal soap when the Japanese tree lilacs are in bloom. The bloom time and egg hatch coincide. Repeat applications two more times at ten- to twelve-day intervals.

- Watch other shrubs for twig blight. The fungal diseases causing twig dieback are most common in cool, wet weather. Remove blighted, brown, and dying branches as soon as they are found. Disinfect tools between cuts.

JULY

- Lightly prune arborvitae, yews, and junipers once the new growth has expanded. Clip stems back to a healthy bud or side shoot to contain growth.

- Touch up your hedges and sheared shrubs when new growth expands. Prune so that the bottom of the plant is wider than the top. This allows light to reach all parts of the plant. Lightly shear summer-blooming spirea to remove faded flowers.

- Healthy shrubs can tolerate most pests in the landscape. When weather conditions favor the pests and not the plants, you may need to lend nature a hand. Check with your local Extension service, botanical garden, or garden center for help with diagnosis.

- Control large populations of aphids and mites with a strong blast of water from the garden hose. Treat shrubs with insecticidal soap if the populations grow and damage is severe.

- Continue monitoring and controlling Japanese beetles. Knock them into a can of soapy water. If you decide to treat, use an environmentally friendly insecticide labeled for this use. Or apply a soil systemic in spring. Don't use traps to control this pest.

AUGUST

- Take a walk through the landscape. Look for those drab, lifeless spots found in every yard. Consider adding a summer-flowering shrub to brighten up those areas. Butterfly bush (*Buddleja davidii*), hydrangeas (*Hydrangea* species), potentilla (*Potentilla fruticosa*), spirea (*Spirea japonica*), and summersweet (*Clethra*) are a few to consider. Find out more about these in the plant profiles.

- This is usually the hottest, driest month of summer. Check all plantings for moisture stress. You may need to prioritize watering needs if water bans are enacted.

- Avoid late-season pruning that can stimulate late-season growth. Finish touchup pruning on sheared plants as soon as possible. Remove only wayward branches. Save major pruning for the dormant season.

SEPTEMBER

- Start transplanting shrubs as the leaves begin to drop and the plants go dormant. Moving large established shrubs can be tricky and heavy work. Replacing overgrown or misplaced shrubs may be easier, cheaper, and more successful.

- If your landscape suffered severe feeding damage from Japanese beetles, some borers, and other pests, check out soil applied systemic insecticides. Use one labeled for these pests in the fall for control next season.

- Note plants covered with a white powdery substance. The powdery mildew fungus is a common problem on lilacs and many other plants. Fortunately the plant will survive; it just looks bad. Thin out overgrown shrubs next spring to increase light and air circulation and to reduce disease problems.

- Rake and compost or recycle fallen leaves. Disease-free leaves can be shredded and left on the lawn, dug into annual gardens, or added to the compost pile. Bury or discard disease-infected leaves. These are a source of infection for the next growing season.

OCTOBER

- Prepare aboveground planters for winter. Find a sheltered location in an unheated garage or enclosed porch to store the planters for winter. Use bales of hay to insulate shrubs in planters left outside.

- Visit your favorite garden center and stock up on repellents if animals have been a problem in the past. Early applications, before feeding starts, appear to be more effective. Reapply repellents after harsh weather and as recommended on the label.

- Wait until early spring to prune evergreens. Pruning now exposes the inner growth that has not been exposed to wind and sun. Fall pruning can increase winter injury.

- Avoid pruning spring-blooming shrubs, such as lilac and forsythia. Dormant season pruning removes flower buds needed for next spring's display. Remove only dead, pest-infected, or damaged branches at this time.

NOVEMBER

- Late purchases can be protected until spring planting season arrives. Find a protected location away from wind and sun. Sink the pots into the ground to insulate the roots from temperature extremes. For added protection, enclose plants in a cylinder of hardware cloth 4 feet high and sunk several inches into the soil to protect the plants from voles, rabbits, and possibly deer. Fill with evergreen boughs or straw for added protection.

- Give special attention to rhododendrons and other broad-leaf evergreens. Use a screen of burlap to cut the winter winds and shade the plants from the drying winter sun. Or circle the plants with a cylinder of hardware cloth several feet tall and sunk several inches into the ground. Fill with straw or evergreen branches to protect the plants. I prefer evergreen boughs—they're much more festive.

- Loosely tie upright arborvitae, junipers, and yews that are subject to splitting. Use strips of cotton cloth or old nylon stockings to tie the multiple stems together or try bird netting. This prevents snow loads and may discourage deer. Tying the stems prevents snow from building up on the plant, causing it to split and bend.

- Make sure new plantings and evergreens are thoroughly watered before the ground freezes. Once the ground is frozen, drain and store the hose until spring.

DECEMBER

- Clean and pack away the tools—another planting season is over. While storing your tools do a quick inventory. Remember the holidays are coming and gardening tools would make a great gift to give—or better yet, to receive! I will take a good pruning saw over a blender any day.

- Check winter protection and make sure it is securely in place—keeping out the animals or protecting the plants from harsh winter weather and deicing salt.

- Carefully add holiday lights to the winter landscape. Do not wrap branches with strands of lights. Drape the lights over the branches or loosely secure the lights to the stems. Remove lights in spring. If left in place the ties can damage fast-growing shrubs. Plus, the wires will quickly dull your saw blades.

- Prune off a few branches of red twig dogwood, juniper, winterberry, arborvitae, and yews. Add these to your indoor or outdoor holiday décor.

TREES
for the Midwest

Trees give structure to our landscape, providing form and year-round interest. They perform a variety of functions from offering privacy and shelter, serving as a habitat for wildlife, and providing a focal point for outdoor plantings. With proper selection, planting, and care, trees can be an integral part of the Midwest gardener's landscape for years to come.

TREE SELECTION

Planting the right tree in the right spot is a vital first step toward keeping it healthy throughout its life. Select the tree that is best suited to the soil, moisture, temperature, and other growing conditions of its location. Look for the most pest-resistant varieties to reduce maintenance and increase your success. Now consider all the features and year-round interest. Look for plants that provide year-round interest with a combination of flowers, fruit, bark, form, and fall color.

And plan for your immediate needs and the future. Fast-growing trees are usually the first to break apart in storms, decline, or die from disease. Use a mix of fast- and slow-growing trees for immediate and long-term enjoyment. The slow growers will take over as the fast-growing trees begin to decline.

Then choose a tree that will fit the available space, making sure the roots and crown will have enough room when they reach full size. Remember to check for overhead and underground utility lines. With the choices narrowed down, the final consideration is selecting a tree appropriate for your landscape's design and function. Trees are available in upright, spreading, weeping, and irregular forms. Use the species and form best suited to your needs.

Locate the planting site and call the free utility locating service at 811 or visit their website at www.call811.com. They will mark the location of any underground utility in the planting area within three working days. Making that call is important for your safety and your pocketbook. Digging into a utility line can be expensive, even deadly.

PURCHASING THE TREE

Now it's time to go shopping. Purchase your trees from a quality nursery or garden center. Trees are available bare root, balled and burlapped, or container grown. Bare-root plants are cheaper but should only be planted in the spring before growth begins. Balled-and-burlapped trees are dug in the spring and fall. They are more expensive and are available for a longer period than bare-root trees. Container-grown trees are planted and grown in pots. They can be purchased and planted throughout the season.

Choose a tree with a straight trunk, good structure, and no signs of insect or disease problems. Smaller trees are easier to handle and recover more quickly from transplanting. A 2½-inch-diameter transplanted tree will soon surpass a 6-inch-diameter transplanted tree, plus, you get the joy of watching it grow.

TRANSPORTING

Give your tree a safe ride home. Transporting the tree in a pickup truck or trailer is easier for you and better for the tree, or you can have it delivered. It is worth the extra effort or delivery cost to get your investment home safely.

Use a tarp to cover the top of the tree to prevent wind damage to the leaves on the trip home. Cover the roots of bare-root trees to prevent drying. With a towel, wrap the trunk where it will rest on the vehicle. And *always* move the tree by the rootball, *not* the trunk, to prevent damage to its roots.

Tie the tree in place and don't forget the red flag for trees that extend 3 feet or more beyond your vehicle. Many nurseries will help; in fact, many will deliver. They have the equipment and staff to handle and move larger trees.

Plant your new trees as soon as possible. Keep them in a cool, shaded location until planting. Mulch bare-root and balled-and-burlapped trees with woodchips to keep their roots moist. Water these and container-grown trees daily or as needed.

PLANTING

Locate the tree's root flare (the bell-shaped area where the roots angle away from the trunk). Plant the tree with the root flare at or slightly above the soil line. Dig a shallow planting hole the same depth as, and three to five times wider than, the root system. Roughen the sides of the planting hole to make it easier for the tree's roots to grow into the surrounding soil.

Remove container-grown plants from the pot. Roll the pot on its side or push on the container to loosen the roots; cut away the bottom of the pot. Set the tree in the planting hole and make sure the root flare is at or slightly above the soil surface. Slice and peel away the pot. Loosen or slice potbound and girdling roots.

For balled-and-burlapped trees, set the tree in the planting hole so the root flare is at or slightly above the soil surface. Remove the twine and cut away the burlap and wire cages. These materials do not decompose in most soils and can interfere with root growth and eventually girdle the tree.

Once the tree is in the hole make sure it is straight, moving it by the rootball, not the trunk, to minimize root damage. Fill the hole with existing soil. Do not amend the backfill. The tree roots need to adjust to their new environment, and amended soils encourage roots to stay in the planting hole instead of moving out into the landscape. Water to settle the soil; mulch. Do not stake balled-and-burlapped or container-grown trees unless they have a large canopy and a small root system or are subject to high winds and vandalism. Stake bare-root plants. Install the stakes in undisturbed soil outside the planting hole. Use a soft strap rather than wire around the tree trunk. Remove the stakes one or two years after planting. (See the planting diagram on the opposite page.)

CARE FOR NEWLY PLANTED TREES

Do not prune newly planted trees. Research shows that the more leaves a tree has, the more energy it can produce, and the quicker it develops new roots and recovers from transplant shock. Do remove broken and damaged branches at planting time. Structural pruning will start in the next few years once the tree has adjusted to its new home.

Water the area near the trunk to beyond the planting hole. The key to success with watering is to water thoroughly but infrequently. Check the soil moisture before watering. It's time to break out the hose when the top four to 6 inches of soil is crumbly and moist. Apply enough water to wet the top 12 inches of soil. A thorough watering once every seven to ten days is usually enough for clay soils. Check quick drying, sandy soils twice a week.

Mulch the soil to conserve moisture, reduce competition from grass, and prevent weeds. Mulch also keeps the tree-damaging mowers and weed whip away from the tree trunk. Apply a 3-inch layer of woodchips or shredded bark on the soil surface. Keep the mulch an inch or so away from the tree trunk.

ONGOING CARE

Do not fertilize newly planted trees. Wait until the following spring to apply fertilizer. Use the amount recommended by soil test results or read and follow label directions on the fertilizer packet. Established trees do not need routine fertilization. They usually get plenty of nutrients from the fertilizers applied to surrounding lawns and gardens.

Overfertilization can reduce flowering, increase the risk of certain diseases and insects, damage tree roots, and actually reduce a plant's health and vigor. Proper watering and mulching are the best care you can give your plants.

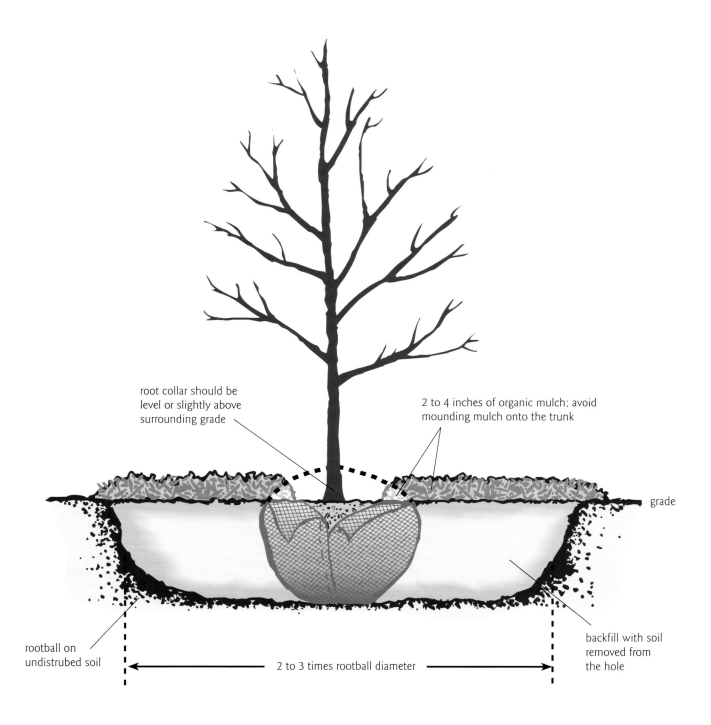

root collar should be level or slightly above surrounding grade

2 to 4 inches of organic mulch; avoid mounding mulch onto the trunk

grade

rootball on undistrubed soil

2 to 3 times rootball diameter

backfill with soil removed from the hole

Everyone wants to know how much fertilizer to add—without a soil test. The proper amount really depends on the health of the tree, its growing location, and our climate. It is better to err on the side of underfertilizing; you can always add more at a later time. Use a slow-release nitrogen fertilizer with little or no phosphorous and potassium. Apply 2 to 3 pounds of actual nitrogen fertilizer for every 1,000 square feet under the tree. This is equal to 20 to 30 pounds of a 10 percent nitrogen fertilizer, or 10 to 15 pounds of a 20 percent fertilizer formula. Get out the calculator to adjust the quantity for the percentage of nitrogen in the fertilizer you select and the size of the area you will be fertilizing.

Apply in spring before growth begins or in fall after the trees are dormant for best results. Fertilizer can be applied over mulch. Water to move the fertilizer through the mulch and down to the tree roots. Place fertilizer in the soil for trees growing in the lawn areas. Remove small cores of soil 6 inches deep and 2 to 3 feet apart throughout the area around the tree. Start digging holes several feet away from the tree trunk. Divide needed fertilizer evenly between the holes. Water thoroughly, moistening the top 12 inches of soil.

PRUNING

Prune young trees to establish a strong framework, keeping the plant's growth habit in mind. Remove crossed, rubbing, and parallel branches. Select branches with wide crotch angles, the angle between the trunk and branch, to form a strong framework. Create a framework of branches that spiral upward around the trunk. Prune out competing central leaders. Pruning young trees results in smaller wounds that close faster. Do not apply pruning paint; it can trap in problems instead of keeping them out.

Remove broken, damaged and hazardous branches as they occur. Consider hiring a certified arborist for help establishing and maintaining healthy and structurally sound trees. Visit www.treesaregood.com to find a certified arborist in your area.

PEST MANAGEMENT

Minimize pest problems by planting the right tree for your location. Trees suited to their environments have fewer pest problems.

Check trees frequently for signs of insects and disease. Look for speckled and discolored leaves, holes, spots, and other signs of insects and disease. Early detection can make control easier and more effective. It may also save your tree.

Despite your best efforts, pest problems may arise. Get a proper diagnosis and control recommendations from the local county university Extension office or a certified arborist (tree care professional).

Many problems that look bad to us are not really detrimental to healthy trees. If treatment is needed, select an effective method that is the safest for you, the tree, and the environment. Your efforts will be rewarded with years of enjoyment.

Let's take a look at a few trees that will add shade, season interest and years of enjoyment to your Midwest landscape.

BALD CYPRESS
Taxodium distichum

Why It's Special—The stately nature and fine texture of this needled tree combined with its adaptability to wet and dry soils make it worthy of attention. Don't be fooled as the needles turn orange-bronze in the fall; this is normal for this deciduous conifer (cone bearing).

How to Plant & Grow—Plant in spring in moist, well-drained soils for best results. Native to swampy areas this tree will tolerate both wet and dry conditions once established. Follow the planting directions in the chapter introduction.

Care & Problems—Knees, oxygen capturing knobby growths, form in wet locations. This is usually not a problem for gardeners growing this tree in a normal landscape setting. Prune young trees to establish a strong framework in early spring. Remove damaged and diseased limbs as needed. Twig blight and canker and a few insects can attack the tree. Proper care and sanitation will usually keep these under control.

Hardiness—Zone 5 (dieback); Zones 4 to 11

Seasonal Color—Orange-brown foliage

Peak Season—Fall

Mature Size (H x W)—Up to 70 ft. x 20 ft.

Water Needs—Bald cypress tolerates wet and dry soils once it's established.

BEECH
Fagus species

Why It's Special—The beech tree is one of the majestic trees of the woods and landscape. These slow-growing trees carefully build a strong framework that lasts for many years. This four-season tree has smooth gray bark, rich brown fall color, and fruit for a variety of birds to enjoy.

How to Plant & Grow—Plant young trees in early spring. European beeches adapt better to transplanting and are more readily available. Beeches must have moist, well-drained soil and grow best in full sun but tolerate partial shade. See the planting directions in the chapter introduction.

Care & Problems—Moist, well-drained soil is the key to success. Create a mulch bed or grow groundcovers under these trees to conserve moisture and eliminate competition from the grass. If planted in the proper location, beech trees are low maintenance and have no real problems, but remember this is a slow-growing plant. Prune young trees to establish a framework.

Hardiness—Zones 4 to 7

Seasonal Color—Golden bronze fall foliage

Peak Season—Fall

Mature Size (H x W)—More than 50 ft. x 35 ft.

Water Needs—Moist, well-drained soil is essential.

BIRCH
Betula species

Why It's Special—The beautiful white bark of paper birch (*Betula papyrifera*) has many gardeners trying to raise this woodland native in their front yard. River birch, *Betula nigra*, is also native but has fewer challenges. Its bark exfoliates (peels off), exposing multiple colors of gray, cinnamon, or reddish brown.

How to Plant & Grow—Plant birch trees in the spring so this slow-to-establish plant has time to root before winter. Cool moist soils are critical for success. Follow the planting directions in the chapter introduction.

Care & Problems—Proper siting and care will reduce pest problems. River birch leaves yellow (chlorosis) in high pH soils. Paper birch is subject to the deadly bronze birch borer. Both are susceptible to leafminers and Japanese beetles. Reduce problems by selecting more landscape tolerant cultivars that resist borer and better tolerate heat. Birch trees will "bleed" when pruned in the spring. It won't hurt the plant; it's just makes for a messy job.

Hardiness—Throughout the Midwest

Seasonal Color—White or cinnamon brown bark; yellow fall foliage

Peak Season—Fall and winter

Mature Size (H x W)—40 to 50 ft. x 20 to 25 ft.

Water Needs—Moist soil is critically important.

BLACK GUM
Nyssa sylvatica

Why It's Special—Black gum is a good alternative to many of the invasive trees that overpopulate our landscapes. Grow this tree where its year-round beauty can be enjoyed. Use as a specimen plant or part of a naturalized or wildlife garden.

How to Plant & Grow—Black gum is a slow grower but give it room to reach its mature size and show off its beauty. In nature it can be found growing in upland drylands and swampy woods. But in the landscape it is more particular. Make sure it has moist, well-drained acidic soil and is sheltered from the wind. See the planting instructions at the beginning of this chapter.

Care & Problems—Chlorosis (yellowing leaves, plant decline, and eventual death) is a problem when these acid lovers are grown on very alkaline (high pH) soils. Daring gardeners in Zones 3 and the northern parts of 4 need to proceed cautiously.

Hardiness—Zones 4 to 9

Seasonal Color—Yellow to orange to scarlet to purple fall color

Peak Season—Fall

Mature Size (H x W)—30 to 50 ft. x 20 to 30 ft.

Water Needs—Moist, well-drained soil is important.

CRABAPPLE
Malus hybrids

Why It's Special—The disease-resistant crabapple species have kept this four-season beauty an important part of the landscape. Look for cultivars with persistent fruit that you and the birds can enjoy for months. Use crabapples as specimen plants or in small groupings.

How to Plant & Grow—Crabapples respond best to spring planting. Grow them in full sun with moist, well-drained soil. See the chapter introduction for planting directions.

Care & Problems—Avoid excess fertilization, which can encourage disease problems and eliminate flowering and fruit. Prune only to establish and maintain the tree's structural framework. Excessive pruning will encourage water sprouts. Remove suckers by pruning just below the soil surface. Prune crabapple trees in late winter for quick wound closure that reduces the risk of disease. Select fireblight- and scab-resistant cultivars to avoid major problems. Watch for and remove tent caterpillars when they're found.

Hardiness—Throughout the Midwest

Seasonal Color—White, pink, and red flowers; red, orange, and yellow fruits

Peak Season—Spring blooms; fall and winter fruit

Mature Size (H x W)—40 to 60 ft. x 20 to 40 ft.

Water Needs—Drought tolerant once established.

ELM
Ulmus species and hybrids

Why It's Special—Memories of tree-lined streets and sitting under the shade of American elms have kept researchers busy looking for Dutch Elm-resistant strains. Progress has been made with introductions like 'Princeton' and 'Triumph' American elms. This, along with pest-resistant and ornamental options like lacebark elm, *Ulmus parvifolia*, make elms a shade tree option for large landscapes.

How to Plant & Grow—Elms adapt well to transplanting. Grow elms in full sun with moist soil, but many will tolerate wet soil and even temporary flooding. Follow the planting directions in the chapter introduction.

Care & Problems—Elms tend to be fast growers and weak wooded. Proper pruning throughout the tree's life will help reduce storm damage. Avoid adding disease-susceptible elms to your landscape. Use a preventative fungicide treatment to protect valuable trees. Contact a certified arborist for proper diagnosis and treatment.

Hardiness—Throughout the Midwest; varies with the species

Seasonal Color—Yellow fall color

Peak Season—Fall

Mature Size (H x W)—30 to 80 ft. x 40 ft.

Water Needs—Established trees tolerate drought and also temporary flooding.

FIR
Abies species

Why It's Special—If you like the look of a blue spruce but are tired of fighting the pests consider the white fir, *Abies concolor*. It has blue-green needles and a pyramidal shape similar to the Colorado blue spruce. It prefers ideal growing conditions but is more tolerant of heat, drought, and urban conditions than other firs. The introduction of new dwarf cultivars is allowing greater use of these finicky trees. Most gardeners can find the perfect microclimate for a small-scale tree.

How to Plant & Grow—Grow firs in full sun or light shade. They prefer moist, well-drained soil in cool, humid locations. Firs do not tolerate hot, dry conditions. See the chapter introduction for planting directions.

Care & Problems—Proper site selection is critical for growing success. A well-placed fir will require little maintenance, have few pest problems, and require minimal pruning. Mulch the soil with wood chips or another organic material to keep the roots cool and moist.

Hardiness—Throughout the Midwest

Seasonal Color—Evergreen needles

Peak Season—Year-round

Mature Size (H x W)—70 ft. x 30 ft.

Water Needs—Moist, well-drained soil is required.

FRINGETREE
Chionanthus virginicus

Why It's Special—Add some fragrance and spring blooms to any size landscape. Use this slow grower as a large shrub or small multi-stemmed tree. The white, lightly fragrant and frilly flowers bring in the butterflies and beneficial insects. And the blue fruit, often masked by the leaves, attract the birds.

How to Plant & Grow—Grow fringetree in moist, well-drained acidic soils for best results. Place in a sheltered location free from late spring frosts to increase growing and flowering success. Plant early in the season for best results. See the chapter introduction for planting guidelines.

Care & Problems—Avoid high-nitrogen fertilizer than can interfere with flowering and fruiting. These plants are low maintenance and fairly pest free. They need minimal pruning, though some gardeners do a bit of thinning to improve the flower and fruit display. Fringetree is late to leaf out so don't be alarmed when nearby plants are fully leafed before this starts showing signs of growth.

Hardiness—Zones 4 to 9

Seasonal Color—White flowers

Peak Season—Spring

Mature Size (H x W)—12 to 20 ft. x 12 to 20k ft.

Water Needs—Moist, well-drained soil is needed.

GINKGO
Ginkgo biloba

Why It's Special—Ginkgo is a beautiful landscape tree. The attractive, fan-shaped leaves add to the overall uniqueness of this plant. Mature specimens are breathtaking, especially in the fall. The leaves turn a clear yellow and, best of all, they all drop from the tree at the same time, making cleanup easier.

How to Plant & Grow—Plant ginkgoes throughout the growing season. This tough tree seems to thrive anywhere. It prefers full sun with slightly moist, well-drained soil. It is very tolerant of salt, pollution, and other urban conditions. Follow the planting directions in the chapter introduction.

Care & Problems—Female ginkgo trees produce smelly, messy fruit with edible seeds inside. Plant male clones to avoid this problem. Otherwise, rake and compost the fruit or find a forager to harvest and use the fruit. Ginkgo's slow growth and open habit eliminate the need for regular pruning. You can speed growth by providing adequate, but not too much, water and fertilizer.

Hardiness—Zones 4 to 8

Seasonal Color—Yellow fall foliage

Peak Season—Fall

Mature Size (H x W)—50 or more ft. x 30 or more ft.

Water Needs—Moist, well-drained soil is important.

HAWTHORN
Crataegus species

Why It's Special—Hawthorns are nice, small trees that provide year-round interest both in small and large settings. Their white spring flowers are followed by orange-red fruit that is quite showy from fall through winter. As the fruit softens over winter, the hungry birds will start eating them.

How to Plant & Grow—Plant throughout the growing season. Early season planting will increase success. Hawthorns prefer full sun and will tolerate a variety of soils as long as they are well drained. Grow them in planting or mulch beds to hide any fallen fruit and eliminate the risk of accidentally walking into a thorny branch. See the chapter introduction for planting tips.

Care & Problems—Avoid excess fertilization and fast-release, high-nitrogen fertilizers that can reduce flowering and fruiting and increase the risk of disease. Prune hawthorns in early spring before growth begins. Hawthorns are susceptible to several major diseases including fireblight, scab, and rust. Select the least susceptible species whenever possible.

Hardiness—Throughout the Midwest

Seasonal Color—White flowers; fall color; winter red-orange fruit

Peak Season—Spring bloom

Mature Size (H x W)—20 to 30 ft. x 20 to 30 ft.

Water Needs—Drought tolerant once established.

HEMLOCK
Tsuga canadensis

Why It's Special—Hemlock's graceful beauty and shade extends the use of evergreens in the landscape. This native evergreen tree is pyramidal when young. They are attractive when grown individually or in small groups. Dwarf cultivars are nice additions to small landscapes and perennial gardens. This is *not* the infamous poison hemlock (*Conium maculatum*).

How to Plant & Grow—Plant hemlocks throughout the season, preferably before October 1. Grow hemlocks in a sheltered location out of wind, drought, pollution, and waterlogged soil. Winter winds and sun can be especially damaging. Follow the planting directions in the chapter introduction.

Care & Problems—Moisture and mulch are the keys to growing healthy, long-lived hemlocks. Stressed trees are susceptible to quite a few pests. Brown needles and branch dieback can occur when the plants are exposed to temperatures over 95 degrees Fahrenheit, drying winter winds, or drought. Prune out damaged branches, eliminate the stress, or move the plants to a more suitable location.

Hardiness—Throughout the Midwest

Seasonal Color—Evergreen foliage

Peak Season—Year-round

Mature Size (H x W)—75 ft. or more x 25 ft. or more

Water Needs—Keep soil moist and well-drained.

HONEYLOCUST
Gleditsia triacanthos var. inermis

Why It's Special—The fast-growing honeylocust is frequently used in difficult growing spots and to shade patios, decks, and lawn areas. The filtered shade is cooling, but not detrimental to the grass below.

How to Plant & Grow—Plant throughout the growing season in moist, well-drained soil. Honeylocust tolerates drought, salt, and high pH. Handle this tree with care and avoid damage when transporting and planting. Wounds create an opening for life-threatening diseases such as nectria canker. Follow the planting directions in the chapter introduction.

Care & Problems—Plantbugs, leafhoppers, and aphids can be a problem in dry springs. Control is not usually needed for the health of the tree. Lower the risk of nectria canker by selecting healthy, disease-free trees and avoiding injuries to the trunk and branches during transplanting and maintenance. Prune and remove sprouts that form on the main trunk in early spring before growth begins. Wait for cool dry weather if you must prune during the growing season.

Hardiness—Throughout the Midwest

Seasonal Color—Yellow fall foliage

Peak Season—Fall

Mature Size (H x W)—40 ft. x 30 ft.

Water Needs—Drought tolerant once established.

HORSECHESTNUT
Aesculus hippocastanum

Why It's Special— Horsechestnuts' large spring blooms appeal to gardeners as well as bees and hummingbirds. Use them as a shade or large specimen tree in expansive lawn areas or on a woodland edge. Consider its close relative, the Ohio buckeye (*Aesculus glabra*). Its smaller size and fall color make it a better fit for most home landscapes. These are *not* the holiday chestnuts that are roasted on an open fire.

How to Plant & Grow—Horsechestnuts are massive trees that need room to showcase their beauty. Avoid planting these over sidewalks where falling fruit can create a messy hazard. Horsechestnuts respond best to spring transplanting. See the chapter introduction for planting directions.

Care & Problems—Use mulch or groundcovers under fruiting trees to minimize cleanup. Use fruitless varieties where you don't want to attract squirrels or provide ammunition for children. Leaf blotch, anthracnose, and powdery mildew can all cause leaves to discolor and drop prematurely. Healthy trees can tolerate these diseases.

Hardiness—Zones 4 to 7

Seasonal Color—White flowers

Peak Season—Late spring blooms

Mature Size (H x W)—50 or more ft. x 40 ft.

Water Needs—Moist, well-drained soil is needed.

IRONWOOD
Ostrya virginiana

Why It's Special—These small trees are a good fit in small landscapes. Plant them in groupings for a bigger impact in larger settings. Ironwood's graceful growth habit helps soften vertical elements in the landscape. Take advantage of ironwood's shade tolerance. Use it in woodland gardens or as an understory plant for your larger shade trees.

How to Plant & Grow—Plant early in the season for best results. They prefer moist, well-drained soil but can tolerate the dry, gravelly, and sandy soils found in our region. See the chapter introduction for detailed directions.

Care & Problems—Finding a plant may be your biggest challenge. Check with specialty nurseries in your area. Though tolerant of dry soil, ironwoods do best when watered during extended drought periods. Ironwood is slow to get started, but starts growing faster once established. Ironwood has no serious pests. Minimal pruning is needed.

Hardiness—Throughout the Midwest

Seasonal Color—Yellow fall leaves; winter bark and fruit

Peak Season—Fall

Mature Size (H x W)—30 ft. x 20 or more ft.

Water Needs—Tolerates dry soils once established.

KATSURATREE
Cercidiphyllum japonicum

Why It's Special—Enjoy the seasonal changes of this delicate beauty. The leaves emerge reddish purple and change to a blue-green for summer. In fall they turn a clear yellow or apricot. The heart-shaped leaves are helped by long petioles (leaf stems) that allow them to "quake" like aspens in the wind. And once the leaves are fully colored you'll notice a brown sugary, cinnamon aroma.

How to Plant & Grow—Plant early in the season so they have more time to establish before winter. Grow in rich, moist well-drained soils for best results. Katsuratrees are adaptable to both acidic and alkaline soils. See the chapter introduction for detailed planting directions.

Care & Problems—Getting this plant through the first few years seems to be the challenge. Once established, specimens can be fairly long lived. These plants need even moisture. Make sure to water these trees during drought. Water thoroughly as needed and mulch to keep roots cool and moist.

Hardiness—Zones 4 to 8

Seasonal Color—Yellow to apricot fall color

Peak Season—Fall

Mature Size (H x W)—40 to 60 ft. x 20 to 60 ft.

Water Needs—Moist, well-drained soils are important.

KENTUCKY COFFEETREE
Gymnocladus dioicus

Why It's Special—This versatile plant tolerates a wide range of conditions while blending into formal and informal landscape designs. It is a close relative to the honeylocust but with fewer pests. Use the large Kentucky coffeetree to provide shade in the summer and an interesting silhouette in winter. Give it time; young plants are quite homely, and need space to grow.

How to Plant & Grow—Spring planting is best, though you can plant throughout the season. Kentucky coffeetrees prefer full sun and moist, well-drained soil but will tolerate wet and dry as well as windy and urban locations. Follow planting directions in the chapter introduction.

Care & Problems—Kentucky coffeetree is a low-maintenance plant with no serious pests. It may be hard to locate, so pick up the phone before you hop in the car. 'Espresso' is a fruitless (male) cultivar. The long leaf stem (rachis) can be messy and annoy more meticulous gardeners.

Hardiness—Zones 3b to 8

Seasonal Color—Yellow fall color; colorful bark in winter

Peak Season—Fall

Mature Size (H x W)—75 ft. x 40 ft.

Water Needs—Established plants tolerate wet and dry soils.

KOREAN SUN PEAR
Pyrus fauriei 'Westwood'

Why It's Special—This small-scale tree is a good alternative for the invasive Callery pear. It has similar ornamental features but is hardier, and with stronger branching. It colors earlier in fall reducing the risk of frost spoiling its colorful season finale.

How to Plant & Grow—Grow this adaptable plant in full sun for the best flowering and fruiting. It prefers moist well-drained soil but is very adaptable and seems to tolerate clay soil and somewhat poorly drained soils. Follow the planting instructions in the chapter introduction.

Care & Problems—Avoid high-nitrogen fast-release fertilizer that can inhibit flowering and fall color and increase the risk of disease. This ornamental pear tends to be widely branched so minimal pruning will be needed. No disease or insect problems have been reported but fireblight on pears is always a threat. The trees tend to produce small quantities of fruit, but so far does not appear to be invasive.

Hardiness—Zones 4 to 9

Seasonal Color—White flowers; reddish orange fall color

Peak Season—Spring and fall

Mature Size (H x W)—12 ft. x 15 ft.

Water Needs—Drought tolerant once established.

LARCH
Larix species

Why It's Special—Larches are good plants for large landscapes and new dwarf cultivars are making them useful in small-scale yards Consider using one of these graceful plants near a pond or water feature. The American larch, *Larix laricina*, is also called tamarack and is a tall pyramidal plant. Larch's needles turn a beautiful golden yellow and drop in fall.

How to Plant & Grow—It may be difficult to find the American larch. Check with local nurseries specializing in native plants. The Japanese larch, *Larix kaempferi*, and European larch, *Larix decidua*, are more readily available, ornamental, not as tolerant of wet soil, and need lots of space to grow and show their beauty. Plant throughout the growing season in moist, well-drained soil. Avoid dry soil and polluted locations. See the chapter introduction for more planting details.

Care & Problems—Properly placed larch trees need little maintenance. Insect and disease problems are few and infrequent. Healthy plants properly watered and mulched usually resist and tolerate any damage.

Hardiness—Throughout the Midwest; varies with the species

Seasonal Color—Yellow fall foilage

Peak Season—Fall

Mature Size (H x W)—75 ft. x 40 ft.

Water Needs—Moist soil is best.

LINDEN
Tilia species

Why It's Special—Fragrant flowers and fall color makes this an excellent shade tree for landscapes. The American linden (*Tilia americana*) is good for naturalized settings or woodland areas. The littleleaf linden (*Tilia cordata*) is frequently used for street trees, planters, and planting beds. Silver linden (*Tilia tomentosa*) has silver undersides and is more tolerant of heat and drought conditions; it's hardy to Zone 5.

How to Plant & Grow—Plant throughout the growing season in full sun with moist, well-drained soil. Most lindens tolerate heavy clay soil (see the chapter introduction for planting details).

Care & Problems—Recent droughts and environmental stresses have increased problems with linden borer. Mulch and proper watering, especially during drought, will help reduce the risk. Littleleaf lindens produce lots of side branches very close together requiring regular pruning. Japanese beetles are a major pest problem. Drought-stressed and specimen trees may benefit from control. Watch for nectria canker on littleleaf lindens. See the honeylocust profile for more details.

Hardiness—Throughout the Midwest; varies with the species

Seasonal Color—Yellow blooms; fall foliage

Peak Season—Summer

Mature Size (H x W)—Up to 75 ft. x 40 ft.

Water Needs—Moist, well-drained soil is needed.

MAGNOLIA
Magnolia species

Why It's Special—Small magnolias can be used as an accent, a flowering specimen, or as a mass display in small or large yards. Include smaller trees near the house and patio or as part of a mixed border. Save the larger magnolias for bigger settings.

How to Plant & Grow—Magnolias do not respond well to transplanting, so plant early in the season for best results. Grow them in moist, well-drained soil. These trees will not tolerate wet or dry conditions. Avoid low spots and other areas subject to late spring frosts that can destroy the spring floral display. See the chapter introduction for planting directions.

Care & Problems—Plants grown in poorly drained soil are subject to yellow leaves, poor growth, and even death. Magnolias are subject to snow and ice damage. Reduce the risk with proper training and pruning. Prune magnolias soon after flowering so you don't interfere with the next season's bloom.

Hardiness—Throughout; varies with species

Seasonal Color—Pink, white, and yellow flowers

Peak Season—Early spring

Mature Size (H x W)—15 to 40 ft. x 30 ft.

Water Needs—Moist, well-drained soil is important.

MAPLE
Acer species

Why It's Special—Maples, with their cooling shade and colorful fall foliage, are one of the most widely used shade trees. Match a maple to your landscape design and growing conditions.

How to Plant & Grow—Plant red and Freeman maples in spring for best results. Other maples can be planted throughout the growing season. Some maples will tolerate wet, dry, or other difficult conditions. See the chapter introduction for planting directions.

Care & Problems—Avoid excess fertilization that can hinder fall color. Avoid planting invasive Norway and Amur maples. Mulch or plant groundcovers under maples to mask and reduce maintenance around shallow roots. Do *not* cut or bury the roots. This can eventually kill the tree. Prune young trees to establish a central leader and sturdy framework. Maple trees will bleed when pruned in the spring but it won't hurt the plant. Verticillium wilt can be deadly. Healthy maples will tolerate the other pests.

Hardiness—Throughout the Midwest; varies with species

Seasonal Color—Red or yellow flowers; yellow-orange and red fall foliage

Peak Season—Fall

Mature Size (H x W)—Up to 75 ft. x 40 ft.

Water Needs—Most prefer moist, well-drained soils.

MOUNTAINASH
Sorbus species

Why It's Special—The small-scale European mountainash (*Sorbus aucuparia*) has long been a favorite tree for Midwest gardens, providing seasonal interest. The fruit display is excellent and attractive to birds. Our native mountain ashes, American mountainash (*Sorbus americana*) and showy mountainash (*Sorbus decora*), are similar in appearance and bird appeal.

How to Plant & Grow—Plant container-grown trees throughout the growing season, preferably early in the season. Grow mountainash in areas with cool, moist, but well-drained soil. They will not tolerate heat, drought, pollution, or compacted soil. Follow the planting directions in the chapter introduction.

Care & Problems—Mountainash trees are susceptible to quite a few disease and insect problems. Sunscald, frost cracking, scab, and fireblight are the most common. Proper siting, regular watering, mulching to keep roots cool, and avoiding excess fertilization can help reduce the risks. Or try Korean mountain ash, *Sorbus alnifolia* (shown), that is equally ornamental and more tolerant of our climate (hardy in Zone 4).

Hardiness—Throughout the Midwest; varies with the species

Seasonal Color—White blooms; colorful fall foliage; pink or orange fruit

Peak Season—Spring and fall

Mature Size (H x W)—30 ft. x 20 ft.

Water Needs—Moist, well-drained soil is needed.

MUSCLEWOOD
Carpinus caroliniana

Why It's Special—Musclewood's small scale and shade tolerance make this a good solution for small and shady landscapes. The fine texture, fall color, persistent fruit, and smooth, gray bark give this tree year-round appeal.

How to Plant & Grow—Musclewood trees do not respond well to transplanting so plant early in the season for best results. Musclewood prefers partial shade and moist soil in the landscape but it will tolerate heavy shade and temporary flooding. See the chapter introduction for more planting details.

Care & Problems—New trees take time to adjust to their new location. Mulch their roots to keep the soil cool and moist. Once established, musclewood requires little maintenance. Although trees are subject to damage from ice storms, properly trained trees will be less susceptible. Prune young trees to establish a structurally sound framework. Minimal pruning should be done after this. There are no serious pests when plants are properly planted and maintained.

Hardiness—Zones 3 to 9

Seasonal Color—Yellow, orange, and red fall foliage

Peak Season—Fall foliage; winter bark

Mature Size (H x W)—Up to 30 ft. x 30 ft..

Water Needs—It needs moist soil and tolerates temporary flooding.

OAK
Quercus species

Why It's Special—Oaks are the majestic trees of nature, and they bring the same feeling to large landscapes. A wider range of oaks is now available thanks to an increased interest in native plants and greater transplanting success. These large trees are medium to slow growing but can still be enjoyed in a lifetime.

How to Plant & Grow—Most oaks are difficult to transplant so plant early in the season for best success. In general, oaks prefer moist, well-drained soil. Some require acidic soil while others will tolerate alkaline soil. Select species adapted to your soil conditions.

Care & Problems—Prune oaks during the dormant season to minimize the risk of oak wilt infection. Apply pruning paint to oaks pruned during the growing season. Anthracnose and galls are common problems but are not harmful. Several oaks, like pin oak, are very intolerant of alkaline (high pH) soil and develop chlorosis, a yellowing of leaves.

Hardiness—Throughout the Midwest; varies with the species

Seasonal Color—Yellow, brown, or red fall foilage

Peak Season—Fall foliage; interesting bark

Mature Size (H x W)—50 to 80 ft. x 50 to 80 ft.

Water Needs—Most are drought tolerant once established.

ORNAMENTAL PLUM AND CHERRY
Prunus species

Why It's Special—Ornamental plums and cherries are grown for their impressive flowers or decorative foliage. These small trees can add early spring interest to both large and small landscapes. Many have decorative bark, nectar for attracting hummingbirds, fruit for the wildlife, and interesting forms.

How to Plant & Grow—Select the most pest-resistant varieties suited to your growing conditions and landscape design. Native cherries and plums are often considered less ornamental but are more suited to our soils and climate. Plant these trees in spring in a sheltered location on the east side of your home in full sun with moist well-drained soils. Follow the planting directions in the introduction.

Care & Problems—Proper siting will help extend the life of these short-lived plants. These ornamental plants have many insect and disease problems. Healthy plants are the best defense against these problems. Avoid excess fertilization that can interfere with flowering. These trees tend to be short lived and also sucker freely.

Hardiness—Throughout the Midwest; varies with the species

Seasonal Color—White or pink flowers

Peak Season—Spring

Mature Size (H x W)—Up to 30 ft. x 30 ft.

Water Needs—Moist, well-drained soil is needed.

PAGODA DOGWOOD
Cornus alternifolia

Why It's Special—Pagoda dogwoods are small-scale trees that provide four seasons of interest and bird appeal. Several members of this group can be used as large shrubs or small-scale trees. Flowering (*C. florida*), Kousa (*C. kousa*), cornelian cherry (*C. mas*), and pagoda (*C. alternifolia*) dogwoods are commonly found at nurseries and growing in landscapes. Select the species and cultivars best suited to your growing conditions.

How to Plant & Grow—In general, dogwoods grow in full sun to partial shade as long as the soil is kept evenly moist. See the chapter introduction for planting instructions.

Care & Problems—Mulch to keep the roots cool and moist. Be patient—dogwoods tend to take a few years to get established before they get growing. Cold winters, late spring frost, and excess fertilization can prevent some dogwoods from blooming. Proper selection, placement, and care will reduce pest problems on all the dogwoods.

Hardiness—Throughout the Midwest; varies with the species

Seasonal Color—Cream, pink, or yellow flowers; red, white, or blue fruit; red to purple fall foliage

Peak Season—Spring flowers

Mature Size (H x W)—15 to 25 ft. x 25 to 35 ft.

Water Needs—Moist, well-drained soil is needed.

PINE
Pinus species

Why It's Special—Pines have long been used in our landscapes as windbreaks, screens, and wildlife habitats. Planted in the right location with sufficient space, pines provide years of beauty. The many dwarf varieties allow even small space gardeners an opportunity to grow them as specimens and in perennial and mixed borders.

How to Plant & Grow—Plant by October 1, when possible, to allow the plants time to adjust before winter. Pines prefer full sun and moist, well-drained soil. Most pines can tolerate dry conditions once established. Follow the planting directions in the chapter introduction.

Care & Problems—Pines need minimal pruning. Remove dead and damaged branches and maintain a central leader. Pines can be pruned to limit new growth by removing one-half or two-thirds of the candles (expanding buds) in spring. There are several fungal diseases and insect problems that can be damaging. Contact your local university Extension office or a certified arborist for diagnosis and treatment recommendations.

Hardiness—Throughout the Midwest; varies with species

Seasonal Color—Evergreen foliage

Peak Season—Year-round

Mature Size (H x W)—Up to 75 ft. x 40 ft.

Water Needs—Most species tolerate dry soil once established.

REDBUD
Cercis canadensis

Why It's Special—The redbud is a small-scale tree with four seasons of interest. The reddish purple buds and rosy pink flowers are a welcome addition to the early spring landscape. Its yellow fall color, attractive bark, and growth habit add to its appeal.

How to Plant & Grow—Select a locally grown or hardier type, such as the Columbus or Minnesota strains, to increase longevity. Redbuds respond best to spring planting, which allows them to start establishing before winter. Grow them in a protected location with full sun to part shade and moist, well-drained soil. Follow the planting directions in the chapter introduction.

Care & Problems—Proper selection, siting, and care will help increase longevity and reduce winter injury and pest problems. Prune young trees to establish a strong framework. Established trees need minimal pruning. Verticillium wilt can be a problem. Do not replace verticillium wilt-killed trees with this or other susceptible plants.

Hardiness—Zones 4 to 9

Seasonal Color—Rosy pink flowers; yellow fall foliage

Peak Season—Early spring

Mature Size (H x W)—Up to 30 ft. x 30 ft.

Water Needs—Moist, well-drained soil is best.

SERVICEBERRY
Amelanchier species

Why It's Special—Serviceberries provide four seasons of beauty, edible fruit, and bird appeal to landscapes small and large. They are native to woodland edges, stream banks, fencerows, and hillsides. This adaptability helps them tolerate a wide range of landscape conditions. Shrub, columnar, and small tree species are available. Look for cultivars known for outstanding fall color and the size and form that best complements your landscape design.

How to Plant & Grow—Plant throughout the growing season in moist, well-drained soil. Serviceberries take time to establish after transplanting. See the chapter introduction for more details on planting.

Care & Problems—Serviceberries don't have serious insect or disease problems. Fireblight can occasionally attack. Remove infested branches beneath the canker and disinfect tools between cuts. Prune young trees to establish a strong framework. Mature trees will need minimal pruning. Late winter or early spring pruning allows wounds to close quickly, reducing the risk of pest problems.

Hardiness—Throughout the Midwest; varies with species

Seasonal Color—White flowers; yellow, orange, and red fall foliage

Peak Season—Spring and fall

Mature Size (H x W)—Up to 40 ft. x 30 ft.

Water Needs—Moist, well-drained soil is best.

SPRUCE
Picea species

Why It's Special—Spruce trees provide a strong, pyramidal silhouette in the garden. Their evergreen needles make a nice backdrop for deciduous trees and shrubs and ornamental grasses. Grow a few dwarf spruce varieties in mixed borders and gardens.

How to Plant & Grow—Plant container-grown trees by October 1 to increase their winter survival. Grow spruce in moist, well-drained soil. Consult the chapter introduction for planting tips.

Care & Problems—Mulch to conserve moisture and to suppress weeds (don't bother growing grass under these trees). Or grow dry shade-tolerant groundcovers like Canadian ginger. Spruce need very little pruning. Touch-up pruning can be done in the spring before growth begins. Make cuts on branch tips above a healthy bud. There's no need to prune off lower branches; this is for the gardener's benefit, not the plant's. Several diseases and insects can reduce the health, vigor, and beauty of these trees. Consult your Extension service or certified arborist for proper diagnosis and treatment.

Hardiness—Throughout the Midwest; varies with species

Seasonal Color—Evergreen needles

Peak Season—Year-round

Mature Size (H x W)—Up to 60 ft. x 30 ft.

Water Needs—Moist, well-drained soil is important.

TRANSPLANTING TREES

- Start transplanting when trees begin dropping their leaves or in spring before growth begins.

- Loosely tie lower branches to prevent damage and keep them out of your way.

- Dig a trench around the tree slightly larger and deeper than the desired rootball. See page 205 for recommendations on the size of rootball to make for the tree being moved.

- Undercut the rootball with your shovel. A sharp spade will make the job easier. Use hand pruners and loppers for larger or tougher roots.

- Slide a piece of burlap or canvas under the rootball. Have several friends lend a hand. Extra hands and strong backs will make the job easier and reduce the risk of dropping the tree and damaging the rootball.

- Set the tree in the prepared hole (wider but same depth as the rootball). Carefully cut away or slide the tarp away from the tree.

- Backfill the hole with existing soil, water, and mulch.

To protect young trees from rabbits and rodents, place a cylinder of ¼-inch mesh hardware cloth around the trunk. The cylinder should extend 18 to 24 inches above the soil and 2 to 3 inches below ground.

HONEYDEW

Have you ever parked your car under a large tree and returned to find the windshield spotted with a clear, sticky substance? It is not tree sap, but honeydew. If you could see into the tree canopy, you would find it full of aphids. These small, teardrop-shaped insects can be green, black, white, or peach in color. As these insects suck out plant juices, they secrete the excess as honeydew.

Occasionally a black fungus, sooty mold, grows on the honeydew. The fungus does not infect the plant, but it does block sunlight, causing leaves to yellow and even drop. Lady beetles often move in and eat the aphids before this pest is even discovered. Other years, you may need to step in with a strong blast of water from the garden hose. Insecticidal soap will help control aphids and remove the sooty mold.

JANUARY

- Work off the winter blues and a few pounds with a walk through a local arboretum, botanical garden, or your neighborhood. Look for trees that provide winter interest with evergreen foliage, interesting bark, fruit, or unique growth habit.

- Monitor and adjust snow removal to minimize winter injury. You can take steps to reduce damage this season and reduce winter injury next year. Check trees for snow and ice damage. Do not try to knock frozen snow and ice off trees. This can cause more damage than the snow and ice. Make notes on next year's calendar to adjust winter protection and prevent future problems.

- Walk through the landscape to check for animal damage and overwintering insects such as egg masses of tent caterpillars and gypsy and tussock moths. A little prevention now can save lots of headaches and extra work this season.

- Trees can be pruned during the dormant season. It is much easier to see the overall shape of the tree and what needs to be removed. Prune oaks in winter to reduce disease problems. See pages 188 and 236 for more pruning tips.

FEBRUARY

- Continue checking trees for overwintering insects. Egg masses of tent caterpillars look like small, shiny blobs of mud on stems. Gypsy and tussock moth egg masses are hairy masses found on tree trunks and branches. Remove these whenever they're found.

- Dormant oil sprays, such as Volck and All Seasons®, can be applied on warm days when temperatures are 40 degrees Fahrenheit or above for at least twelve hours. Dormant oil sprays are used to control many gall-causing insects (for aesthetic reasons only), some scales, aphids, and mites. Galls cause bumps on leaves while scale, aphids, and mites cause discolored and brown leaves. Make sure you have a problem before using this or any chemical.

- Save branches from flowering trees such as crabapples, magnolias, and pussy willows for indoor bloom.

MARCH

- Late winter and early spring are the best times to transplant trees. Moving trees can be tricky and heavy work. Save large, expensive, and special trees for professionals. They have the experience and equipment to move larger plants successfully. For more details, see page 202.

- Check the base of plants for girdling by rabbits and voles. Damage appears as a lighter area on the trunk. The damage interrupts the flow of water and nutrients between the roots and leaves. Severe damage (feeding around most of the trunk) can kill trees. When in doubt, wait and see if the tree will survive.

- Gardeners using tree wraps should remove them as temperatures warm. Research has shown wrapping tree trunks is not beneficial and can even be harmful to trees. If you use tree wraps, remove them in spring.

- Cankerworms are voracious insects that eat the leaves of oaks, elms, apples, crabapples, and many other trees. These brown or green wormlike insects can be seen munching on tree leaves. Fortunately, birds and weather usually keep these pests under control. Severe infestations can be controlled. Apply sticky bands around the trunks of trees that were severely defoliated the previous season. Use a band of fabric treated with a sticky material, such as Tangle-foot®, to avoid injury to the tree. Put sticky traps in place in spring and fall.

- Prune out black knot cankers. The cankers start out as swollen areas on the branches of flowering almonds, ornamental and edible plums, and cherries. Removing the cankers now reduces the risk of future infection.

- Complete pruning before trees leaf out. Pruning during leaf expansion increases the risk of trunk and branch damage. Birches, walnuts, and maples can be pruned in late winter. The running sap does not hurt the tree; it just makes the job messy.

APRIL

- Plan a special Arbor Day event for your family, friends, neighborhood, or school group. Arbor Day is the last Friday in April.

- Spring—before growth begins—is a good time to fertilize established trees. Let the plant and a soil test be your guides. Trees often get nutrients from decomposing mulch, lawn fertilizers, and grass clippings left on the lawn.

- Start checking crabapples, birches, and other ornamental trees for signs of eastern tent caterpillars. These wormlike insects build webbed nests in the crotches of tree branches. Remove or destroy the tent to control this pest.

- Birch leaf miners are insects that feed between the upper and lower surface of the leaves. Their feeding causes the leaves to turn brown. They do not kill the tree but add to the stress, making the white-barked birches more susceptible to borers. A soil systemic labeled for use on birches to control leaf miner can be applied in fall to prevent infestations.

- Apple scab is a common problem on crabapples and apples. This fungal disease causes black spots and eventual leaf drop. Raking and destroying infected leaves will reduce the source of disease. Fungicides labeled to control apple scab on crabapples will help reduce infection on susceptible trees. Consider hiring an arborist with the training and equipment to do the job safely. Better yet, replace susceptible trees with a more disease-resistant cultivar.

- Dead branches on spruce are often caused by cytospora canker. Remove branches that are infected and disinfect tools with rubbing alcohol or a solution of one part bleach to nine parts water. Mulch the soil under the tree and water during dry periods. Rhizosphaera needle blight has become a major problem. Consult a professional if you plan to treat it.

MAY

- Honeylocust plantbugs and leafhoppers begin feeding soon after buds break. This causes new growth to be distorted and sparse. Once the insects are done feeding, the trees will leaf out and be fine. Patience and proper care is the best control.

- Watch for signs of gypsy moth larvae. These wormlike insects eventually grow to 2 inches long and have two rows of red and blue warts on their backs. Catch caterpillars as they crawl down the tree trunk looking for shade during the day. Wrap a 12- to 18-inch-wide strip of burlap around the tree trunk at chest height. Tie a string around the burlap 6 inches from the top. Let the top 6 inches of burlap flop over the string. Check under the burlap every day between 2 and 6 p.m. Use gloves to remove caterpillars; drop them in soapy water to kill the insects.

- European pine sawflies are wormlike insects that feed in colonies. They will do a little dance for you when you get too close. Check mugo and other common landscape pines for feeding colonies of this insect. Even in large numbers, they are easy to control. Slide on a leather glove and smash the insects. Or prune out the infested branch and destroy the insects.

- Phomopsis blight is a fungal disease that attacks junipers. It is most prevalent in cool, wet springs. The infected branches turn brown and die. Remove infected branches and disinfect tools between each cut.

- Fireblight is a bacterial disease that infects susceptible crabapples, pears, and some of their relatives. Infected leaves to turn black and branch tips to curl. Avoid pruning crabapple trees during wet periods. Prune out infected branches 12 inches below the canker (sunken, discolored area) on the stem. Disinfect tools between cuts with rubbing alcohol or a solution of one part bleach to nine parts water.

JUNE

- Summer storms can leave you with broken branches and uprooted trees. Proper care and preventative pruning can help reduce storm damage to trees. Consider contacting a certified arborist (tree care professional) to evaluate the health and soundness of your trees. Together you can develop a long-term plan to maintain or improve your tree's storm resistance.

- Start watching for Japanese beetles. The small, metallic green beetles feed on over 300 species of plants. The beetles skeletonize the leaves by eating the leaf tissue and leaving the veins intact. The Japanese beetle population is growing and additional outbreaks are appearing throughout the Midwest. Stressed trees or those repeatedly defoliated by Japanese beetles would benefit from treatment. Consider applying a soil systemic in fall or early spring to reduce damage.

- Rake anthracnose-infected leaves as they drop from trees. This fungal disease causes brown spots on lower leaves of oak, maple, ash, black walnut, and sycamore. Though annoying, the disease is usually not life threatening. Sycamores may benefit from future preventative treatments.

JULY

- Monitor the landscape for opportunities to reduce maintenance and improve plant health. Create planting beds by joining several isolated trees together into one large garden. Fill the space with shrubs and perennials. Larger beds mean less mowing and eliminate the need for hand trimming around individual trees.

- Summer often means hot, dry weather. You may need to lend nature a hand as the temperatures rise and the summer rains cease.

- Aphid and mite populations can explode during hot, dry weather. They suck out plant juices, causing leaf discoloration and distorted growth. Nature usually keeps them in check with rains and natural predators. In dry seasons, use the garden hose and a strong blast of water to dislodge the insects and reduce the damage. The predaceous lady beetles are a great aphid control.

AUGUST

- Do not fertilize. Late-season fertilization can stimulate late-season growth that can be damaged or killed by cold winter temperatures.

- Surface roots are those roots that grow slightly above the soil and dull your mower blades as you cut the grass or interfere with the grass growing under your trees. Do not get out the axe. Those roots are important to the support and well-being of your tree. Mulch or plant groundcovers in the existing soil.

SEPTEMBER

- Fall is for planting. The cooler temperatures mean less watering for you and an easier time for the trees to get established. See October for a list of plants to avoid for fall planting. See the "Planting" section of the chapter introduction for planting details.

- This is the second-best time to transplant trees. Wait until the leaves drop and the trees are dormant. Remember, moving trees can be tricky and heavy work. Save large, expensive, and special trees for professionals. They have the experience and equipment to move larger plants successfully.

- As the beautiful fall leaves start dropping to the ground, the cry for raking help can be heard throughout the neighborhood. Before you start to grumble, consider recycling your leaves. It saves you work and improves the landscape.

RECOMMENDED ROOTBALL SIZE FOR TRANSPLANTING

TREE DIAMETER AT CHEST HEIGHT (SIZE IN INCHES)	ROOTBALL DIAMETER	ROOTBALL DEPTH
1/2	14	11
3/4	16	12
1	18	14
1¼	20	14
1½	22	15
1¾	24	16
2	28	19

- Fall, after the trees are dormant, is a good time to fertilize established trees. Let the plant and a soil test be your guide. Trees often get sufficient nutrients from decomposing mulch, lawn fertilizers, and grass clippings left on the lawn.

OCTOBER

- Fall is a great time to plant most trees and shrubs. But avoid planting trees that are slow to root. Wait until next spring and summer to plant the following:
  - *Acer rubrum* (red maple)
  - *Betula* species (birches)
  - *Crataegus* species (hawthorn)
  - *Gleditsia triacanthos* var. *inermis* (honeylocust)
  - *Liriodendron tulipifera* (tulip tree)
  - *Magnolia* species (magnolia)
  - *Malus* species (crabapples and apples)
  - *Nyssa sylvatica* (black gum)
  - *Populus* species (poplar)
  - *Prunus* species (ornamental and edible plums and cherries)
  - *Pyrus calleryana* (Callery pear)
  - *Quercus* species (oaks)
  - *Salix* species (willows)
  - *Tilia* species (lindens)
- Water as needed until the ground freezes. New plantings, moisture lovers, and evergreens benefit from a thorough watering before the ground freezes.
- Start installing animal fencing around new plantings, fruit trees, euonymus, and other animal favorites. Place a 4-foot-tall

cylinder of hardware cloth (reinforced wire screen) around these trees. Sink it several inches into the soil. This will keep voles and rabbits away from tree trunks.

- Fall pesticide applications can still be made for preventing damage from spruce galls, birch leaf miners, Japanese beetles, gypsy moths, and several other pests. Only treat trees that have suffered severe damage in the past.
- Install cankerworm traps if these voracious insects have caused repeated defoliation of oaks, elms, apples, crabapples, and many other trees. Apply sticky bands around the trunk of trees that were severely defoliated the previous season. Use a band of fabric treated with a sticky material, such as Tanglefoot®, to avoid injury to the tree. Place sticky traps in mid-October and remove in December.

NOVEMBER

- Consider having large tree additions made over winter. Some nurseries dig the rootball (leaving the tree in place) in fall. Once the rootball freezes, they move the tree to a pre-dug hole in its new location. The success rate has been good. It is expensive, but is one way to get an instant tree.
- Planning on having a living Christmas tree this holiday season? Dig the hole now before the ground freezes. Cover the hole with a board or fill it with mulch. Cover the soil to prevent freezing, making winter planting easier.
- Wrap arborvitae and upright junipers with strips of cotton, old nylon stockings, or bird netting. This will prevent the snow load damage that frequently occurs.
- Do not use tree wraps for winter protection. Research has shown that they do not protect the plant and can cause damage if left on the tree too long.
- Move containers to a garage without heat for the winter. Water the soil whenever it is dry. Or protect the roots of plants left outdoors by surrounding them with bales of hay.

DECEMBER

- Shovel first and salt last to minimize salt damage to landscape plants. Install barriers to protect roadside plants from salt spray.
- Keep the roots of living Christmas trees moist at all times. Minimize the time inside to maximize your chance of success. If the tree begins to grow, you are stuck with a big houseplant until next spring.
- Be careful when hanging holiday lights on trees and shrubs. Make sure the lights are made for outdoor use. Loosely attach the lights to the tree branches and trunks. Remove lights in spring before growth begins. Tightly wrapped lights can girdle a tree in one season.

VEGETABLES &
HERBS
for the Midwest

Why should you grow your own food? Besides saving money, you will improve the flavor, increase the nutritional value, and add some fun to your meals. Try your hand at growing the ingredients for some of your favorite recipes. It is wonderful to be able to walk out your backdoor and harvest tomatoes, eggplants, basil, or whatever herbs and vegetables you need to make dinner. And nothing improves your recipe better than the flavor of fresh vegetables and herbs from the garden.

You can use herbs and vegetables to brighten up the landscape. Select plants with colorful fruits, fragrance, and other decorative features. Mix purple ruffle basil with classic zinnia, create an edge with parsley and alyssum, or fill a spring or fall planter with chard, pansies, and colorful lettuce.

Once you harvest your bounty, share with those less fortunate. Plant an extra tomato, row of beans, and more for the hungry. Your surplus produce can provide the hungry in your community with nutritious food. Contact Garden Writers of America at www.gardenwriters.org and click on Plant a Row, or call 877-492-2727 for more information.

PLANNING

Start with a plan before you dig up your backyard. Everyone is eager to plant, but you may find yourself all alone weeding in July—though that can be a nice escape from life's pressures and frustrations!

Take some time to meet with the family and friends who will help plant, maintain, and use the produce. Consider their eating habits, likes, and lifestyles as you plan your herb and vegetable additions.

Make sure the vegetables are suitable for our climate and your garden location. The vegetables need to tolerate the weather and start producing with time to harvest within your growing season.

SELECTING A GROWING LOCATION

Find an area that receives full sun and has moist, well-drained soil. You may need to be creative if you have a small or shady yard or one with poor soil. Carve out small areas or use containers for your garden.

Fruiting and flowering vegetables, such as tomatoes, broccoli, and squash, as well as most herbs, need full sun. These produce best when they receive eight to twelve hours of full sun. Plant root crops, such as radishes and beets, in full sun to part shade. They need at least six hours of sunlight to flourish. Save leafy crops, such as spinach and lettuce, these prefer full sun but tolerate shadier areas. They can get by with as little as four hours of sun.

Use a traditional garden style if space is not an issue. Plant vegetables in rows running east/west. Place the tallest vegetables in the back (north side) to reduce the shade cast on other, shorter plants.

Try some of the space-saving techniques described on page 228 to get the most produce from your garden. Grow peas and beans on trellises, lettuce in blocks, interplant short-season crops with long-season plants, or plant three different crops in one row. All of these techniques can be used in large or small gardens.

Give container gardening a try. It's great for those with small spaces or if you want to keep a few of your favorite veggies handy for you or your guests to enjoy. Grow a pot of your favorite summer herbs and grow it next to the grill. Or plant mint in a pot so guests can pluck a leaf for their ice tea or mojito.

SOIL PREPARATION

Once your plan is in place and snow has melted you can start preparing your garden space. For new beds, you'll need to remove or kill the grass and any weeds. Cut out sod and reuse it to fill in bare areas in the lawn. Or kill the grass using chemical or non-chemical methods. Edge the garden with a

Herb gardens can be pretty as well as practical.

spade or edger. Use a total vegetation killer containing glyphosate, such as Roundup®, to kill the existing grass or weeds. Read and follow all label directions before using this or any chemical. Or cover the garden with clear plastic for six to eight weeks during the hottest part of the summer to kill grass and weeds without the aid of chemicals.

Take a soil test to determine how much and what type of fertilizer you should use on your garden. Contact a state certified lab or your local university Extension service for details on taking and submitting a soil sample. The results will tell you how much and what type of fertilizer to add. If soil test information is not available, incorporate 1 pound of a low-nitrogen fertilizer or 3 pounds of a slow-release fertilizer per 100 square feet in spring.

In fall or spring, add several inches of organic matter, such as peat moss or compost, to the top 12 inches of soil. Organic matter helps improve the drainage of heavy clay soils and the water-holding capacity of sandy soils.

Always check soil moisture before digging in. Grab a handful of soil and gently squeezing it into a ball. Tap the ball with your finger. If it breaks apart, it is ready to work. Otherwise, wait a few days for the soil to dry. Working wet soil results in clods that last all season.

And don't overlook the free resources in your own backyard. Use shredded fall leaves to improve the soil. Shred fallen leaves with your mower. Dig them into the top 12 inches of soil each fall. These will decompose over the winter.

Consider creating raised beds in poorly drained soils or for easier access. Use existing soil or bring in new soil to create the raised bed. Order a quality garden mix from a reliable topsoil provider. Raised beds can be fancy or strictly utilitarian. Raising the soil improves drainage and helps warm soils faster in the spring.

Make raised beds at least 6 to 8 inches high for better results and 3 to 5 feet wide for easier access. Use long-lasting timbers, plastic lumber, interlocking block, or other edible plant-friendly material to hold the soil in place. (Edible plant-friendly material means no creosote-soaked wood or anything else that can leach chemicals into your food garden.)

Straw bale, lasagna, and Square Foot gardening are other ways to deal with problem soil with quicker results. Visit the library or bookstore and check out Mel Bartholomew's book *All New Square Foot Gardening*; *Straw Bale Gardens: The Breakthrough Method for Growing Vegetables Anywhere, Earlier and with No Weeding* by Joel Karsten; and *Lasagna Gardening* by Patricia Lanza.

STARTING PLANTS INDOORS

Extend your gardening season and plant selection by starting plants from seed. This may be the only way to get transplants of new and unusual plants and cultivars.

Start by locating an area where you can place flats of plants and artificial lights. It can be next to a window on a table or on shelves in the basement. Always use clean containers, flats, and starter mix to prevent problems with damping off. Disinfect used containers with a solution of one part bleach to nine parts water.

Keep the growing mix warm and moist until the seeds sprout. Cover seed trays with plastic or mist the soil to keep it moist during the germination process. Remove the plastic once the seeds sprout. Water flats and containers thoroughly. Pour off any excess that collects beneath the container. Check seedlings every day.

Move containers to a well-lit location as soon as any green starts to show. A southern window will work for some plants, but artificial lights will give you better results. Keep artificial lights 4 to 6 inches above the tops of the seedlings.

Keep the soil moist, but not waterlogged. Excess water can lead to damping off (a fungal disease) and root rot. Check plants daily to make sure they do not dry out. Seedlings do not develop well and often die if exposed to dry conditions.

Check the seed packets and plant profiles for planting times. Most packets will give you information on when to start seeds indoors or when to plant them outdoors.

EXTEND THE GROWING SEASON

Get a jump on the season by using some of the homemade or commercial season-extending devices. Gardeners have long used glass bottles, plastic, cold frames, and other devices to trap heat and protect plants from frost.

Start a month or more earlier than normal by warming the soil. Prepare the garden and cover it with clear plastic for two weeks. This warms the soil and helps germinate annual weed seeds. Lightly cultivate to remove weeds without bringing new weed seeds to the surface.

Plant seeds and transplants in the warm soil. Cover with a polypropylene row cover fabric, such as Reemay®, All-Purpose Garden Fabric, or Harvest-Guard. These products let air, light, and water in while trapping heat near the plants. Drape the fabric over your garden bed or plantings. Leave enough slack for plants to grow. Anchor the edges with stones, boards, or wickets.

Leave the row cover in place until both the day and night temperatures are warm. Covering plants through the early weeks of the growing season can keep them warm on those cool nights, speed up growth, and reduce the time until harvest.

PLANTING

Memorial Day is traditionally the biggest planting date. The worst of the cold weather has passed and the soil has started to warm for those gardening in the north. Those gardening in southern areas of the Midwest have been gardening for a while. Adjust your planting times to better match the weather and crops you are planting.

Cool-weather crops, such as broccoli and cabbage, can be planted outdoors earlier. These plants tolerate cooler air and soil temperatures. They also taste better if they can be harvested before the heat of summer or harvested in fall.

Wait until both the air and soil warm to plant eggplants, peppers, melons, and other warm-weather crops.

Whether you're planting early or at the traditional time, you will need to help transplants adjust to their home outdoors. Many garden centers do this for us. But if you grew your transplants or purchased plants direct from the greenhouse, you will need to "harden off" these tender plants.

Start this process two weeks prior to planting. Stop fertilizing and allow the soil to dry slightly before watering again. Move the plants outdoors into a cold frame, sheltered location, or under season-extending fabric.

Gradually increase the amount of direct sun the plants receive each day. Start with one to two hours per day until it is comparable to its final planting location. Cover or bring the plants indoors during cold nights and days.

Once your transplants are hardened off you're ready to move them into a properly prepared garden. Gently squeeze the sides of the pot and slide, don't pull, the plant out of its container. Tease tangled roots apart to encourage them to grow into the surrounding soil. Plant at the same depth they were growing in the containers. Tomatoes are the exception. Trench or plant tall leggy tomato transplants deeper to encourage roots to develop along the stem. See the tomato profile for detailed directions.

Transplants growing in peat pots and other biodegradable pots are handled just a bit differently. Remove the lip of the pot so it does not protrude above the soil. Remove the bottom and consider slicing through the sides to speed up rooting. Plant transplants grown in these types of biodegradable containers, pot and all. Check the manufacturer's label for any other specific planting guidelines.

Sow seeds of beans, peas, cucumbers, and other vegetables directly in the garden. Dig a furrow in properly prepared soil. Set seeds at proper depth, usually twice the seed's diameter, at the spacing recommended on the seed packet.

Small seeds can be challenging. Mix them with sand or vermiculite to help properly space the seeds. Some gardeners like to mix radish and carrot seeds. You'll harvest the quick-maturing radishes first, leaving room for the carrots to grow. Or purchase seed tapes. The fine seeds are "glued" onto a strip of paper or other biodegradable material. Dig the planting furrow, roll out the tape, cover with soil, and water.

Once the seedling develop a set of true leaves, start thinning. Remove or trim seedlings to their final spacing. This is the amount of space the plants will need to reach full size. Use thinned greens of radishes, turnips, and beets to dress up salads and sandwiches.

WATERING

Proper watering is essential in growing healthy productive plants. Excess water can lead to root rot and other fungal diseases. Drought stress causes stunted growth and low productivity.

Check seedlings and new plants several times a week. Water often enough to keep the top 3 to 4 inches moist. Reduce watering after the first few weeks as the root systems expand.

Water established plants when the top 3 inches begin to dry. Water enough to moisten the top 6 to 8 inches where the roots are growing. This is usually done by applying 1 inch of water each week. Water gardens growing in clay soil once a week. Apply half the needed water twice a week in sandy soils. Always adjust watering to fit the soil, weather, and plant needs.

Save water and reduce the risk of disease by watering early in the morning, if possible. This reduces water lost to evaporation in the heat of the day and disease problems caused by wet foliage at night.

Mulch the soil with evergreen needles, shredded leaves, grass clippings (herbicide-free), straw, or other organic material. A 2- to 3-inch layer will help conserve moisture and reduce weeds. Till the mulch into the soil each fall to improve drainage in clay soils and water-holding capacity in sandy soils.

FERTILIZING

Start with a soil test. Take representative samples, 4 to 6 inches deep, from several areas of the garden. Send it to a state certified lab or contact your local university Extension service for details. The results will tell you how much and what type of fertilizer to add.

Or add a yearly total of 3 pounds of low-nitrogen fertilizer per 100 square feet. This can be applied in one or several applications. Use a slow-release formulation if applying all 3 pounds in the spring. Or add 1 pound at planting and follow-up applications one and two months later.

Use a fertilizer spreader to apply needed nutrients to large gardens. Try a smaller hand spreader or perforated coffee can for small areas. Or sprinkle fertilizer by hand onto small areas.

Add several inches of organic matter to the top 6 to 12 inches of soil. This can be done in the fall or spring. Spring applications of organic matter and fertilizer can be tilled into the soil at the same time.

PESTS

A healthy plant starts with proper care. Prepare the soil, and grow herbs and vegetables in the best possible location.

Avoid problems by selecting the most pest-resistant varieties available. New introductions of more pest-resistant varieties are made each year. Check the catalogs and your university Extension service for the most up-to-date information.

Rotate crops to reduce the buildup and risk of disease and insects. Switch out planting locations with unrelated plants. For example, move tomatoes and their relatives, such as peppers and eggplants, to an area where you grew cabbage last year. Move the cabbage and its relatives to the area where you had beans last year. Those with very little space may just be able to move their tomatoes to opposite ends of the garden each year. Do the best you can.

Adjust planting times to avoid pests. Planting beans and corn too early results in poor germination and more risk of seed corn maggot damage. Their feeding causes poor germination and deformed seedlings that fail to develop. Wait for the soil to warm to avoid this problem.

Mix things up to reduce pest problems. Plant unrelated crops near one another. Crops tend to have different pest problems, so this helps reduce the buildup of insects and disease. At the least, it makes the insects work a little harder for their favorite foods.

Go vertical. Trellises and teepees help increase the light and air reaching pole beans, squash, and other vine crops. This improves the growing conditions and reduces the risk of mildew, anthracnose, and other diseases.

Mulch the soil to keep soilborne fungi away from the plants. It also suppresses weed growth. Weeds not only compete with plants for water and nutrients, but they also harbor insects and diseases that can infect your herbs and vegetables.

Apply water directly to the soil, minimizing wet foliage and risk of disease. Use a watering wand to extend your reach and get the water to the soil. Or try a soaker hose or drip irrigation to make the job easier.

Continual cleanup reduces insect and disease problems. Remove weeds and debris that can harbor pests. Clean the garden each fall to prevent disease and insects from overwintering in the garden.

Once pests occur, you will need to decide on a course of action. First, have the pest properly identified. Contact your local garden center or Extension office for help. They can tell you whether control is needed. Always consider the most eco-friendly method when trying to manage garden pests.

Remove small infestations of insects or infected leaves. This is often enough to limit damage and still have a productive harvest.

Use yellow pans filled with soapy water to trap aphids, whiteflies, and other common insect pests. Cover plantings with fine netting or row covers to keep out unwanted insects.

Consider using some of the more environmentally friendly products on the market if more intervention is needed. Soaps, Neem oil, *Bacillus thuringiensis*, and others control specific pests, while reducing the risk to beneficial insects, wildlife, and people.

Use a pesticide as your last resort. Read and follow label directions carefully before applying any chemical—remember, you plan to eat part of the plant you are treating. Leave sufficient time between the last application and harvest.

Now that you know the basics you can grow just about any herb or vegetable suited to your climate. Here are a few of the more popular you may want to include in your garden.

ASPARAGUS
Asparagus officinalis

Why It's Special—This perennial vegetable provides years of tasty harvests. Small space gardeners can grow it as a backdrop to their flowers. Those with more room may want to dedicate one end of their vegetable garden to this plant.

How to Plant & Grow—Plant one- or two-year-old asparagus roots 12 inches apart in trenches 36 inches apart. Dig the trenches 6 to 8 inches deep and 9 to 12 inches wide. Set the asparagus in the trench, spreading the roots away from the crown of the plant. Cover with 2 inches of soil. Gradually add soil throughout the season until the trench is filled. Water thoroughly whenever the top few inches of soil are crumbly and slightly moist.

Care & Problems—Once established asparagus is pretty drought tolerant. Remove perennial weeds and mulch the bed to prevent them. Handpick any common and spotted asparagus beetles and their worm-like larvae found feeding on the plants, and drop them into a can of soapy water.

Harvest & Best Selection—Start harvesting stems the following year for one month or six to eight weeks if you planted two-year-old crowns. Snap by bending or cutting 6- to 8-inch-long spears off just below the soil surface. Allow the ferny tops to grow after harvesting and stand throughout winter. 'Mary Washington' is still a favorite. But consider one of the male varieties, like 'Jersey Giant' and 'Jersey Supreme', that produces more spears than the female plants.

BASIL
Ocimum basilicum

Why It's Special—Whether it's pesto, ratatouille, or pizza that's your specialty, planting and using your own basil can add to the convenience of cooking and flavor to the dish. Mix this annual herb with ornamental and edible flowers in the garden or containers.

How to Plant & Grow—Grow basil in moist well-drained soil. Purchase plants or start seeds indoors about six weeks before the last spring frost or directly in the garden after about a week of 50-degree temperatures. Move hardened off transplants into the garden after the danger of frost has passed.

Care & Problems—Seedlings are very sensitive to cool temperatures and dry soils. Once the plants are chilled they never seem to recover. Mulch the soil to conserve moisture, suppress weeds, and improve the soil.

Harvest & Best Selection—Basil reaches maturity in seventy to eighty days. Remove individual leaves or harvest short stems as needed. Regular harvest will encourage more growth. Harvest just before flowering for maximum flavor and midday for drying. Sweet basil is one of the most commonly grown. 'Purple Ruffles' has deep purple frilly leaves, making it a good choice for edible ornamental gardens and containers. 'Spicy Globe' forms tight mounds of small leaves. 'Crispum', also known as lettuce-leaf basil, produces large leaves perfect for sandwiches, pizza, and salads. 'Magical Michael' is an All-America Selections winner with purple stems and flowers.

BEAN
Phaseolus species

Why It's Special—After a winter of frozen or canned green beans most gardeners can't wait to pick a few snap beans to eat right in the garden. Those with limited space, bad backs, or arthritis should consider going vertical. You'll save space, but you'll also get an extra picking from pole beans, while making picking much easier.

How to Plant & Grow—Grow beans in the garden or container, or even a hanging basket. Or try the Native American companion planting of corn, pole beans, and squash known as "Three Sisters." Plant snap or dry bean seeds directly in the garden after the danger of frost has passed and the soil has warmed. Planting in cool, wet soil increases the risk of poor germination and corn maggot attacks. Space bush beans 3 to 4 inches apart and space pole beans 6 to 10 inches apart.

Care & Problems—Wait for the soil to warm to avoid problems with seed corn maggots. Cover beans with a row cover to prevent damage or treat with an insecticide if bean beetles are a problem.

Harvest & Best Selection—Beans are ready to harvest in fifty to eighty days, depending on the variety. Harvest snap beans when the shell is tender and before seeds swell and show. Wait for the outer shell to dry when harvesting dry beans. 'Scarlet Runner' beans have colorful flowers and edible pods. 'Burgundy' produces purple pods that turn green when they're cooked.

BEET
Beta vulgaris

Why It's Special—All parts of a beet are edible. Use the greens cooked or serve them fresh in a salad. Bake, pickle, or grill the swollen root, and save some juice for making cold Russian borscht.

How to Plant & Grow—Plant beets as soon as the soil is workable. Plant every three to four weeks to harvest fresh beets all season long. Plant these small seeds ½ inch deep and 1 inch apart. Thin to 3 inches.

Care & Problems—Beets almost always need thinning. Poor germination is a problem if the soil surface dries or crusts over. Try planting, moistening, and covering the row with a wooden lath. Remove this small narrow board as soon as the seeds sprout. Proper thinning, well-drained soil, and raised beds will encourage root development. Cover plants with row covers if you're eating the greens. Spinach leafminer has been a problem. Dislodge aphids with a strong blast of water or use insecticidal soap.

Harvest & Best Selection—Beets mature in fifty to sixty days. Harvest the greens when the leaves are 4 to 6 inches. Harvest both the greens and beets when the roots are 1 to 1½ inches in diameter. Harvest when the beets are 1½ to 3 inches in diameter if only using the roots. 'Detroit Dark Red' remains a favorite. 'Sweetheart' is an extra-sweet red. Try 'di Chioggia' that's bright red outside with bands of red and white inside. Grow 'Green Top Bunching' for superior greens.

BROCCOLI
Brassica oleracea var. *italic*

Why It's Special—Broccoli is one of the most nutritious vegetables and is relatively easy to grow in a garden or container. Eat it fresh on a relish tray or in a salad, add to soups, or steam and serve it as a side dish.

How to Plant & Grow—This cool-weather vegetable thrives and tastes best when it's grown and harvested in cool Midwest springs and falls. Start seeds indoors or purchase plants for a late spring harvest. Plant vigorous transplants outdoors in early spring. Plant seeds in midsummer and set transplants in the garden in summer for a fall harvest. Plant seeds ½ inch deep and thin seeds or plant seedlings to 18 inches apart.

Care & Problems—Transplants left in their containers too long often fail to form a full-sized head. High temperatures and dry conditions can cause bitter flavor. Aphids and cabbageworms can be problems. See the monthly entries for management options.

Harvest & Best Selection—Broccoli is ready to harvest in sixty to seventy days. For the best flavor, harvest when the flowerhead is purplish green, full-sized, and before the buds open revealing the yellow blooms. Mature plants will tolerate a light frost that can improve the flavor. Remove the flowerhead leaving the plant intact to form smaller side shoots. Harvest and enjoy as long as they keep producing and flavor is desirable. 'Green Comet' matures in fifty-five days and is heat tolerant. 'Cruiser' tolerates dry conditions, and 'Green Giant' is tolerant of extreme conditions.

BRUSSELS SPROUTS
Brassica oleracea var. *gemmifera*

Why It's Special—You love 'em or you hate 'em. But the delicious flavor of grilled Brussels sprouts has put this vegetable on the menu of many restaurants and perhaps your table. Use this tall edible as a background in your flower beds, a vertical accent in large containers, or in blocks and rows in the vegetable garden.

How to Plant & Grow—Purchase transplants or start from seed. Plant seeds four to five weeks before moving transplants into the garden. Place hardened-off plants in the garden in early summer, at least 100 days before the average first fall frost. Space 24 inches apart.

Care & Problems—You can speed up the development of the sprouts by removing the growing tip about three weeks before harvest. It develops a bitter flavor in hot and dry conditions. Time planting for a fall harvest. The cooler temperatures, even a light frost, result in better flavor. Cabbage worms and aphids can be a problems.

Harvest & Best Selection—Don't let the catalog pictures fool you. You don't need to pluck off the leaves as you harvest the sprouts. Keep in mind the more leaves on the plant, the more energy they produce and the bigger the sprouts will grow. Harvest sprouts from the bottom up when they are about an inch in diameter and firm. 'Jade Cross' and 'Valiant' are available at most garden centers and produce in ninety days. 'Bubbles' is heat tolerant, resists rust, and matures in eighty-two days. 'Prince Marvel' produces sweeter sprouts.

CABBAGE
Brassica oleracea capitata

Why It's Special—Whether your favorite is slaw, sauerkraut, or stuffed cabbage leaves you will enjoy growing, harvesting, and cooking your own homegrown cabbage. Use the bold texture and form of this plant to create a focal point in large containers and flower beds. Or plant in mass.

How to Plant & Grow—Purchase plants or start from seed. Sow seeds indoors six to eight weeks before the last spring frost. Or plant seeds directly in the garden as soon as the soil is workable for an early season harvest or plant midsummer for a fall harvest. Move transplants into the garden in early spring. Hardened-off plants can tolerate a light frost. Space 12 inches apart.

Care & Problems—Time planting for early-season and late-season harvests when the temperatures are cool. Provide ample moisture and watch for cabbageworms and aphids. Splitting can occur when the cabbage heads are mature and after a heavy rain. Look for cultivars that resist splitting and harvest in a timely manner to reduce the risk of splitting (cracked heads).

Harvest & Best Selection—Harvest when the heads are full sized and firm, in 60 to 100 days. Remove just the head, leaving the rest of the plant in place. Four or five buds will sprout and develop into small size cabbages. 'Savoy Queen' is heat tolerant and has crinkled leaves. 'Ruby Bail' is a red cabbage; it's slow to crack and both heat and cold tolerant.

CARROT
Daucus carota

Why It's Special—Packed full of vitamin A, this nutritious root crop comes in a rainbow of colors and various sizes and shapes. You can find yellow, orange, red, and purple carrots that are long and thin, short and stout, or round like a radish!

How to Plant & Grow—Sow seeds directly in the garden two to three weeks before the last spring frost or in midsummer for a fall harvest. Plant seeds ¼ inch below the surface. Cover with a wood lath or clear plastic to secure seeds and keep them moist. Remove it as soon as the seeds sprout. Some gardeners mix quick-maturing radish seeds to help mark the rows and better space the carrot seeds. Space 2 to 3 inches.

Care & Problems—Proper soil preparation and thinning are critical for straight, quality carrots. For better root development, grow short and half long types in heavy or rocky soils and when growing in containers.

Harvest & Best Selection—Carrots mature in sixty to seventy days and can be dug when they are ½ to 1 inch in diameter. Leave some of your fall harvest in the garden for winter storage. Mulch after the ground freezes and harvest as needed or during a winter thaw. 'Scarlet Nantes' is 6 inches long, crisp, and sweet; 'Orbit' is round; 'Purple Haze' is an All-America Selections winner that is purple on the outside orange on the inside. The purple color fades when it's cooked.

CAULIFLOWER
Brassica oleracea var. *botrytis*

Why It's Special—Cauliflower is not just the white vegetable your mother put on your plate. Colorful varieties can brighten a salad or vegetable tray.

How to Plant & Grow—Cauliflower is a close relative of broccoli and cabbage but a bit more sensitive to its growing environment. You'll have the best luck growing these from transplants. Plant hardened-off plants in the garden in spring no sooner than two to three weeks before the last spring frost. It is more cold sensitive than its relatives. Plant in mid- to late summer for a fall harvest. Space 12 inches apart.

Care & Problems—Cauliflower can be challenging to grow. Heat, cold, and drought can prevent the plant from forming a full-sized head. Keep soil evenly moist. Blanch the head when it is about the size of a quarter. Tie leaves over the head to block out the sunlight. The leaves of self-blanching varieties naturally fold up over the head to help block the sunlight.

Harvest & Best Selection—Cauliflower is ready to harvest in fifty to sixty days when the heads are 6 to 8 inches in diameter. This is usually five to twelve days after blanching begins. 'Snow King' is very heat tolerant, 'Violet Queen' (actually a type of broccoli) needs no blanching and has purple heads that turn green when cooked, and 'Green Goddess' broccoflower hybrid is lime green and easy to grow.

CHARD
Beta vulgaris spp. *cicla*

Why It's Special—This edible beauty, also known as Swiss chard, leaf beet, and spinach beet, will brighten your dinner table and landscape. You'll get the best flavor and nutritional value when you harvest this easy-to-grow vegetable from your own garden.

How to Plant & Grow—Purchase plants or sow seeds directly in the garden in early to mid-spring when the soil temperatures are about 50 degrees. For many in the northern Midwest a spring planting, properly harvested, can last through fall. Or plant in midsummer for a fall harvest. Sow seeds ½ inch deep and 4 inches apart. Thin seedlings to 8 to 12 inches or remove every other plant when they reach 6 to 8 inches. Use thinned ones for greens and allow the remaining plants to reach full size.

Care & Problems—Avoid the bitter flavor that occurs with hot weather by growing chard as a spring and fall crop.

Harvest & Best Selection—Chard is ready to harvest in about forty to fifty days. Remove only the outer leaves when a plant is 8 to 12 inches tall. Chard will continue to produce throughout the season. 'Rainbow', 'Bright Lights', and the Australian heirloom 'Five Color Silverbeet' are popular for their colorful stems of red, orange, yellow, and white. 'Neon Lights' ups the color intensity a notch. 'Rhubarb' is favored for their red stems, and 'Fordhook Giant' has sweet and tender flavor that has made it a traditional favorite.

CHIVES
Allium schoenoprasum

Why It's Special—This hardy perennial herb with attractive and edible purple flowers is easy to grow. Use it in a container, flower gardens, or the corner of your vegetable garden.

How to Plant & Grow—Start from seeds, sets (like onions), plants, or divisions. Plants can be added to the garden anytime during the growing season.

Care & Problems—Choose a permanent site in full sun to light shade with well-drained soil. Chive is a vigorous self-seeder. Pick off flowers when they start to turn brown to prevent having hundreds of seedlings next year. Divide clumps every three to four years to keep plants vigorous. To extend the season, pot up a small clump in fall about a month before the first frost and bring it inside once winter hits. Chive has no serious pest problems and rarely needs additional fertilizer.

Harvest & Best Selection—Harvest throughout the season. Use a sharp knife or garden scissors to cut leaves above 2 inches above the ground once plants have reached a height of 6 inches. If you cut back an entire clump, allow it several weeks to regenerate before harvesting again. Harvest the spring flowers when they're fully colored. Break apart and use them to add a little flavor and color to your dishes. The species (*Allium schoenoprasum*) is usually grown for cooking use. There are some cultivars selected for their showier flowers. 'Forescate' has bright rose-red flowers.

CILANTRO/CORIANDER
Coriandum sativum

Why It's Special—One plant—two names. When grown for its leaves, this annual plant is called cilantro. You'll recognize its strong flavor in salsa and other Mexican dishes. When grown for its dried brown seeds, it goes by coriander. Coriander is commonly used in Indian dishes

How to Plant & Grow—Sow seeds in spring after frost danger, ½ inch deep where you want the plants; seedlings do not transplant well. Sow seeds every three weeks until late summer to have a regular supply of leaves. Plants dry out easily, so plan to water as needed. Plants grow quickly, eventually reaching about 18 inches in height, and go to seed in about two months.

Care & Problems—Seeds need adequate water to germinate, so keep soil moist. Plants will bolt (go to seed) quickly in hot weather, after which the foliage is not as tasty. If you want seeds for coriander, allow plants to go to seed. Let a few plants self-sow. There are no real pest problems.

Harvest & Best Selection—Pinch off leaves as needed for cilantro. Seeds ripen in late summer or fall; collect them before they fall to the ground for coriander. 'Delfino' is an All-America Selections winner with finer fern foliage. 'Caribe', 'Slo Bolt', 'Santo', and 'Leisure' all tend to go to seed slower than the species.

CUCUMBER
Cucumis sativus

Why It's Special—This versatile warm-season vegetable can be pickled or used fresh in salads, on a relish tray, or added to a glass of water or other favorite summer beverages. Save space or add vertical interest to the garden by growing vining types up a trellis or on a fence.

How to Plant & Grow—Sow seeds directly in the garden after the danger of frost has passed and soil has reached 65 degrees. Or start seeds indoors about three weeks before the last frost date for an earlier harvest. Make a midsummer planting for a fall harvest. Plant in rows, beds, or in hills, spaced according to the package.

Care & Problems—Plants need warmth and ample water to produce. Use floating row covers to jump-start the season and protect plants from cucumber beetles that carry bacterial wilt. Remove the row covers when plants set flower for pollination to occur. Bacterial wilt causes plants to suddenly collapse. Discolored foliage and malformed fruit are caused by moisture stress and nutrient deficiencies. Watch for anthracnose and powdery mildew.

Harvest & Best Selection—Plants start bearing in fifty to sixty days. Pick fruit when it's 1½ to 2½ inches long for sweet pickles, 3 to 4 inches for dills, and 6 to 8 inches for slicers. Large fruits are generally seedy and bitter. Burpless are the exception; they can be picked when they're 10 to 12 inches long. Try 'Northern Pickling' and 'Liberty' (pickling); 'Marketmore 76', and 'Fanfare' (slicing); and 'Salad Bush' and 'Spacemaster' (containers).

EGGPLANT
Solanum melongena

Why It's Special—New colorful and compact varieties make eggplant a great choice for edible landscapes, containers, and the traditional vegetable garden.

How to Plant & Grow—Purchase transplants for the greatest success. You can start seeds indoors when starting tomatoes and peppers, eight to ten weeks before the last expected spring frost. Eggplant is very frost sensitive. Wait for soil and air to warm before planting hardened-off transplants outdoors. Space 18 to 24 inches.

Care & Problems—Cover with row covers to protect them from frost and keep them warm on those chilly nights early in the season. This will speed fruiting and increase productivity. Planting too early when the soil and air are cold is the biggest problem. Flea beetles and verticillium wilt can also be problems.

Harvest & Best Selection—Harvest when fruit is full sized and eggplant's skin is glossy. Once the fruit is spongy and skin is dull the texture and flavor have greatly declined. Use the thumb test to check for ripeness. Gently press on the fruit with your thumb. If it bounces back, yet leaves a small impression, it is ready to harvest. The All-America Selections winner 'Hansel' and 'Gretel' are fingerling types that hold their flavor and texture longer than most. 'Fairy Tale' has small purple eggplants with cream or lavender markings. Large oval cultivars 'Black Beauty is purple and 'Ghostbuster' is white and a bit sweeter. 'Ichiban', 'Slim Jim', and 'Little Fingers' have elongated fruit.

GARLIC
Allium sativum

Why It's Special—This popular herb is used in a wide range of dishes. You'll find two types. Softnecks, most often found at supermarkets, have pliable stems and store well. Hardnecks have stiff central stems that curl at the top. They are more cold hardy but do not store as well. You can save some of your largest homegrown cloves for replanting the next fall.

How to Plant & Grow—Plant individual cloves outdoors about six weeks before the soil freezes, around early October. Plant cloves, pointed end up, 2 inches deep, spaced 5 inches apart.

Care & Problems—Mulch after planting to retain soil moisture. Apply a second layer of winter mulch after the ground freezes. Plants need well-drained soil. Stop watering once the foliage begins to turn yellow or fall over. Cut off flower stalks to encourage bulb development. It has no pest problems.

Harvest & Best Selection—Bulbs can be harvested when about three-fourths of the tops have yellowed. Carefully dig up a couple plants to see if the bulbs have well-developed cloves that are beginning to separate. Spread plants, including roots, in a single layer on a screen in a warm, dry, airy location to dry. After two to three weeks, when bulbs are dry, remove excess dirt, roots, and tops, leaving 1 inch of stem. 'Spanish Roja' and 'Carpathian' are hardneck types that send up a scape that can be harvested and eaten when it's immature. 'Inchhelium Red', Idaho Silverskin', and 'Persian Star' are softneck types.

KALE & COLLARDS
Brassica oleracea

Why It's Special—Nutritious, cold tolerant, and easy to grow make kale and collards a good choice for in-ground gardens and containers. The blue-green smooth, crinkled, or fringed foliage adds to its beauty.

How to Plant & Grow—Plant kale in early spring or midsummer for a fall harvest. Hardened-off transplants can be moved into the garden three to four weeks before the average last spring frost. Start plants indoors eight to ten weeks before the last spring frost. Space 12 to 18 inches apart. Sow seeds of collards directly in the garden in early spring and again in midsummer. Sow 6 inches apart.

Care & Problems—Thin collards (really, an early harvest) as plants touch. Leave 18 inches between plants. Cabbageworms, aphids, flea beetles, and a few diseases can be problems. Prevent insect damage with row covers and rotate plantings to minimize disease problems.

Harvest & Best Selection—Harvest the outer leaves of both when they are 10 to 12 inches long. Plants will continue to produce new leaves so you can continue to harvest. Some gardeners prefer to harvest a whole collards plant and just use the tender center leaves. A light fall frost not only won't hurt the plants, it *improves* the flavor. Try 'Blue Ridge' (curled), 'Winterbor' (curled), 'Nagoya Garnish Red' (red leaves with green fringe), and 'Red Russian' kale cultivars. 'Champion' (good cold tolerance), 'Flash' (early with good heat tolerance), and 'Vates' (low growing with smooth leaves) are good collards varieties to try.

LETTUCE
Lactuca sativa

Why It's Special—Cool-season leaf lettuce is easy to grow and gives such fast results even the most impatient gardener is happy. Plus, the colorful leaves make nice additions to container gardens and flower beds.

How to Plant & Grow—Leaf, butterhead, and Romaine are the most popular in the home garden. Leaf and butterhead lettuces perform best in cooler weather, but modern breeding has produced cultivars that are more heat tolerant and slow to set seed (bolt). Plant the small seeds on prepared soil and press them lightly into the soil. They need light to germinate. Sow seeds as soon as the soil can be worked, and again in mid- to late summer for a fall crop. Make successive sowings every ten days to extend your harvest.

Care & Problems—Lettuces require an even supply of water. Once hot weather arrives, most lettuces will bolt and need to be removed. Fence your garden or use other tactics to prevent rabbit damage. Watch for aster yellows, slugs, aphids, and signs of other insects and diseases

Harvest & Best Selection—Begin harvesting the outer leaves of leaf lettuce in about forty days when they are 4 to 6 inches tall. The plants will continue producing new leaves so you can keep harvesting. Pick head lettuces when they're firm and fully formed. 'Oakleaf' and 'Red Sails' are heat-resistant leaf types. 'Parris Island' and 'Valamaine' are Romaine types. 'Buttercrunch' is a butterhead type.

MELON & WATERMELON
Cucumis species & *Citrullus lanatus*

Why It's Special—You can't beat the flavor of freshly picked muskmelon or the fun of growing your own watermelons. Just make sure to select a variety that will ripen before your area's first fall frost.

How to Plant & Grow—Wait for the danger of frost to pass and soil to warm before planting seeds and hardened-off transplants in the garden. Start seeds indoors three to four weeks before the last expected frost date for an earlier harvest. Plant in raised hills to increase soil warmth, placing three plants in a hill. Plants can be trellised, but you'll need to provide support for each melon.

Care & Problems—Melons do best in warm soil. Black fabric mulches and floating row covers will help warm the air and soil. Remove the row cover once the plants start blooming so pollination can occur. Possible problems include mildews, leaf spots, fusarium wilt, cucumber beetle, aphids, squash bugs, and flea beetles.

Harvest & Best Selection—Harvest muskmelons when just a little pressure on the stem separates it from the fruit. Harvest watermelons when the fruits are full sized, dull colored, and the portion touching the ground changes from white to cream. Check the tendrils nearest the fruit for confirmation. These will curl and dry when the fruit is ripe. 'Sugar Baby' and 'Yellow Doll' are short-season watermelons. 'Bush Star', 'Burpee Hybrid', and 'Earli-Sweet' are just a few of the muskmelons suited to the Midwest.

ONION
Allium cepa

Why It's Special—Onions are a major food staple around the world. You probably include them in soups, stews, and meat and vegetable dishes.

How to Plant & Grow—Onions are day-length sensitive. Midwest gardeners should grow long day onions that will set and grow large bulbs in this region. Grow and harvest onions for green onions (scallions), slicing (dry), or to store for later use. Onions can be started from seed, sets, or plants. Start onion seeds indoors eight to ten weeks prior to planting outdoors. Plant sets in the garden about four weeks before the last spring frost. Place sets in the soil with the pointed end up even with the soil surface, spaced 2 (for green onions) to 6 inches (dry) apart. Wait a few weeks to place hardened-off transplants into the garden.

Care & Problems—Proper selection, soil preparation, thinning, and care will help ensure bulbs develop. Remove any plants that form a flower stalk and use immediately. Watch for onion maggots and thrips.

Harvest & Best Selection—Harvest green onions when the tops are about 6 inches tall. Bulbs can be dug as soon as they're big enough to use. Wait till tops fall over and dry for to harvest storage onions. After harvesting, spread onions in a single layer for two to ten days to cure. 'White Sweet', 'Yellow Sweet Spanish', and 'Southport Red Globe' are the most common onions found in the garden center.

OREGANO
Origanum vulgare var. *hirtum*

Why It's Special—This popular herb has been used for centuries. You have tasted or seasoned your pizza, pasta, soups, and other dishes with oregano. It is grown as a perennial in Zone 5, and as an annual in colder regions. Grow the Greek oregano with white flowers; it has the best flavor for cooking. Taste a leaf or two before you buy a plant to make sure it has good flavor. Others are best used as ornamentals though they're often aggressive.

How to Plant & Grow—Start with nursery-grown plants and plant hardened-off transplants in the garden after all danger of frost has passed.

Care & Problems—Mix oregano with perennial flowers or place this perennial herb in the corner of a vegetable or perennials section of your herb garden where it won't be disturbed. Once established, oregano is easy to grow, drought-tolerant, and trouble-free. Plants will self-sow, but the offspring are often flavorless. Watch for spider mites in hot dry weather.

Harvest & Best Selection—Leaves are most flavorful before plants flower. Pick leaves as soon as the plant is large enough to be harvested. You can also cut back entire plants when they are about 6 inches tall, again just before they begin to flower, and a third time in late summer. 'Compactum' stays 2 to 3 inches tall and has good flavor.

PARSLEY
Petroselinum crispum

Why It's Special—Parsley's bright green, tasty leaves add flavor to your meals and texture to container, flower, vegetable, and herb gardens. It will also attract butterflies by providing food for the swallowtail butterfly larvae.

How to Plant & Grow—Parsley is a biennial grown as an annual. Flat-leaved parsley is also called Italian parsley and has the best flavor for cooking. Curly parsley can be used for cooking and is often used as a garnish. Purchase plants or start seeds indoors six to eight weeks before the last spring frost. Soak seed in warm water for twenty-four hours before planting to improve germination. Be patient, it can take three weeks for seeds to sprout. Move hardened-off transplants into the garden in spring. They will tolerate spring and fall frosts. Space plants 8 inches apart

Care & Problems—Parsley is usually problem-free, but watch for crown rot in wet or poorly drained soils. Just plant extras for the swallowtail caterpillars to enjoy. Once they are done feeding your plants will recover and you will be rewarded with beautiful butterflies.

Harvest & Best Selection—Harvest leaves by cutting rather than pulling as soon as they are large enough to use. Plants will survive the winter in most areas, but the flavor is not as good the second year. 'Pagoda' and 'Plain Italian' are good flat-leaved cultivars. Sherwood' is a curly-leaved type (*P. crispum*, Crispum group) with good heat resistance.

PEA
Pisum sativum

Why It's Special—Peas are one of the first vegetables to go into the garden, marking the start of the long-awaited planting season. Garden peas are grown for their seeds; snow and snap peas are grown both for seeds and pods.

How to Plant & Grow—Peas tolerate cold temperatures but seeds will rot in wet, cold soil. Direct-seed up to five weeks before the last spring frost, in single or double rows. Put stakes in place at planting. Smaller types can be grown without supports. Plant every ten days to spread out the harvest. Plant again in late summer for fall harvest.

Care & Problems—Cover new plantings with row covers or netting to prevent birds from harvesting seedlings. Late spring plantings will decline in the heat of early summer. Powdery mildew is often a problem. Growing plants in full sun and staking will help reduce the risk.

Harvest & Best Selection—Pods are usually ready to harvest about three weeks after plants flower. Use a small pair of scissors to cut off the pods. Garden peas should have filled pods and still be bright green, not dull. Snow peas can be picked as soon as the pod is full-sized but before the seeds begin to swell. Snap peas should be picked after the seeds have filled out but before the pods are large and hard. Harvest daily. 'Knight', 'Maestro', 'Green Arrow', and 'Wando' are garden types. 'Mammoth Melting Sugar' and 'Oregon Sugar Pod' are snow peas. 'Sugar Snap' and 'Sugar Ann' are snap peas.

PEPPER
Capsicum annuum

Why It's Special—Sweet bell peppers are great fresh, cooked, and stuffed. Most bell peppers start out green and turn red or orange when mature, but there are also yellow, purple, and even brown cultivars. You can grow jalapeño, Serrano, and poblano types for use in Mexican cooking.

How to Plant & Grow—All peppers like warm weather so choose short-season cultivars for the best results. Most do well in containers and are quite ornamental. Sow seeds indoors eight to ten weeks before the last frost or purchase plants. Place hardened-off plants 12 to 18 inches apart in the garden after the soil has warmed and the danger of frost has passed.

Care & Problems—Keep soil evenly moist but not wet. Blossoms will drop in cold and hot temperatures. Stake tall types that need support at time of planting. Peppers are fairly pest free, although you may experience problems with blossom end rot, tomato hornworm, cutworm, sunscald, aphids, and flea beetles.

Harvest & Best Selection—Keep plants picked to extend the harvest. Peppers can be picked at the immature green stage or allowed to ripen to their next color. Hot peppers can be picked green, but they will continue to increase in flavor and heat as they mature. Use a pair of scissors to cut fruits from plants. If frost is forecast, pick all remaining fruits.

POTATO
Solanum tuberosum

Why It's Special—Potatoes are high in vitamin C and potassium and only contain 110 calories apiece, if you leave off the butter and sour cream. And they are fun to grow. It is like discovering buried treasure when you dig and discover your gardening efforts were successful. Grow them in the garden or in a large container.

How to Plant & Grow—Potatoes are started from pieces of potatoes called seeds. Always buy certified seed, free from disease. Cut these into pieces with at least one eye. Plant in spring two to four weeks before the last frost date or when soil has warmed to 40 degrees F. Potatoes do best in cooler temperatures. Plant 4 inches deep and 12 to 15 inches apart.

Care & Problems—When potatoes reach 6 to 8 inches cover the lower (leafless stem) with soil. Repeat until the hill is 6 to 8 inches tall. Or mulch with 6 inches of weed-free straw. This reduces the risk of green, bitterly flavored tubers. The main pest problem is the Colorado potato beetle. Watch for early and late blights, wilts, and a few other problems. Floating row covers will greatly reduce insect problems.

Harvest & Best Selection—"New" small potatoes are harvested seven to nine weeks after planting. Wait for the tops to die to harvest full-sized potatoes or for storing. Use a garden fork or your hands, working carefully to avoid damaging the tender skins. 'Superior', 'Yukon Gold', 'Kennebec', 'Norland', and 'Pontiac' are ones to try.

RADISH
Raphanus sativus

Why It's Special—Quick and easy growing makes radishes a good choice for kids, beginner gardeners, and those who like quick results.

How to Plant & Grow—Sow seeds outdoors four to six weeks before the last expected frost. Make successive sowings every seven to ten days until the weather is consistently above 65 degrees F. Short-season radishes mature quickly, making them perfect for intercropping with slower-maturing vegetables. Seeds can be sown again in late summer for a fall crop. Long-season radishes should be planted in spring or summer depending on the cultivar. Winter-storage types should be planted to mature around the first frost.

Care & Problems—Thin seedlings to 2 to 4 inches or you won't get nice round globes. Maintain an even moisture. Water-stressed plants can get bitter and tough. There are few problems, but watch for club rot, cabbage root maggots, and flea beetles.

Harvest & Best Selection—Begin pulling spring radishes as soon as they are large enough to use. Their quality quickly goes downhill as they get larger. Winter types can be harvested as soon as they are large enough use, but a mild frost or two will improve their flavor. There are several colors and types. The most familiar is the red globe, or spring radish, that is ready for the table in a month. Long-season, or winter radishes, include the Asian radishes (daikon, Oriental, Japanese, Chinese, and lo bok); they are larger and mature in two months or more.

RHUBARB
Rheum

Why It's Special—This long-lived, easy-to-grow perennial vegetable has stood the test of time as a favorite in Midwest gardens and on the dessert table in the form of rhubarb pie.

How to Plant & Grow—Proper soil preparation is key since rhubarb will remain in its location for many years. Start new plantings from roots, potted plants, or division in early spring. Dig and divide in spring as new growth begins. Set plants at the same depth they were growing in the garden or container. Plant roots with the crown bud 1 to 2 inches below the soil surface.

Care & Problems—Rhubarb has few problems when grown in well-drained soils. Fertilize with well-rotted manure in the spring before growth begins or a low-nitrogen slow-release fertilizer after harvest. Plants grown in poorly drained soil and heavy shade produce spindly stems. Remove any flower stalks as soon as they appear.

Harvest & Best Selection—Do not harvest new plantings of rhubarb. Harvest two-year-old plants for one or two weeks. Harvest older, established plantings for eight to ten weeks. Pull or cut the leafstalks from the plants when they are 12 to 15 inches high, thick, and crisp. Remove the leaf (it is toxic) and just use the stem. Eating summer rhubarb stalks is not harmful to you (they are not poisonous; just the leaf parts). 'Canada Red' and 'McDonald' are the easiest to find. 'Valentine', 'Ruby', 'Strawberry', and 'Cherry' are also good choices.

SAGE
Salvia officinalis

Why It's Special—This culinary herb adds texture to herb and flower gardens as well as containers. A hardy perennial in much of the Midwest (parts of Zone 4 and warmer) it can be grown as an annual and in colder regions. All gardeners may want to try growing it indoors for winter.

How to Plant & Grow—Plant hardened-off transplants outside after all danger of frost has passed. Grow in well-drained soil for best results. Space 12 to 24 inches apart.

Care & Problems—Poorly drained or wet soil can lead to root rot and winter kill. Sage tolerates partial sun and drought once established. In colder areas where sage doesn't overwinter, take cuttings in late summer to overwinter indoors. Water as needed to keep soil moist, but not wet. Cut plants back by one-third each spring to promote new growth. Replace woody plants every three to four years to keep them healthy and vigorous. Sage has no serious pest problems.

Harvest & Best Selection—Pinch leaves off as needed, but stop in early fall to harden plants for winter. For storage, dry leaves in a single layer in a dry location out of sunlight. There are several cultivars that have showier leaves, including 'Aurea', 'Kew Gold', 'Tricolor', and 'Purpurea', but they are not as hardy. Pineapple sage (*S. elegans*) is a tender perennial with pineapple-scented leaves that can be used in the kitchen.

SPINACH
Spinacia oleracea

Why It's Special—This cool-season vegetable adds flavor and nutrition to spring and fall meals. The smooth types have thin, tender leaves that are good for salads. Savoyed types have broader, thicker, crinkled leaves and hold up better in cooking.

How to Plant & Grow—Sow seeds directly in the garden four to six weeks before the last expected frost. Seeds can be started indoors a few weeks earlier, or planted in containers or under row covers to jump-start the season. Sow seeds every two weeks in spring to get a continuous harvest and then start again in late summer for a fall crop. Cover fall planting to extend your harvest even later in the season.

Care & Problems—Thin seedlings to 6 inches, using the thinnings for salads. This quick-maturing crop is good for succession planting and interplantng with broccoli and cabbage. Plants will bolt when planted too closely, when day length exceeds twelve hours, or when exposed to extremely high or low temperatures. Use row covers to manage the infrequent pests.

Harvest & Best Selection—Spring spinach is usually harvested by picking the entire plant before it bolts, but you can cut individual leaves at any time, starting with the outside leaves and moving inward. Fall crops can be harvested either way. 'Tyee', 'Bloomsdale Long Standing', and 'Correnta' are all slower to bolt.

SQUASH & PUMPKIN
Cucurbita species

Why It's Special—These vegetables may generate memories of eating pumpkin pie at Thanksgiving, dining on butternut squash ravioli, or picking pumpkins with your family. Try growing these to create some new memories.

How to Plant & Grow—Pumpkins and squashes are in the same group of plants and require the same growing conditions and care. Wait until the soil and air are warm and danger of frost has passed to plant these warm-season vegetables. Plant three to five seeds in hills spaced 3 to 4 feet apart. They don't respond well to transplanting. If you start seeds indoors use biodegradable pots and start just as few weeks prior to planting outside.

Care & Problems—Plants need plenty of room, and adequate spacing reduces disease problems. Small-fruited plants can be trained on a trellis, but the heavy fruited ones will need to be supported with a cloth sling. Squash vine borer and squash bugs are major pests. Anthracnose, powdery mildew, and wilt can also affect these plants.

Harvest & Best Selection—Harvest summer squash in fifty to sixty days when the fruits are 6 to 10 inches long or 3 to 6 inches diameter. The seeds will be small, the rind soft, and the flavor at its best. Winter squash, including pumpkins, are ready in 90 to 120 days when they're full sized, the rind is hard, and the portion touching the ground is cream or orange color. 'Gold Rush' and 'Sunburst' are summer squashes; 'Table Ace' and 'Sweet Mama' are winter squashes. 'Lumina' and 'Big Max' are pumpkins to try.

TOMATO
Lycopersican esculentum

Why It's Special—Nothing tastes better than fresh-from-the garden tomatoes. Plus, one plant yields lots of fruit for eating fresh, slicing, and cooking.

How to Plant & Grow—Wait for warm soil and air to move transplants into the garden or jump-start the season with the help of row covers. Plant tall, leggy tomatoes deeply or in a trench to encourage rooting. Grow them sprawled on the ground, staked, in towers, hanging, or in 3- to 5-gallon containers. Space 24 to 36 inches apart.

Care & Problems—Determinant tomatoes grow a certain height and stop growing, making them great for containers and small supports. They tend to have a large harvest in a shorter time. Indeterminant varieties grow flowers and fruits until frost kills them, or you pinch out the growing tip (in September). This speeds ripening of the tomatoes that have already formed. You'll need tall supports for indeterminant types. Their fruit is produced over a longer period of time. Blossom end rot (see page 231), septoria leaf spot, early and late blights, and tomato hornworm can be problems.

Harvest & Best Selection—Tomatoes are ripe in sixty-five to eighty-five days when the fruit is fully colored. Leave them on the plant for an extra five days for better flavor. Unfortunately, the critters tend to snatch the fruit while you wait. Harvest green tomatoes to enjoy or ripen indoors before the first fall frost. Select disease-resistant cultivars that best suit your needs. Paste types are for cooking, cherry tomatoes are for salads and snacking, and medium-sized fruit is for slicing.

BEWARE BLACK WALNUTS

Did your tomatoes wilt, beans die, or garden perform badly? Check surrounding yards and your own for black walnut trees. The roots, leaves, and nuts of these trees contain juglone. This substance is toxic to many plants, including vegetables. The roots can travel hundreds of feet beyond the tree, killing any susceptible plants in their way.

- Avoid planting black walnut trees in small landscapes where you are trying to grow other trees, flowers, and vegetable gardens.

- Plant vegetable gardens at least 50 feet, preferably farther, from these trees.

- Grow vegetables in containers or create a raised-bed garden. Cover the ground and inside of the raised-bed walls with weed barrier fabric. Fill with 8 to 12 inches of soil. This will help keep the tree roots out of the raised bed garden.

- Do not use black walnut leaves to amend soil. Compost them until they are unidentifiable.

- Consider removing the black walnut tree for long-term, not short-term, benefits. It takes five to ten years for the roots and debris to decompose and become nontoxic.

MAKING YOUR "FAVORITES" LIST

- List the vegetables your family likes to eat. Be sure to include the ingredients for your favorite recipes. Star the ones that taste best grown in the garden or that are more expensive to buy. Also consider the work involved compared to the price. I love to grow beans, but when life is busy I would rather pay the growers at the farmer's market to do all the picking. But I always find time for growing tomatoes.

- Consider the space each plant needs. One tomato plant produces lots of fruit, but one corn plant produces one, maybe two ears. Plus, you will need at least a 4-by-4 block for pollination and fruit production. But nothing beats the taste of freshly harvested corn.

- Evaluate how much of the various vegetables your family will eat. I like the look and flavor of okra, but my family does not. This means one plant takes care of all our needs.

- Make a list of herbs you use for cooking, crafts, and gifts. Flavored vinegars and oils are easy to make and great to give as gifts. Consider using bunches of dried herbs for decorations, deodorizers, or potpourri.

- Decide how many vegetables and herbs you need for fresh use and preserving. Most vegetables can be canned or frozen for later use. Consider purchasing a food dryer to dry vegetables and herbs. Or let nature, the oven, and microwave dry herbs for later cooking and crafts.

- Always add a few fun vegetables for the children in your family and neighborhood. Try growing popcorn, pumpkins, and watermelons to get the kids interested in gardening. Do not forget to grow radishes, Bibb lettuce, and other short-season vegetables that will give quick results.

- Try something new and different. Check out the garden catalogs to find a new tomato, more heat-tolerant lettuce, or hot pepper. Look for new colors, shapes, and sizes to add interest and fun to the garden.

- Make sure the vegetables are suited to our climate and your garden location. The vegetables need to thrive in our weather and be able to reach maturity and produce within our short season.

SPACE-SAVING TECHNIQUES

Do not panic if your garden plans are bigger than the available planting space. Try these space-saving techniques:

- Grow plants in blocks or wide rows instead of single rows. Blocks can be several feet wide. Make sure you can easily reach all the plants for maintenance and harvest. Space plants just far enough apart to allow for the mature plant size. Make the aisles wide enough for you to work the surrounding rows.

- Make the most of all available space. Try growing pole beans, cucumbers, and other vine crops on fences, trellises, and other vertical structures. Growing vertical not only saves space, it can help reduce disease and make harvesting easier.

- Consider planting short-season crops, such as radishes and beets, between long-season crops of tomatoes, peppers, and broccoli. The short-season plants will be ready for harvest just about the time the long-season plants need the extra space. Interplant lettuce for added shade from heat and sun that can give the lettuce a bitter flavor.

- Grow several crops throughout the season in the same row. Start with cool weather-tolerant crops, such as radishes or leaf lettuce. Harvest the first plant and replace it with a second planting. Try growing an unrelated crop (to reduce the risk of disease), such as beans or cucumbers. Plant a third crop if time allows.

MAKE GROWING VEGETABLES FUN FOR EVERYONE!

If the kids help plan, plant and tend they are more likely to eat their vegetables.

- Start with a fun planning activity. Get out some paper, scissors, old catalogs, and glue. Have each family member cut out pictures of the vegetables they want to grow and eat.

- Create a teepee made of stakes and pole beans. Use them to shade lettuce planted in the center. Or better yet, make it a hiding place in the garden.

- Include a sunflower maze to add mystery in the garden. Plant sunflowers in narrow rows and patterns to create a mazelike walkway through the garden. Use the maze to direct children from planting to planting or from one side of the garden to the other.

- Try designing and planting theme gardens. The pizza garden is a favorite. Include all the fresh ingredients you will need to make your own pizza—except for the cheese and pepperoni, of course!

- Give your children a little gardening space of their own. Let them plan, plant, and harvest their own garden. I did this for my daughter when she was seven years old. She chose the seeds and plants for her own plot. Then she asked for a 10-foot-high fence—to keep her parents, not the rabbits, out!

Kids of any age can enjoy working in a vegetable garden.

JANUARY

- It's time to plan this year's vegetable garden. Gather the family and review last year's harvest. Make a list of all the vegetables you want to grow again. Adjust the number of rows and plants to include favorites. Reduce the number of those vegetables that were more productive than you needed or not very popular with family and friends.

- Plan some kid-friendly features in this season's garden. It is a great way to get your children, grandchildren, or neighborhood kids to share your passion. Make gardening fun for everyone involved. See page 229 for ideas.

- Gather and organize seed-starting equipment and supplies if you plan on starting seeds indoors. Find an area where you can place flats near a window or under artificial lights.

- Create a planting chart. List all the vegetables and herbs you plan to grow. Check seed packets, plant profiles, and frost maps to help determine the best time to plant in your part of the Midwest. Record this information in your garden journal or Planting Chart.

- Harvest herbs from your windowsill herb garden as needed for cooking. This will encourage branching and more growth for harvest. You may need to add some extra artificial light during these short, dark days of January. Harvest carrots and parsnips that have been stored in the garden for winter. Dig carefully to avoid damaging these root crops. Enjoy their sweet flavor.

FEBRUARY

- Visit your local garden center to purchase seeds you'll need for starting indoors. Order any unusual or hard-to-find seeds from a reliable company. Select one with a good reputation by asking family, friends, and fellow gardeners.

- Continue to harvest carrots and parsnips stored in the garden for winter. Try digging them during a winter thaw for easier access. Then enjoy their sweet flavor.

- Finish your garden plan. Take a look at your plan and available growing space. Plan and locate needed expansions. Consider mixing a few vegetables and herbs in with your flowers and shrubs. Decide what type of soil preparation is needed. Locate sources for topsoil, compost, and other amendments you might need. Calculate the amount needed before you go shopping. See page 234 for help calculating soil and mulch needs.

- Repair, locate, or replace cold frames, row covers, and other season-extending materials if you plan an early start to the season.

MARCH

- Get busy adding to your indoor garden. Fill clean flats or small containers with sterile seed-starting mix. Plant seedlings in rows in flats or place one or two seeds in each container. Check the seed package for planting recommendations. Most seeds like to be planted twice as deep as they are thick.

- Start cleaning up and preparing your garden for planting. Take advantage of any snow-free days to remove debris, take a soil test, and get started. The soil can be worked anytime it is not frozen and is only slightly moist. See "Soil Preparation" in the chapter introduction for more details.

- Get a jump on the growing season and this year's weeds. Prepare the garden for planting as soon as the soil thaws and can be worked. Cover the garden with clear plastic. Wait two to three weeks for the soil to warm and the weed seeds to sprout. Remove the plastic and lightly cultivate. Avoid deep hoeing that can bring new weed seeds to the surface. You will have both removed many weeds and warmed the soil for early planting.

- Trim onions that are getting long and leggy. Continue to harvest and trim back your windowsill herbs.

APRIL

- Harvest three-year and older asparagus when spears are 6 to 8 inches long. Snap or cut the spears off below the soil surface. Harvest three-year-old plantings for just one month. Four-year and older planting can be harvested for six to eight weeks.

- Do not harvest new plantings of rhubarb. Harvest two-year-old plants for one or two weeks. Keep harvesting older, established plantings for eight to ten weeks. Pull or cut the leafstalks from the plants when they are 12 to 15 inches high, thick and crisp. Remove the leaf (it is toxic) and just use the stem.

- Spread well-rotted manure around rhubarb in the spring before growth begins. Or wait until after harvest (June) to apply fertilizer.

- Fertilize young asparagus plantings (one to three years old) with the rest of the garden. Add 1 pound of a low-nitrogen fertilizer per 100 square feet of garden. Wait until after the final harvest to fertilize four-year and older plantings.

- Protect new plantings from birds and animals. Spread bird netting or season-extending fabric over the garden. Anchor the sides securely. This will keep birds out and may discourage other animals.

- Install a fence around the garden to keep rabbits out. Use chicken wire or hardware cloth to make a fence. Sink the bottom several inches into the soil. Make the fence at least 4 feet high to keep out rabbits. Bury at least 12, preferably 18, inches of the fence beneath the ground to discourage woodchucks.

• Examine lavender, sage, and thyme for winter damage. Look for healthy buds (firm and plump) and pliable branches. Wait for new growth to begin. Remove dead tips and trim as needed. Always leave some healthy buds for new growth.

MAY

• Refer to your planting chart. Make additions to the garden based on vegetables you are growing and the average date of the last spring frost. Keep harvesting asparagus when the spears are 6 to 8 inches long.

• Remove all flower stalks as soon as they appear on rhubarb plants. Cut them back to the base of the plant. These typically appear during unseasonably hot weather, in overcrowded plantings, on old plants, or in infertile soil. Correct the cause to reduce the problem in the future.

• Stake or cage tomatoes at or just after planting. Going vertical helps reduce disease and soil dwelling insects. It also makes harvesting easier.

• Avoid seed corn maggot damage on corn and beans by waiting until the soil warms for planting. Quick-germinating seeds are less susceptible to this damage. Seed corn maggots feed on germinating seeds, preventing germination or causing deformed seedlings that never develop.

• Cover broccoli, cabbage, turnips, and radishes with season-extending fabric. They prevent harmful insects from reaching the plants.

• A thorough spring cleanup will reduce problems with the asparagus beetle. These orange-and-black beetles feed on emerging spears. Handpick and destroy or use an insecticide labeled for use on beetles in asparagus.

• The yellow-and-green striped or spotted cucumber beetles can be found on vine crops in spring or late summer. Remove and destroy these insects as soon as they appear. The cucumber beetles not only feed on leaves and fruit, but also transmit a deadly bacterial disease to the plant.

JUNE

• Remove suckers (side shoots) that form between the leaf and stem on staked tomatoes. This gives you an earlier, but smaller harvest. Cut or snap the small shoots off by hand when they are 1 to 2 inches long. No need to do this on caged or sprawling plants.

• Handpicking is the best control for the Colorado potato beetle. Many insecticides do not provide adequate control. Watch for yellow-and-black striped beetles or the red humped larvae feeding on the leaves.

• Set out shallow, covered containers of beer or place boards between rows to capture slugs. The slugs will crawl into the beer and drown. Or they will hide under the board in the morning so you can remove and destroy them.

• Watch for squash vine borer. This orange-and-black day-flying moth lays its eggs at the base of vine crops. Remove and smash any that are found. Check for sawdust-like material and holes at the base of the plant. This means the borers have entered the stem and are causing damage. Slice the stem lengthwise and kill any borers you find. Bury this portion of the stem, keep the soil moist, and hope it develops new roots. Reduce damage with three weekly applications of an insecticide to the base of the plant when the adults can be seen and are laying eggs.

JULY

• The garden season is well under way, but there is still plenty of time to plant. Add seeds and transplants to the garden. Use vacant spots and harvested rows for these late additions. Grow crops that will reach maturity and be ready for harvest before the first fall frost.

• Blanch celery and cauliflower to keep the stems and flowers white and the flavor less bitter. Many cauliflower cultivars are self-blanching. The leaves naturally fold over the flower bud, blocking the light. You need to lend a hand for the other types. Start blanching when the flower bud is about 2 inches in diameter. Tie the outer leaves over the center of the plant. It will be ready in five to twelve days when the head is 6 to 8 inches in diameter. Cover stems of celery with soil or cardboard to block out the sunlight.

• Keep harvesting vegetables as they reach their peak. You'll have the best flavor and nutritional value. See individual profiles for specifics.

• Be patient when dealing with blossom end rot. The blackened ends of fruit are caused by a calcium deficiency. Do not add calcium unless directed by a soil test. Most of our soils have plenty. Instead, avoid root damage caused by late staking and cultivating. Mulch the soil to keep it consistently moist, and wait. Once the soil moisture is consistent, the plants will adjust and the remaining fruits will be fine. Cut off the black portion and eat the rest. See August for more on tomato troubles.

• Pick herbs as needed. Cut short pieces off the ends of the stem. Make the cut just above a set of leaves. It looks neater, and the plant recovers faster. Wait until the plants start blooming for the most intense flavor. Preserve this flavorful harvest for later use.

- Fertilize, if needed, leafy vegetables, sweet corn, and root crops when they are half their mature size. Fertilize tomatoes, peppers, cucumbers, beans, and vine crops when they have started producing fruit. Use a low-nitrogen fertilizer to avoid damaging the plants during hot dry weather.

- Protect ripening melons and the fruit of other vine crops from rot. Slide a downturned plastic lid under each fruit or mulch the soil under the fruit.

- Keep harvesting to keep plants producing. See individual profiles for harvesting tips.

- Keep picnic beetles out of the garden with timely harvest. These ¼-inch, black-with-four-yellow-dots beetles do not harm the fruits, but they are attracted to overripe or damaged fruits. Attract them with a mixture made of 1 cup water, 1 cup dark corn syrup, one cake of yeast, and a spoonful of vinegar. Place the mixture in a container outside the garden. Use it to attract the beetles away from the garden, trap, and drown them.

- Watch for signs of aphids, leafhoppers, and tarnished plantbugs. These insects suck out plant juices, causing the leaves to yellow and bronze. Severe damage can stunt plant growth. Use several applications (five to seven days apart) of insecticidal soap to treat these pests.

- Check the lower leaves of tomatoes for yellowing and brown spots. Septoria leaf spot and early blight are common causes of these symptoms. Remove and destroy infected leaves as soon as they are found. Fall cleanup, proper spacing, staking, and full sun will reduce the risk of these diseases, as will sterilizing tomato cages from year to year. Regular applications of a fungicide, labeled for use on vegetables, can be used to prevent the spread of this disease, if cleanup and sanitation haven't worked. Look for and select more environmentally friendly products.

- Watch for mildew (white or gray film on the leaves) and leaf spots on vine crops. Try growing them on trellises or fences to increase light and air flow and to reduce disease problems. Remove infected leaves as soon as they appear. You can use a fungicide labeled for use on vine crops to prevent further spread of these diseases as a last resort.

SEPTEMBER

- Plan to extend the season using cold frames, hotcaps, and season-extending fabrics. A little frost protection on those first frosty nights can extend the harvest through the warm weeks that always follow. Or let nature end the season with the first killing frost. Use this as an excuse to end a troublesome growing season full of insects, disease, and weeds. Then you can start planning for next year's garden.

- Take cuttings of oregano, rosemary, sage, marjoram, mints, and winter savory for your indoor winter herb garden. Take 3- to 4-inch cuttings from healthy plants. Stick the cut end in moist vermiculite or perlite. Keep the vermiculite moist and the plant in a bright, not sunny, location. Plant the rooted cutting in a small container of moist, sterile potting mix. Grow them in a sunny window.

- Store leftover seed in an airtight jar in the refrigerator. The controlled environment will help keep the seeds viable for next season.

- Remove and destroy all pest-infested plant debris in fall. A thorough cleanup is your best defense against insects and disease. Do not compost pest-infested material unless you have an active compost pile that reaches 160 degrees. Contact your local municipalities for disposal options.

- Prune out the stem tips on tomato, squash, and melon plants early this month. This will allow the plant to expend its energy on ripening the existing fruits instead of producing more fruits that will not have time to mature.

- Leave ferny asparagus leaves and stems standing for the winter. The standing stems help capture snow that will insulate the roots for winter.

OCTOBER

- Start a windowsill garden for fresh seasonings all winter long. Try oregano, thyme, parsley, and sage in small individual pots or planted together in a larger container.

- Plant annual rye, oats, or buckwheat as a green manure crop. These plants will provide a green groundcover for the winter garden. Dig or till these plants into the top 6 inches of soil next spring. They add nutrients and help improve the soil.

- Move rosemary, sweet bay, and other tender herbs indoors. Place them in a bright, sunny window or under artificial lights for the winter. Keep the soil moist, but not too wet.

- Pick mature green tomatoes when the blossom end is greenish white, or showing color before the tomato plants are killed by frost. Ripen these tomatoes indoors for an added enjoyment. Store unripe tomatoes in a 60- to 65-degree Fahrenheit location. Spread them out on heavy paper so that the fruits do not touch. Or wrap each one in newspaper if they have to touch in storage. They will ripen over the next few weeks. Speed up the process by moving a few tomatoes to a bright, warm location a few days prior to use. You can also use green tomatoes to make relish or fried green tomatoes.

- Check stored vegetables during the fall and early winter. Discard any damaged or rotting fruit. One bad apple, onion, or squash really does spoil the bunch.

- Make sure perennial herbs and vegetables are well watered before the ground freezes.

NOVEMBER

- Start a compost pile. You do not need anything fancy. Remember, the compost bin is just a structure meant to contain and hide your pile from view. It should allow easy access and be large enough to hold your materials. Buy or build your own compost bin. All you need are discarded pallets, chicken wire, lattice, or just some space to pile green garbage and let it rot. See "Composting" in the book's introduction for more details on building and using a compost bin.

- Mulch carrots, parsnips, and other root crops left in the garden for winter storage. Cover the lightly frozen (crunchy) soil with straw or evergreen branches. This insulates the soil, protecting the vegetables and making it easier to harvest in winter.

- Finish cleanup and start preparing the garden for next spring. Shred fallen leaves with your mower or leaf shredder. Dig a 3- to 4-inch layer of shredded leaves into the top 6 to 12 inches of soil. These will decompose over the winter, improving the drainage of heavy clay soils and the water-holding capacity of sandy soils.

DECEMBER

- Keep gardening throughout the winter. Try growing sprouts or microgreens. These plants are ready to harvest in less than a week. And all you need are seeds, containers, sprouting mix, and a bit of counter space.

- Or start a windowsill herb or vegetable garden. It is a great distraction for the whole family. Use leftover seeds or scour the garden centers for their leftover inventory. Leafy crops, such as lettuce, do well in the low light indoors. Mix in radishes and miniature carrots for some zing. Onions, parsley, basil, chives, and other herbs are always good suggestions for indoor gardens.

- Monitor herbs and other indoor plants for aphids and mites. These insects suck out plant juices, causing them to yellow and brown. You may see a clear, sticky substance on the leaves. Spray infested plants with insecticidal soap. You may need to make several applications one week apart for adequate control. This is safe for the herbs and all who eat them.

- Watch for fungus gnats and whiteflies. These insects can be seen flitting around the plants. Try catching them with yellow sticky traps. Buy them at a garden center or make your own by coating pieces of yellow paper with Tanglefoot® or another sticky substance. Place them near the plants.

Floating row covers can be used to protect plants against insect pests.

ORDERING SOILS AND MULCH

GARDEN SIZE IN SQ FT	CUBIC YARDS OF MATERIAL NEEDED TO COVER GARDEN SPACE DEPTH OF DESIRED MATERIAL			
	2"	4"	6"	8"
100	½	1+	2	2½
200	1+	2½	3½	5
300	2	3½	5½	7½
400	2½	5	7½	10
500	3+	6	9	12
600	3½	7½	11	15
700	4+	8½	13	17
800	5	10	15	20
900	5½	11	17	22
1000	6	12	18½	25

PEAT MOSS BALE SIZE	AREA THAT CAN BE AMENDED WITH	
	1"	2"
1 cubic ft.	24 sq. ft.	12 sq. ft.
2.2 cubic ft.	50 sq. ft.	25 sq. ft.
3.8 cubic ft.	90 sq. ft.	45 sq. ft.

Or calculate what you need:
Multiply the area (length times width measured in feet) by the desired depth (in feet) of mulch or compost. Convert this volume from cubic feet to cubic yards by dividing by 27 (the number of cubic feet in a cubic yard). This is the amount of material you will need to order.

SPACING CHART

Use this chart to calculate the number of plants you'll need. Divide the square footage of the garden by the spacing factor. The result is the number of plants you'll need.

SPACING (INCHES)	SPACING FACTOR	PLANTS NEEDED			
		25	50	75	100
4	0.11	227	454	682	909
6	0.25	100	200	300	400
8	0.44	57	114	170	227
10	0.70	36	72	107	143
12	1.00	12	50	75	100
15	1.56	16	32	48	64
18	2.25	11	22	33	44
24	4.00	6	13	19	25
30	6.25	4	8	12	16
36	9.00	3	6	8	11
48	16.00	2	3	5	6
60	26.00	1	2	3	4

PRUNING

Prune plants to create a strong framework and structure that withstands our adverse weather. Improve the look and ornamental appeal of your plants through proper pruning. Increase flowering and fruiting, encourage new colorful bark and maintain an attractive form. Remove hazardous and broken branches as they appear.

Minimize your workload by selecting the right plant for the location. You will prune often if you are trying to prune a 40-foot tree to fit a 20-foot location. This is hard on you and the plants.

Here are some basics on pruning various plants. Be sure to check out the pruning recommendations in each chapter and plant profiles as well.

TREE PRUNING

As always, prune with a purpose in mind. Strive to maintain the plant's natural shape. Prune young trees to establish a strong framework. Use proper pruning to maintain a strong structure and healthy growth, as well as to improve flowering and fruiting on established trees.

The best time to prune is usually when trees are dormant. You can see their silhouette better, and the chances of disease and insect problems are reduced.

PRUNING FOR STRUCTURE

- Wait two to four years after planting to start pruning for structure. The more top growth (branches and leaves), the faster the trees will recover from transplanting.
- Remove any branches that are crossed, sprouting from the same area on the trunk, or growing parallel to one another.
- Remove any branches that are growing straight up and competing with the main trunk.
- Remaining branches should be more horizontal (perpendicular to the trunk) than upright.
- Make sure branches are well spaced from top to bottom and around the tree trunk. See figure below.

MAINTENANCE PRUNING

- Well-trained trees will need minimal pruning.
- Consider hiring a certified arborist for large jobs. They have the training and equipment to do the job safely and properly.
- Start by removing dead and damaged branches.
- Next, prune out watersprouts (upright shoots on branches) and suckers (upright shoots at the base of the trunk) as close to their bases as possible.
- Remove any branches that are crossed, rubbing, or parallel.
- Only prune off lower branches for safety and clearance. The lower limbs are the tree's best defense against disease and old age.

236

PERFECT PRUNING CUTS

Do not make a flush cut at the trunk. Rather, make a smooth cut at the outside edge of the collar; the swollen area where the branch meets the trunk.

By keeping the collar you will encourage callus tissue to form and heal over the cut, keeping out disease organisms from entering the cut surface.

How you remove a branch is as important as deciding which branch to remove. Improper cuts create perfect entryways for insects and disease.

- Make the pruning cut flush with the branch bark collar. Pruning cuts flush with the trunk are slow to close and make a great entryway for pests and decay. Stubs left behind look unsightly and also increase pest problems.
- Remove branches where they join the trunk or other branches. This will help maintain the tree's natural form and encourage balanced growth.
- Larger branches (2 inches in diameter or greater) should be double-cut to prevent branch splitting and bark tearing.

- Make the first cut on the bottom of the branch about 12 inches from the final cut. Cut about one-fourth of the way through the branch.
- Make the second cut on top of the branch within 1 inch of the first cut. Continuing cutting until the branch breaks off.
- The final cut should be flush with the branch bark collar.
- Do not apply pruning paints or wound dressings to pruning cuts. Research shows that these materials actually trap moisture and disease in rather than keeping them out. Oaks pruned during the growing season are the only exception.

REPAIRING EVERGREENS

Snow, ice, and winter winds can often damage or destroy the main leader of spruce and other evergreen trees. The loss of the central leader causes a tree to lose its nice pyramidal shape. As other branches compete for the lead position, the tree tends to flatten out. You can help restore the shape by giving nature a helping hand.

TO CREATE A NEW CENTRAL LEADER:

1. Cut off the damaged leader, leaving a 1½-inch stub.
2. Select one of the shorter side shoots to serve as the new leader.
3. Tie the side shoot to the remaining stub. Over time, this branch will start to grow upright and become the new leader.
4. Remove the tie after one year.
5. Several side shoots may begin to grow upward. Prune out all but the leader trained to be an upright growing stem.

PRUNING SHRUBS

Your landscape does not need to be filled with green rectangles, gumdrops, and tuna cans. Instead, prune shrubs in their natural form to maximize their beauty and improve their health and longevity. Proper pruning can help you maintain size, improve flowering and fruiting and bark color, or remove damaged or diseased branches. When and how you prune is equally important. More details and specific plant recommendations can be found in the shrub chapter introduction and individual plant profiles.

Prune spring-flowering shrubs, such as lilac and forsythia, in spring right after flowering. Spring bloomers flower on the previous season's growth. Pruning in late summer or winter removes the flower buds and eliminates the spring display.

Trim summer-blooming plants during the dormant season. Hills-of-snow hydrangeas, potentilla, and summer-blooming spireas flower on the current season's growth.

When cutting a branch back to an outward facing bud, make the cut ¼ inch past the bud and angle the cut upward at a 45-degree angle to avoid damaging the bud. If the plant has opposite buds, you can make the cut straight across.

Remove dead, damaged, or disease-infected branches whenever they are found. Disinfect tools between cuts to prevent the spread of disease. Use rubbing alcohol or a solution of one part bleach to nine parts water as a disinfectant.

Make pruning cuts on a slight angle above a healthy bud, where a branch joins another branch, or where a branch joins the trunk. These cuts heal quickly and reduce the risk of insects and disease entering the plant. The location of the pruning cut also influences the plant's appearance and future growth.

Use thinning cuts to open up the plant and reduce the size while maintaining its natural appearance. Prune off branches where they join the main stem or another branch. Thinning cuts allow air and light to penetrate the plant improving flowering, fruiting, and bark color. It also helps reduce some disease problems.

Use heading cuts to reduce the height and spread of shrubs. Limit the number and vary the location of heading cuts to maintain the plant's natural appearance. Prune branches back to a shorter side shoot or above a healthy bud. Excessive heading can lead to a tuft of growth at the end of a long, bare stem.

Reserve shearing for only the most formal settings. This technique is easy on the gardener but hard on the plant. Shearing makes indiscriminant cuts, leaving stubs that make perfect entryways for insects and disease. Prune so that the bottom of the plant is wider than the top. This allows light to reach all parts, top to the bottom, of the plant.

Use renewal pruning to manage overgrown shrubs, contain growth, and stimulate new, healthy, and more attractive stems. Start by removing one-third of the older (larger) canes to ground level. Reduce the height of the remaining stems by one-third if needed. Repeat the process the next two years for overgrown shrubs. By the end of the third year, the shrub will be smaller, more attractive, and healthier. Continue to remove older canes as needed throughout the life of the shrubs.

Use rejuvenation pruning to manage the size of some fast-growing and overgrown shrubs. Make sure the plant will tolerate this severe pruning. Cut all stems back to 4 inches above the soil line during the dormant season. Late winter through early spring before growth begins is the best time. The plant will soon begin to grow and recover.

Shrubs that have numerous stems coming out of the ground can be thinned by cutting some stems all the way to the ground.

Shrubs or small trees with only a few main stems or trunks should be thinned by cutting branches back to a crotch rather than to the ground.

CREATING PLANTING BEDS

Reduce maintenance and improve plant health by creating large planting beds around trees and shrubs. The larger bed eliminates competition from grass and damage caused by weed whips and mowers that get a little too close to the plants.

1. Start by outlining the bed. Select the size and shape that complements your design. You can always add more shrubs, perennials, and other plants to fill in the voids.
2. Lay out the garden hose to mark the area. Use a shovel or edger to create the outline of your new planting bed.
3. Remove the existing grass. Peel it off with a sod cutter and use this grass to repair problem areas. Or cut the grass short and cover with several layers of newspapers or a layer of cardboard and several inches of woodchips. The grass and woodchips will eventually decompose. Or use a total vegetation killer to kill the existing grass and weeds. Keep these chemicals off desirable plants. Cover the dead turf with mulch.
4. Mulch the planting bed. A 2- to 3-inch layer of woodchips or bark will help reduce future weed problems. Do not put plastic or weed barriers under wood mulch. As the mulch decomposes, it creates the perfect environment for weeds. Weed seeds blow in, nearby turf spreads in, and soon the garden is full of grass and weeds that are growing through the weed barrier.
5. Reserve weed barriers for use under rock. The weed barrier helps keep the rock from working into the soil. This reduces the need to replenish the settled mulch and makes it easier for you to make changes to the area. Only use fabric weed barriers that allow air and water through. Do not use plastic that prevents water and nutrients from reaching the roots. Better yet, reserve stone mulch for non-planting areas and use organic mulches around plants to improve their growing environment.

CREATING A RAISED BED

Raised beds are good choices for growing vegetables and herbs, especially where soil conditions or drainage problems make gardening difficult. Raised beds allow you to create a rich, well-drained soil in any area. Raised beds also warm up earlier in spring, allowing for earlier planting. They are easier to tend and weed, as long as they aren't too wide. And, they look nice!

A raised bed can range from a simple mound of soil to an elaborate bed framed with wood, plastic, or concrete blocks. Raised beds created by hilling up soil are inexpensive and it's easy to change their sizes and shapes. The downside is that they have to be built every year, which can be quite a bit of back-breaking work each spring.

Permanent enclosed raised beds cost more up front, but most gardeners find they are worth the investment because they require less maintenance and are easier to tend. Soil in raised beds does not get compacted from foot traffic so the soil tends to stay loose and is better for root growth. You'll find fewer weeds in enclosed raised beds and they are easier to tend because they are up off the ground.

Raised beds should be no wider than 4 feet to allow you to easily reach from one side to the middle without stepping inside. Orient your beds north to south, if possible, to maximize sun exposure. If you are using wood, be sure to use a naturally long-lived wood such as cedar or redwood. Avoid using treated wood where you will be growing food crops. If you are plagued by gophers or moles, you can line the bottom of your bed with wide-mesh hardware cloth to create a barrier. A weed barrier fabric may be laid at the bed base to help prevent tree roots from infiltrating the bed.

In addition to being very handy, well-designed raised beds can also become an attractive part of a garden.

HOW TO BUILD A SIMPLE RAISED BED

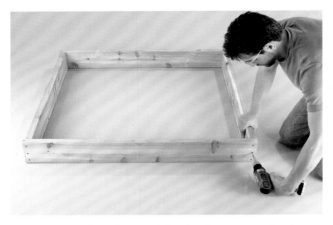

Cut the wood and assemble the frame upside down on a flat surface. Drive deck screws through pilot holes at the corners.

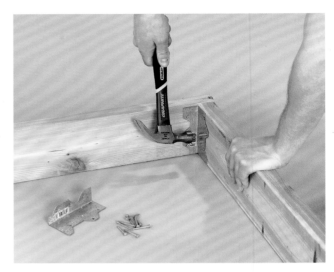

Reinforce the corners by nailing metal corner brace hardware. Use galvanized joist hanger nails to fasten the braces.

Position the bed frame in your garden location. Bury the bottom at least 2 inches below grade.

Fill the bed with a suitable planting soil and rake smooth. The surface of the soil should be at least an inch or two below the top edges of the frame.

DEALING WITH TREE SURFACE ROOTS

Surface roots are those roots that grow slightly above the soil and dull your mower blades as you cut the grass or interfere with the grass growing under your trees. Do not get out the axe. Those roots are important to the support and well being of your tree.

Keep these points in mind:

- Consider mulching under the tree canopy. A 2- to 3-inch layer of mulch provides a good environment for the tree and keeps those surface roots under cover.

- Do not build a raised bed around your tree. Burying tree roots can kill many species of trees. The roots of those that do not die will soon reach the surface again.

- Plant perennial groundcovers under the tree. These plants help insulate the roots, but do not out-compete with the trees for water and nutrients.

- Do not rototill or add soil to the planting area.

- Kill the grass by covering it with newspaper and mulch or with a total vegetation killer. Read and follow all directions carefully.

- Select plants suited to the growing conditions. See the Groundcovers and Vines chapter for plant suggestions.

- Space the plants throughout the area.

- Dig a hole slightly larger than the root system of the groundcover.

- Amend the small planting holes with peat, compost, or other organic matter. Plant, mulch, and water.

- Weed control is critical for the first few years. Once the groundcovers fill in, your weeding chores will be minimal.

Shredded wood and bark is a good choice for mulch, but it does break down, improving the soil but requiring regular refreshing.

ZONE MAPS

ZONE	Average Minimum Temperature
2 A	-45 to -50
2 B	-40 to -45
3 A	-35 to -40
3 B	-30 to -35
4 A	-25 to -30
4 B	-20 to -25
5 A	-15 to -20
5 B	-10 to -15
6 A	-5 to -10
6 B	0 to -5
7 A	5 to 0
7 B	10 to 5
8 A	15 to 10
8 B	20 to 15
9 A	25 to 20
9 B	30 to 25
10 A	35 to 30
10 B	40 to 35
11	40 and Above

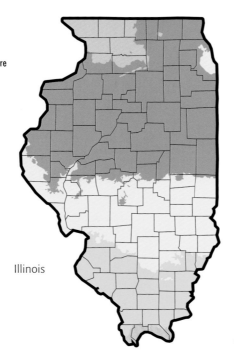

Illinois

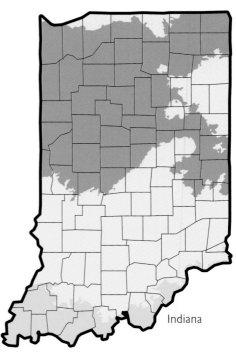

Indiana

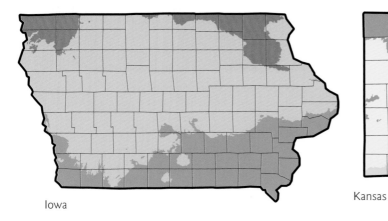

Iowa

Kansas

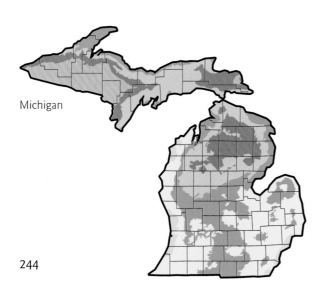

Michigan

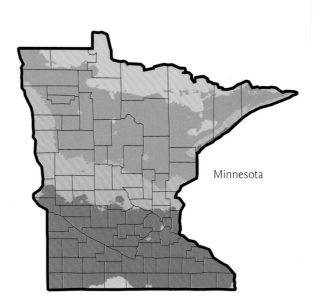

Minnesota

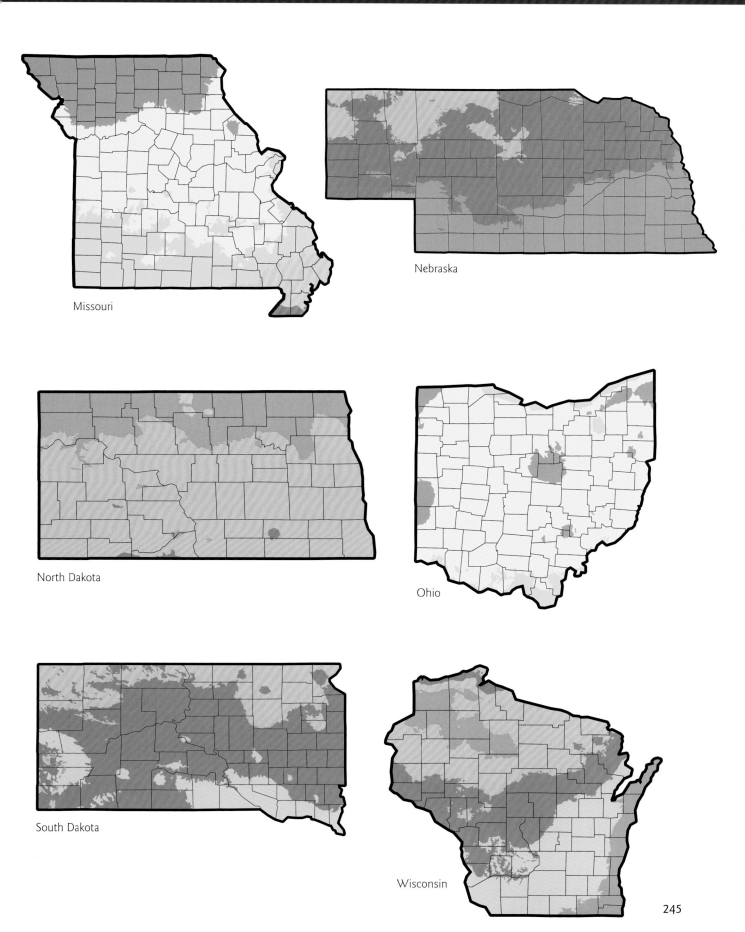

Missouri

Nebraska

North Dakota

Ohio

South Dakota

Wisconsin

245

GLOSSARY

Acid soil: soil with a pH less than 7.0. Acid soil is sometimes called "sour soil" by gardeners. Most plants prefer a slightly acid soil between 6 and 7 where most essential nutrients are available.

Alkaline soil: soil with a pH greater than 7.0, usually formed from limestone bedrock. Alkaline soil is often referred to as sweet soil.

Annual: a plant that completes its entire life cycle in one season. It germinates, grows, flowers, sets seed, and dies within one year.

Balled and burlapped: describes a large tree whose roots have been wrapped tightly in protective burlap and twine after it is dug. It is wrapped in this manner to protect it for shipping, sales, and transplanting.

Bare-root: trees, shrubs, and perennials that have been grown in soil, dug, and have had the soil removed prior to sales or shipping. Mail-order plants are often shipped bare-root with the roots packed in peat moss, sawdust, or similar material and wrapped in plastic.

Barrier plant: a plant that has thorns or impenetrable growth habit and is used to block foot traffic or other access to an area in the landscape.

Beneficial insects: insects or their larvae that prey on pest organisms and their eggs. They may be flying insects such as ladybugs, parasitic wasps, praying mantids, and soldier bugs; or soil dwellers such as predatory nematodes, spiders, and ants.

Berm: a low, artificial hill created in a landscape to elevate a portion of the landscape for functional and aesthetic reasons such as added interest, screening, and improved drainage.

Bract: a modified leaf resembling a flower petal, located just below the true flower. Often it is more colorful and visible than the actual flower, as in poinsettia.

Bud union: the place where the top of a plant was grafted to the rootstock; a term frequently used with roses.

Canopy: the total overhead area of a tree, including the branches and leaves.

Cold hardiness: the ability of a perennial plant (including trees, shrubs, and vines) to survive the minimum winter temperature in a particular area.

Complete fertilizer: powdered, liquid, or granular fertilizer with a balanced proportion of the three key nutrients—nitrogen (N), phosphorus (P), and potassium (K).

Composite: an inflorescence (cluster of flowers) also referred to as a head container petal and disk-like flowers. They are often daisylike with a flat (disk-like flowers) center and petal-like flowers surrounding the outside.

Compost: decomposed organic matter added to the soil to improve its drainage and ability to retain moisture.

Corm: a modified bulb-like stem. It is swollen, short, solid, and located underground. Crocus and gladiolus are two such plants.

Crown: (a) the point where the stems and roots meet. Located at, or just below the soil surface. (b) the top part of the tree.

Cultivar: a CULTIvated VARiety. A unique form of a plant that has been identified as special or superior and has been selected for propagation and sale.

Deadhead: to remove faded flowers from plants to improve their appearance, prevent seed production, and stimulate further flowering.

Deciduous plants: trees and shrubs that lose their leaves in the fall.

Desiccation: drying out of foliage, usually due to drought or wind.

Division: splitting apart perennial plants to create several smaller rooted segments. The practice is useful for controlling a plant's size and for acquiring more plants.

Dormancy: the period, usually the winter, when perennial plants temporarily cease active growth and rest. (The verb form is "dormant.")

Established: the point at which a newly planted tree, shrub, or flower has recovered from transplant shock and begins to grow. Often indicated by the production of new leaves or stems.

Evergreen: perennial plants that do not lose their foliage annually with the onset of winter. Needled or broadleaf foliage will persist and continues to function on a plant through one or more winters, aging and dropping unnoticed in cycles of one, two, three, or more.

Foliar: of or about foliage—usually refers to the practice of spraying foliage with fertilizer or pesticide for absorption by the leaves.

Floret: a small individual flower, usually one of many forming an inflorescence considered the blossom.

Germinate: to sprout. Germination is a fertile seed's first stage of development.

Graft (union): the point on the stem of a woody plant where a stem or bud of a desirable plant is placed onto a hardier root system. Roses, apples, and some ornamental trees are commonly grafted.

Hardscape: the permanent, structural, non-plant part of a landscape; such as walls, sheds, pools, patios, arbors, and walkways.

Herbaceous: plants having fleshy or soft stems that die back with frost; the opposite of woody.

Hybrid: a plant produced by crossing two different varieties, species or genera. Usually indicated with a × in the name such as Acer × fremanii.

Inflorescence: a cluster of flowers occurring at the tip of a stem. This includes such arrangements as umbels (Queen Anne's lace), composite or head (daisy), spike (salvia), raceme (snapdragon) and panicle (coral bells).

Mulch: a layer of material used to cover bare soil to conserve moisture, discourage weeds, moderate soil temperature, and prevent erosion and soil compaction. It may be inorganic (gravel, fabric) or organic (wood chips, bark, pine needles, chopped leaves).

Naturalize: (a) to plant seeds, bulbs, or plants in a random, informal pattern as they would appear in their natural habitat; (b) to adapt to and spread throughout natural areas and appear as if native to that location (a tendency of some non-native plants).

Nectar: the sweet fluid produced by glands on flowers that attract pollinators such as hummingbirds and honeybees for whom it is a source of energy.

Organic material, organic matter: any material or debris that is derived from plants.

Peat moss: organic matter from peat sedges (United States) or sphagnum mosses (Canada) often used to improve soil drainage and water holding abilities.

Perennial: a flowering plant that lives over two or more seasons. Many die back with frost, but their roots survive the winter and generate new shoots in the spring.

pH: a measurement of the relative acidity (low pH) or alkalinity (high pH) of soil or water based on a scale of 1 to 14, with 7 being neutral. Individual plants require soil to be within a certain range so that nutrients can dissolve in moisture and be available to them.

Pinch: to remove tender stems and/or leaves by pressing them between thumb and forefinger. This pruning technique encourages branching, compactness, and flowering in plants.

Pollen: the yellow, powdery grains in the center of a flower. A plant's male sex cells, they are transferred to the female plant parts by means of wind, bees, or other animal pollinators to fertilize them and create seeds.

Raceme: an arrangement of single stalked flowers along an elongated, unbranched stem.

Rhizome: a swollen energy-storing stem structure, similar to a bulb, that lies horizontally in the soil. Roots emerge from its lower surface and stems emerge from a growing point at or near its tip, as in bearded Iris.

Rootbound (or potbound): the condition of a plant that has been confined in a container too long, its roots are forced to wrap around themselves and even swell out of the container. Successful transplanting or repotting requires untangling and trimming away some of the matted roots.

Root flare: the transition at the base of a tree trunk where the bark tissue begins to differentiate and roots begin to form just before entering the soil. This area should not be covered with soil when planting a tree.

Self-seeding: the tendency of some plants to sow their seeds freely around the yard. It creates many seedlings the following season that may or may not be welcome.

Semievergreen: tending to be evergreen in a mild climate but deciduous in a harsher one.

Shearing: the pruning technique whereby plant stems and branches are cut uniformly with long-bladed pruning shears (hedge shears) or powered hedge trimmers. It is used when creating and maintaining hedges and topiary.

Slow-acting (slow-release) fertilizer: fertilizer that is water insoluble and releases its nutrients when acted on by soil temperature, moisture, and/or related microbial activity. Typically granular, it may be organic or synthetic.

Succulent growth: the sometimes undesirable production of fleshy, water-storing leaves or stems that results from overfertilization.

Sucker: a new growing shoot. Underground plant roots produce suckers to form new stems and spread by means of these suckering roots to form large plantings, or colonies. Some plants produce root suckers or branch suckers as a result of pruning or wounding.

Tuber: a thickened portion of underground stem used for energy storage and reproduction. Irish potato is a tuber.

Tuberous root: a swollen root with one point of growth where stem joins the root. Sweet potatoes and dahlias grow from tuberous roots.

Variegated: having various colors or color patterns. The term usually refers to plant foliage that is streaked, edged, blotched, or mottled with a contrasting color, often green with yellow, cream, or white.

White grubs: fat, off-white, worm-like larvae of Japanese and other beetles. They live in the soil and feed on plant (especially grass) roots until summer when they emerge as beetles to feed on plant foliage.

Wings: (a) the corky tissue that forms edges along the twigs of some woody plants such as winged euonymus; (b) the flat, dried extension of tissue on some seeds, such as maple, that catch the wind and help them disseminate.

BIBLIOGRAPHY

American Horticultural Society, The, Christopher Brickell and Judith Zuk, ed. *A-Z Encyclopedia of Garden Plants*. New York, NY: DK Publishing, Inc., 1997.

American Horticultural Society, The, Christopher Brickell and David Joyce. *Pruning and Training*. DK Publishing, Inc., New York, NY, 1996.

Brickell, Christopher and Judith D. Zuk, ed. *The American Horticultural Society: A-Z Encyclopedia of Garden Plants*. DK Publishing, Inc., New York, NY, 1997.

Brickell, Christopher, and David Joyce. *The American Horticultural Society: Pruning and Training*. DK Publishing, Inc., New York, NY, 1996.

Browne, Jim, William Radler, and Nelson Sterner, ed. *Rose Gardening*. Pantheon Books, New York, 1995.

Dirr, Michael A. *Manual of Woody Landscape Plants, 5th edition*. Stipes Publishing Co., Urbana, IL, 1998.

DiSabato-Aust, Tracy. *The Well-Tended Perennial Garden*. Expanded Edition, Timber Press, Portland, Oregon, 2006.

Harris, Richard, et al. *Arboriculture: Integrated Management of Landscape Trees, Shrubs and Vines*. Upper Saddles River, NJ: Prentice Hall, 1999.

Johnson, Warren T. and Howard H. Lyon. *Diseases of Trees and Shrubs*. Ithaca, NY: Cornell University Press, 1987.

Johnson, Warren T. and Howard H. Lyon. *Insects that Feed on Trees and Shrubs*. Ithaca, NY: Cornell University Press, 1991.

Reilly, Ann. *Park's Success with Seeds*. Geo. W. Park Seed Co., Inc., Greenwood, South Carolina, 1978.

Rodale's Illustrated Encyclopedia of Herbs. Emmaus, PA: Rodale Press, 1987.

Schneider, Donald. *Park's Success with Bulbs*. Geo. W. Park Seed Co., Inc., Greenwood, South Carolina, 1981.

Still, Steven M. *Manual of Herbaceous Plants, 4th Edition*. Stipes Publishing Company, Urbana, IL, 1994.

INTERNET RESOURCES

All-America Selections
www.all-americaselections.org

Bailey Nurseries
www.baileynurseries.com

Ball Horticultural Company
www.ballhort.com

Great Garden Plants
www.greatgardenplants.com

Iowa State University Extension and Outreach
www.extension.iastate.edu

Kansas State University
www.he.k-state.edu

Michigan State University, Gardening in Michigan
www.migarden.msu.edu

Missouri Botanical Garden
www.missouribotanicalgarden.org

Monrovia Nursery
www.monrovia.com

North Dakota State University Publications
www.ag.ndsu.edu

Ohio State University Plant Facts
www.plantfacts.osu.edu

Perennial Database
www.perennials.com

Perennial Plant Association
www.perennialplant.org

Plant Delights Nursery, Inc.
www.plantdelights.com
Proven Winners
www.provenwinners.com

Purdue University Garden Publications
www.hort.purdue.edu/ext

Renee's Garden Heirloom and Gourmet Seeds
www.reneesgarden.com

Seed Savers Exchange (heirloom seeds)
www.seedsavers.org

South Dakota State University Extension
www.sdstate.edu/sdsuextension

Trees Are Good International Society of Arboriculture
www.treesaregood.com

United States Department of Agriculture Natural Resources
    Conservation Service plants.
www.usda.gov

University of Illinois Extension
web.extension.illinois.edu/state/hort.html

University of Minnesota Extension
www1.extension.umn.edu/garden

University of Minnesota Landscape Arboretum
www.arboretum.umn.edu

University of Missouri Extension
www.extension.missouri.edu

University of Nebraska-Lincoln Extension Publications
www.ianrpubs.unl.edu

University of Wisconsin Extension Learning Store
www.uwex.edu

Walters Gardens Perennial Nursery
www.waltersgardens.com

COMMON NAME INDEX

BOTANICAL NAME INDEX

PHOTO CREDITS

MEET MELINDA MYERS

Nationally known gardening expert, TV and radio host, author, and columnist Melinda Myers has more than thirty years of horticulture experience. She has written more than twenty gardening books, including *Can't Miss Small Space Gardening, The Garden Book for Wisconsin, Minnesota Gardener's Guide, Month-by-Month Gardening in Wisconsin,* the *Perfect Lawn* Midwest series, as well as the upcoming *Midwest Gardener's Handbook* and *Michigan Getting Started Garden Guide.*

In addition to authoring books, Myers hosts the nationally syndicated "Melinda's Garden Moment" segments that air on over 115 TV and radio stations throughout the United States. She is also the instructor for *The Great Course How to Grow* DVD series. Myers is a columnist and contributing editor for B*irds & Blooms* magazine and writes the twice monthly "Gardeners' Questions" newspaper column. She also has a column in *Gardening How-to* magazine and *Wisconsin Gardening* magazine. Melinda hosted *The Plant Doctor* radio program for over twenty years as well as seven seasons of *Great Lakes Gardener* on PBS. She has written articles for *Better Homes and Gardens* and *Fine Gardening* magazines, and was a columnist and contributing editor for *Backyard Living* magazine. Melinda has a master's degree in horticulture, is a certified arborist, and was a horticulture instructor with tenure. Melinda Myers's many accomplishments include starting the Master Gardener program in Milwaukee County and winning two Garden Media Awards (a Garden Globe Award for radio talent and a Quill and Trowel Award for her television work), both from the Garden Writers Association. She has also won the American Horticultural Society's B.Y. Morrison Communication Award for effective and inspirational communication. Melinda was the first woman inducted into the Wisconsin Green Industry Federation Hall of Fame.

Visit with Melinda at her website www.melindamyers.com.